C000166077

MICKY STEWART

and the Changing Face of Cricket

To Tony,

All Good Wishes &

Happy Birthday,

Micky Stewart

MICKY STEWART

and the Changing Face of Cricket

Stephen Chalke

FAIRFIELD BOOKS

Fairfield Books
17 George's Road, Bath BA1 6EY
Tel 01225-335813

Text © Stephen Chalke
Photographs appear by permission, as follows:
Getty Images: pages 227, 259 and 275
PA Photos: pages 85 and 136
Surrey County Cricket Club: pages 93, 102, 119 (top), 133 and 206
The other photographs have come from Micky Stewart's collection

First published 2012

ISBN: 978 0 9568511 2 3

Jacket design by Robert Taylor

MIX
Paper from
responsible sources
FSC
www.fsc.org
FSC® C023561

Printed and bound in Great Britain by
Butler Tanner and Dennis, Frome, Somerset

CONTENTS

PREFACE

by Micky Stewart

It was eleven years ago that I first met Stephen Chalke. He was writing a book on Geoffrey Howard, a former Secretary of Surrey in the 1960s and 1970s, a great visionary in the game. At that initial meeting Stephen asked me if I had ever been interested in doing a book, to which I replied "Not really". I had been asked the question a number of times some years earlier when I had retired from the England manager's job, and I had always given the same reply. I was still working in the game, and also son Alec was only beginning the second stage of his career with Surrey and England.

In spite of my negative answer Stephen's badgering was non-stop as the years rolled on, during which time I read with great interest his books on Geoffrey Howard, Tom Cartwright and Bob Appleyard, all of which won awards.

I began to reconsider my negative reply when I realised what a tremendous change I had seen in the game of cricket, at all levels, since I had first picked up a bat and ball as a youngster, then graduated to the first-class game as player, captain, coach, manager with Surrey and England, then finally for the last five years before retirement as the ECB's Director of Coaching and Development of Excellence.

It will be close on 75 years since I first picked up a cricket bat. My father advised me to enjoy whatever work I did, and cricket has allowed me to do that. The game of cricket, with all its qualities, has given me great pleasure, and it has provided me with so many friends for life. None of this would have been possible without the unselfish support of my wife Sheila, who has given me a wonderful family. I have been doubly lucky in experiencing not only my own great pleasure in cricket but that of my two sons, Neil and Alec, who in their different ways have known great joy and achievement in the game.

I still have memories as an eight-year-old of playing with my friends across the street and over the park when not even World War Two and the Battle of Britain could stop us. That was my introduction to the game, and we did it all ourselves. It is often said that in my generation every state school played cricket which is totally untrue. Up to the age of eleven I played just one game before I was lucky enough to go to Alleyn's School, Dulwich, to whom I owe a great deal, particularly to the cricket master Geoffrey Charnley.

A major change in the south of England was the introduction of league cricket. In Surrey it began in 1968 and has attracted overseas players and seen payments to players at certain clubs in order to win some silverware. My club was West Surrey, for whom I played from the age of 13 years, and they never batted me lower than number four in the order. They played a major part in my progress in the game, and I often wonder if things would have been different if league cricket had existed then.

During my career I have seen the abolition of 'amateurs' and 'professionals' in the first-class game, and in 1963 I was appointed the first professional captain of Surrey. I have seen the introduction of limited-over cricket: first the Gillette Cup, then the Sunday League, then the Benson and Hedges Trophy and now Twenty20 cricket, the game that has had the greatest impact in attracting spectators and revenue both at home and abroad. It has been a real money-spinner, but it has little in common with the traditional game of the county championship, the breeding ground for Test cricket.

I have seen the introduction of the cricket manager, both at county clubs and in the international game. I was England's first team manager, and I have watched as the role has developed in the twenty years since my retirement.

The biggest change in the financing of cricket came with the introduction of *Sky* TV to the international game. Their first coverage was England's 1990 tour of the West Indies, when I was team manager. The *Sky* revenue has benefited the game enormously, allowing the introduction of central contracts for England players, the building of the National Academy at Loughborough and the development of the National Coaching Scheme with all the technology involved, right down to the grass roots of the game. However, the downside has been the programming of both our international and domestic cricket, with particular damage done to the county championship.

I hope that this book describes clearly the changes I have seen during my life in cricket. That has been my intention in agreeing to work with Stephen on it. I also hope that it conveys the great pleasure the game has given me. Cricket has changed in so many ways, but in one way it has not changed at all. It is still the greatest game in the world.

1

INTRODUCTION

I first met Micky in the autumn of 2001 when I was working on a book with Geoffrey Howard, the far-sighted cricket administrator who had two spells with Surrey County Cricket Club: as Assistant Secretary in 1947 and 1948, then as Secretary from 1965 to 1975. Geoffrey was 92 years old, living in the Cotswolds, and I drove him to the Oval to meet up with three of the men with whom he had worked most closely during his years as Secretary. Two were leading lights on the committee, Derek Newton and Bernie Coleman. The third was Micky, Surrey's captain for much of that time.

Our meeting was scheduled for 13 September, two days after the destruction of the Twin Towers in New York, and we considered postponing it. But Geoffrey was adamant that life must go on, and we sat in the Committee Room and took our minds back to 1947 when Geoffrey started as Assistant Secretary.

Micky related to us how in the spring of that year his father had sent him to the Oval with ten shillings and sixpence, the price of junior membership of the county club. He was 14 years old and, when he arrived, his application was rejected with unsympathetic abruptness: "You need a proposer and a seconder." He was standing there bewildered – "I didn't even know what a proposer and a seconder were" – when Geoffrey appeared out of the General Office and, with typical kindness, took him under his wing. He found him a pair of sponsors – Errol Holmes, the Surrey captain, and Bob Gregory, the senior professional – and Micky began an association with the club that continues to this day. It is hard to think that anybody in the past sixty years has given more to Surrey.

Geoffrey's great age and his remarkable memory made the writing of his book a magical journey for me. He had first attended cricket at the Oval in August 1919, in that summer after the Great War when they experimented with two-day games. At lunchtime, he recalled, he and his father went for a stroll: "We walked behind the pavilion, and it just so happened, as we passed the players' entrance, Jack Hobbs was standing outside. He was wearing his MCC touring cap and his blazer, as he always did. I got as near to him as I could, and I touched him. I just touched his blazer. He was obviously going to be a great hero of mine."

After the book had been published, another moment from that lunchtime popped out of his memory: "After I had seen Jack Hobbs, we walked round to the Vauxhall End. Where the stands are now, there were stables for the horse that pulled the roller. I remember stretching up and stroking the horse's head. It was probably a big Clydesdale horse. They were commonplace, doing the work of the world. They wore big leather overshoes, covering their hooves, to make sure they didn't leave any marks. It was one of the items in the annual expenditure: 'repair of, or purchase of, new shoes for horse.' Four substantial, hand-made overshoes. They wouldn't have been cheap."

The horse had gone by the time Geoffrey became Surrey's Assistant Secretary, but the roller was still there. "It was called The Bomber. It was six foot or more in diameter, with great shafts, and it needed a whole gang to pull it. I can see the wonderful wave of water it pushed in front of it as the liquid top dressing was rolled in."

"I'd have put that in the book," I told him.

"Never mind," he said. "We can always do a second volume."

We never did, of course, though in some ways this book is the sequel. Geoffrey spanned the years from 1919 to 1975; now Micky spans the years from 1947 onwards. How appropriate that the join of the stories should be that moment of kindness outside the General Office, for Geoffrey was a generous, caring man and so is Micky.

Geoffrey took me to a world I am too young to have known. I loved his story of going out to bat as an amateur for Middlesex at Lord's in 1930. After he had been in for some minutes the Gloucestershire captain Bev Lyon turned to Wally Hammond at slip: "Take over for half an hour, will you, Wally? I've got a haircut appointment."

Micky's memories do not go back as far as Geoffrey's. Yet eleven years have passed since that book, and Micky is now almost the last survivor of Surrey's all-conquering side of the 1950s, the greatest county side of them all. They played in an era of uncovered pitches, adapting to an extraordinary range of surfaces and conditions, and that will seem as prehistoric to younger readers as the overshoes of the old Clydesdale horse seem to me. I am not old enough to have known a county game in which an amateur captain could feel free to disappear for a haircut, just as today's cricketers will have no experience of a world in which a young Micky could be advised kindly that he would find it rather too expensive if he kept getting his flannels dirty by diving for the ball.

Cricket has changed greatly during the past sixty years. That is one of the themes of this book. Micky, through his long involvement in the game, has seen those changes as closely as anybody alive. He is also one who, during more than thirty years as captain, manager and administrator, has pioneered some of the changes: the rise of physical fitness training, the greater emphasis on fielding and on team work, the move towards more professional structures.

Pat Pocock first played for Surrey as a 17-year-old in 1964, Micky's second year as captain, and he retired at the end of 1986, when Micky left his post as Surrey manager to become England's first team manager. "Micky is dateless," he says. "He was ahead of his time when he played, and he's still ahead of his time now. And he's classless. Whether he's mixing with cockneys or kings, he treats everybody exactly the same way."

*

It was not easy to persuade Micky to undertake this book. At that first meeting I put it to him that he had a fund of fascinating memories and insights, but he was not at all convinced that he wanted to have them committed to paper. Whenever we ran into each other, I would raise the subject afresh, and I am fairly sure that others, notably Derek Newton, were badgering him on my behalf.

After about five years I decided to drop the matter. The next time I met him, at the launch of a book about Sir George Edwards, I didn't raise the subject. Yet, as he said goodbye, he turned back and put his hand on my arm. "I will do that book with you," he said and left.

I wrote to him, outlining how I liked to work. He rang me on Friday afternoon, promising to think it through over the weekend and to give me a final answer on the Monday. It was almost 18 months before I heard from him again.

By then I was greatly overstretched with various projects. Sue, my partner, was getting fed up with the constant crises over impossible deadlines, and one morning she sat me down and told me to make a list of all the books I had undertaken to write or, through Fairfield Books, to publish. There were far too many, and she forced me to jettison several till the list was down to five or six titles. "Now promise me," she said, "that you won't say yes to anything else till we've worked through all these." I promised.

We were still sitting there, mulling over our decisions, when the telephone rang. "Stephen, it's Micky here. I've been thinking, and I'd like to get started on that book."

How could I say no?

*

11

I have written several books with individuals in the world of cricket. With Geoffrey Howard the principal strand of the writing lay in the witness he bore to events across so many years at the heart of our national game. With Bob Appleyard, the indomitable Bradfordian, the focus was more on the remarkable life he has lived, his strength of character in overcoming setbacks that would have broken a lesser man. With Tom Cartwright, the car worker's son from Coventry, I wanted, above all else, to record his opinions which challenged so refreshingly the orthodoxies of our age.

Here with Micky there is something of all three. At times he is witness, at other times protagonist and also somebody with a distinctive set of views. So the book is neither biography nor autobiography, neither survey of the past nor blueprint for the future – but something of all of these.

The story of this book follows the conversations I have held with Micky, but I have also threaded into the narrative the voices of others: some from interviews, some from books, some from the newspapers and magazines of the time. It is not intended to be a wholly objective biography; it is largely driven forward by Micky's memories and perceptions. However, it is not an autobiography, either, in that it presents other points of view.

Micky and I have been meeting regularly for three years, usually in the bar of the Grosvenor Hotel in Stockbridge in Hampshire. There we will talk away from eleven in the morning till four in the afternoon, fascinating conversations in which time seems to fly.

In one digression we were discussing 'The Spirit of Cricket', and I asked Micky to name three cricketers whom he had played with or against who best represented what he thought this 'Spirit of Cricket' thing meant. He sat for a long time in silence. Then he offered me three names, none of them from the traditional elite with which so many associate the game's highest ideals: Tom Clark, his first opening partner at Surrey, Jack Birkenshaw of Leicestershire and England, a man who has given so much in later life as a coach, and ... Tom Cartwright. As a coach Tom was a lovely mix, a disciplinarian with a natural kindness, and he always upheld the best values of the game. I can see the similarities with Micky.

*

A friend, who has been asking me regularly about the progress of this book, said to me one day, "I think of Micky Stewart as the Bobby Robson of cricket." I asked him what he meant by that, and he explained that as managers they both had a great ability to get the best out of their players and they both had a deep love of, and respect for, their sport.

The next time I saw Micky I said to him, "A friend of mine paid you a great compliment last week."

Micky is not one to lap up gushing praise. If I'd said, "He thinks you did a great job in difficult circumstances" or some such pleasantry, he would have batted it away with a joke and moved the conversation on.

"He said he thinks of you as the Bobby Robson of cricket."

There was a gulp and a silence. Then eventually: "That *is* a compliment."

Bobby and Micky were great friends, going back to the time in the early 1960s when their boys attended the same nursery. Bobby lived in a Fulham Football Club house in Worcester Park, Micky nearby in New Malden, and they met up regularly, along with George Cohen and Alan Mullery, two other stars of Fulham. They came round and played in the back garden with Micky's boys, Neil and Alec: Dad's friends the England footballers.

Bobby Robson loved his cricket, opening the batting in summer for Worcester Park Cricket Club. In later years he would sometimes attend international matches at the Oval where, if he was being wined and dined in the Committee Room, he would always be back in his seat for the first ball after the interval.

Micky loved his football, playing for top-level amateur clubs, then as a professional for Charlton Athletic. For some in the world of cricket Micky had a bit too much of football about him. Jim Swanton in the *Daily Telegraph* was one, referring on one occasion to 'the dreaded football culture' which Micky was importing into cricket.

"I was livid," Micky recalls. "I had a go at him. I said, 'There's no greater gentleman in English sport than Bobby Robson.'"

"Oh, Micky," Swanton replied. "I'm generalising."

Robson, a miner's son from County Durham, was five months younger than Micky, but they shared common values. Both had a burning competitive spirit, allied to an unflinching commitment to the highest standards of sportsmanship, a determination never to do their two sports any disservice. Both had a great respect for the players, and both knew how lucky they were to be working at something which they loved.

Robson was manager of Ipswich from 1969 to 1982, moving on to become England manager for eight years. In 1986 he took the national side to the quarter-finals of the World Cup in Mexico, where they lost to Maradona's 'hand of God' goal.

"It wasn't the hand of God," Robson said later. "It was the hand of a rascal. That day Maradona was diminished in my eyes forever."

Four years later in Italy England reached the semi-finals, where in his last game in charge they lost in a penalty shoot-out to West Germany.

In 1972 Micky retired as a cricketer, to work for the sports equipment firm Slazenger. He was invited back to Surrey in 1979 in the newly created post of Cricket Manager, and he hesitated long before accepting. Such was his success at Slazenger that he was about to join the board, and it was not clear how the role of Cricket Manager would develop.

Micky made his decision after spending a weekend with Bobby Robson. He attended Ipswich's home match against Arsenal, and they talked for hours about their lives. "Do what you love doing," was the theme of Robson's advice, an echo of what Micky's father had always told him.

Eight years later, while his great friend was England football manager, Micky became England's first cricket manager. In the summer of 1988, following a disastrous European Football Championship, the tabloids screamed 'ROBSON MUST GO'. Then, as English cricket lurched from crisis to crisis, getting through four captains in a five-Test series against the West Indies, they went on to pillory Micky. 'ROBSON MUST GO' became 'STEWART MUST GO'.

"Don't take any notice," Bobby would tell Micky on the telephone. "You're doing a good job. Believe in what you're doing."

Micky sometimes tells the story in after-dinner speeches, adding an imaginary further line from Robson: "Don't give up. You're taking a hell of a lot of pressure off me, you know."

*

We have called the book *Micky Stewart and the Changing Face of Cricket*. The inspiration for this was a most perceptive article by Simon Barnes of *The Times* when Micky stepped down as England manager.

> *Cricket, like everything else, has changed since the war. It is just that cricket has been slower to realise this than most other concerns. Stewart has not changed the face of cricket, but he has forced the England team to come to terms with the fact that the face of cricket has changed forever.*

The book is about Micky Stewart, the story of a life, and it is also about the changing face of cricket, the story of what he has witnessed in that life.

2

NEVER BE AN ALSO-RAN

"We'll be all right here," I say to Micky as he reads the parking notice on the lamp post of the quiet side street. "We're only going to be five minutes – and, if anybody comes along, we'll see them."

The sun is shining, and we wander along the two-storey, late Victorian terrace to number nine, a downstairs maisonette with its own front door, a sash window and a small unkempt front garden.

"I broke my arm falling out of that window," he tells me. "When I was about five years old. I arrived home, rang the bell and there was no answer. I tried to climb in, and I fell backwards."

For only the second time in thirty years Micky is back in the South London street where he grew up, on the street where – before the cars arrived – he played football and cricket all day, outside the rented flat where as a young man he returned each night from the Oval until he married in 1957.

In the early years he slept in the front room in a put-you-up bed. Then, when his older sister Jacquie moved out, he moved to the back bedroom beyond the kitchen and scullery. There was no hot running water, and heating was a coal fire. It was not luxury, not by the standards of life today, but for the Stewarts it was a step up from the flat they had rented in Coldharbour Lane, where Micky had been born in September 1932.

Coldharbour Lane, running from Brixton to Camberwell Green, was a busy thoroughfare. The tall houses, built for large families with servants, had long been broken up into flats, and all sorts lived cheek by jowl: the theatrical folk who took advantage of the late trams from the West End that terminated in Brixton, the larger-than-life personalities who sold their wares in the market and the occasional dubious characters who wove in and out of the crowds. It was rough in places – but rough in the cheerful way of south London in those years.

Micky has driven me through Brixton and down Coldharbour Lane, pointing out the sights he remembers. There is the town hall where he used to meet Sheila at weekends – "She says I always used to be late." Then there is the old Empress music hall where he saw Max Miller, the Cheeky Chappie, and a young Tommy Trinder, the fast-talking comedian with the catch-phrase "You lucky people". Displays of nakedness were illegal on the stage, unless the bodies were entirely motionless. "So there used to be these standstill nudes. When they appeared, my mother used to cover my eyes." Then we pass the arcade where at the age of ten his father bought him his first proper cricket bat. "It was war time, and they didn't have any rubber grips. The guy had two moulded tennis racquet grips, and he put one above the other."

At busy traffic lights beside Loughborough Junction railway station he turns into Herne Hill Road, following the journey his parents took when he was two years old. The move to Oakbank Grove was barely half a mile, but it was a half mile away from the noise and bustle of Coldharbour Lane, uphill towards the leafier, more genteel world of Dulwich.

When in his teens Micky started bringing school friends home, his mother would advise him not to take the 35 bus to Loughborough Junction, the closest stop. "Bring them on the 68, dear, and walk down from the top of the hill."

"There used to be a big hedge here," he says, looking at the front of his old home, "and flowers in the garden."

Then he leads me back to the end of the road where a blank brick wall stands before us.

"For hours I used to play by myself in front of this wall – with all sorts of balls: old tennis balls, table tennis balls, various types of rubber ball. Working out how they bounced differently. Setting myself tasks and tests like hitting a particular brick. Seeing the pace of the ball, how far it would come back. Where I had to throw it to gain the greatest distance on the rebound. Starting at a reasonable distance, then getting closer and closer and still catching the ball. Right hand, left hand, both hands."

Micky was the best close catcher of his generation. In the summer of 1957, in 34 matches, he took 77 catches, just one short of Wally Hammond's all-time record, and 54 years on we stand together before the wall where it all began. Then he starts to explain how they chalked a wicket on the bricks and bowled from the pavement across the road. But at this point he glances back towards his car and catches sight of a warden writing out a parking ticket.

"Oh no, no, no. Hold on, hold on," he cries in horror, breaking into a half-run. "Please don't do that."

"I thought it might be your car," the man says impassively, "but you took no notice of me."

"We're only stopping for a minute," Micky pleads, but there is no sign of the warden relenting.

"He grew up in this road," I weigh in, trying to appeal to his softer side. "It's the first time he's been back for years." I can tell that my words are making no difference so I try a different tack. "I'm writing a book about him. He's a famous cricketer. You're a West Indian. You like cricket, don't you?"

I am all set to tell him how Micky managed England to Ashes victory in Australia. I might even try the line Micky used one time when a chap interrupted us in a bar, asking who he was: "I'm Alec Stewart's father." But the warden puts a swift end to that.

"No," he says. "I'm a tennis man."

Then, just as all seems lost, he snaps his book shut. "Well, don't stay much longer," he instructs us. He returns to his bicycle, remounting it and disappearing round the corner.

I linger for one last moment in front of number nine, imagining them seventy years earlier huddled in the Anderson shelter in their garden, listening to the bombs falling around them; imagining them at Christmas in the front room, gathered around the upright piano as his mother accompanied the song his father loved to perform: *Underneath the Arches*, Flanagan and Allen's Cockney song of the homeless during the Depression years:

> *Pavement is our pillow,*
> *No matter where we stray.*
> *Underneath the Arches,*
> *We dream – our – dreams – away.*

It is another time and another world – though there is little nostalgia in Micky's description of it all. He has only come back here for my sake.

*

Hector McDonald Stewart, Micky's father, was born in 1900, the son of Matthew Stewart, a Glaswegian who for a while was a song-and-dance man, touring America, alongside Charlie Chaplin, with the Fred Karno Troupe. In that golden age of music hall before the First World War the troupe was so popular that before departure they were driven through the streets of south London in horse-drawn coaches, with the local folk all leaning out of windows to cheer them. Chaplin went on to Hollywood fame while Matthew Stewart travelled north to Canada where he became a professional cyclist with Rudge Whitworth. Some in the family think he may have ridden in the Tour de France, though in time he returned to London, where he became a taxi driver. That's how Micky remembers him.

He had five children: three girls and two boys. Hector's older brother Jack was killed in the war, but Hector himself was too young to see much action, serving in the Army of Occupation on the Rhine. "I joined the King's Rifles," he told Micky, "because they had black buttons. You didn't have to polish them."

The daughters – Tressie, Amy and Sadie – all went on the stage. Sadie was in the cast of the 1920s hit musical *No, No, Nanette* at the Palace Theatre, while Amy, with her long red hair, played Cinderella at the Finsbury Park Empire, before teaming up with the ukulele-playing Charlie Carr. For a while in the '20s and '30s they were stars of the music hall, earning big money and touring the States.

The Stewarts were an enterprising family, not people who would settle easily for the routine of office or factory life. After his military service Micky's father Hector started out on his own as a salesman. At the British Empire Exhibition of 1923 he did well, selling pens off a stall at the newly built stadium at Wembley. Then, when greyhound racing came to Britain in 1926, he saw his opportunity. The first race meeting was held in Manchester and, when the sport arrived shortly afterwards in London, he was immediately in operation as a tic-tac man, the youngest on the circuit.

The sport rapidly caught the popular imagination, finding a star in Mick the Miller, an Irish-born dog that won the Greyhound Derby in both 1929 and 1930. He would have won in 1931, too, but the race was ordered to be re-run and he was exhausted. The controversy, however, enhanced his legendary status, and he was signed up to appear in a film with Flanagan and Allen. In the words of one greyhound newspaper, he was 'as idolised as any horse, cinema star, footballer or boxer in history'.

Hector married Rosie Smith. He had met her at a dance, though he was never much of a one for dancing. She was three years his junior, a bright woman who had left school at 14 in the latter stages of the war, when she was directed to work in a munitions factory in the Midlands.

Their first child, Jacqueline, born in 1925, was named after Hector's lost brother Jack. By 1932, when their second arrived, Hector's life revolved around horses and greyhounds, and the boy was christened Michael. His mother stuck to Michael, the world came to know him as Micky, but to his father he was always Mick. After Mick the Miller.

By the age of four, Micky had learnt all the tic-tac signals that laid off bets between the various bookmakers on the course. "They'd never wear a wrist watch. If you did and you laid five to four, you'd smash it."

Hector and Rosie Stewart at Micky's wedding, 1957

Micky at London Zoo

"I'm not sure about including this photo," he says. "I know what everybody's going to say: 'Which one is Micky?'"

Then there were all the fast-moving calculations they made – fifty pounds at thirteen to eight, twenty pounds at nine to four on – and the quick decisions to lay off some of the larger bets, all done with fast-moving sign language about the course. "I learned my mental arithmetic by going through his card when he came home. Fifteen times ninety-eight: fourteen hundred and seventy. It's just fifteen times a hundred less thirty. That's how I learned."

At the race course or dog track thousands of pounds of bets would be placed with no hint of a signature. "There was never a problem. Such was the code of conduct that, if anybody tried it on, he would never be included again."

It was a vibrant world, full of life and colour. As a boy Micky sometimes accompanied his father, and he experienced it as a joyful, happy environment, welcoming and friendly – "though my father always made me aware that there were some doubtful characters about." Pick-pockets moved at the horse-racing courses amidst the loud, self-confident people from the upper ranks of society, and there were gangs, the Hills and the Richardsons. It was an era in which protection rackets were rife.

Hector retained his integrity. "In the profession he was in," Micky's sister Jacquie says, "to remain as he did, it was wonderful. Even Mummy would say that. There was a lot going on that bordered on the illegal, and he always kept on the right side of the line."

He hardly ever drank, and he upheld the highest of standards when ladies and children were present. "He might be having a chat with his friends at the races," Micky recalls, "and one of them would come out with a swear word. And, straightaway, seeing me there, he'd say, 'I'm sorry, Hector, I'm so sorry.'"

He was a smart dresser, buying his hats from Lock's in St James's Street, his shirts from Herbert's in Leicester Square and his suits from Charles Wilson, the Brixton tailor who supplied all the local show-business people.

"He had a terrific personality," Jacquie says. "Everybody liked him. And he idolised the two of us. There was nothing he wouldn't do for us."

He and Micky called each other 'best mate', and without doubt he was the rock of his boy's early life, a man with a great strength of character who inculcated values which have stayed with Micky all his life.

For Jacquie, though, it was their mother who had the greater influence. "Daddy had strong principles," she says, "and he was a great believer in discipline. But Mummy had the stronger character. She did all the bringing up. A woman's life could be tough in those days, but she was always so fair, so sensible about everything."

"He might not get home till eleven at night," Micky remembers, "and she'd cook him a fresh meal when he got in."

Hector did not limit himself to running the tic-tac at race courses. At a time when off-course betting was illegal except if you had an account, he was a partner in a turf accountants' business, taking telephone bets at a shop in Coldharbour Lane. He was also a shrewd placer of a bet himself. He was, in fact, a professional gambler, deriving the majority of his income in this way. "He gambled at cards as well," Micky recalls. "Mainly poker. And he played snooker. He was the champion at the Camberwell Green Snooker Hall."

"If you were going to go into this, Mick," he told Micky when he was in his teens, "I'd teach you all I know. But if you don't and you ever put more than five shillings on a horse, I'd consider I'd brought up the biggest mug there's ever been."

He was not especially religious, and he did not engage in politics. But he had an uncompromising set of values and he passed them on to his children – honesty, a hatred of hypocrisy and a belief that the best people, if they worked hard, could rise to the top.

"You won't win every fight," he would tell Micky, in the language of the boxing ring. "But always look to be the Guv'nor." Or, as Micky's mother might have put it, "Be respectful – but never subservient."

For all the uncertainty of his income Hector Stewart always seemed to bring home enough money, and Rosie was a level-headed woman who made sure the two children never went short. "She was a typical London lady," Micky says, "and she *was* a lady. She had grown up in the Old Kent Road. She always had a smile and a laugh, but she was a strong lady. Everything had to be right. Good manners, respect, looking the part, integrity. She was always preaching about good manners and being respectful."

One evening, when Micky was a small boy, he was sitting in the front room of their maisonette in Oakbank Grove when his father came home from a successful day at the races.

"Where's Mummy?" he asked with a hint of conspiracy in his voice.

"She's just nipped out."

"Quick."

Unusually he was carrying a bag, and he opened it to reveal a great stash of money. In no time he and Micky had covered every flat surface of the room, including the floor, with notes: not just ten shilling and pound notes but the large white five and ten pound ones, too.

They heard the key turn in the front door, and Micky ran out.

"Mummy," he said with excitement. "Daddy wants to see you."

She entered the room and stared briefly at the display.

"Oh well," she said. "At least I've *seen* this lot," and walked back out.

On another occasion, when Micky was about six years old, his father came home from the races with plenty. A difference of opinion about money developed, and his father handed Micky a ten-pound note.

"Take that, Mick. Now go and throw it in the fire, will you?"

"What *are* you doing?" Micky's mother exclaimed.

"Throw it in the fire," he repeated.

Micky did as he was told. An orange flame caught the white paper, and it was gone in an instant. Ten pounds – at a time when most workers earned three or four pounds a week.

"Never let money be your god," his father said.

The words have stayed imprinted on Micky's brain. "In those years everybody was scrambling about to earn a bob or two to exist. His philosophy was that you should work at what you enjoy and earn your living from that. 'Whatever you do in life,' he would say, 'the more you enjoy it, the better you will be doing it. And the money will come. Don't do it just for the money.'"

Doing what you enjoy was not just about having fun, however. It was also about the pursuit of excellence, as he made clear in another piece of advice that has stayed with Micky all his life, advice that he couched in the language he used every day, the language of the race course.

"Let me tell you this, Mick. Never spend your time as an also-ran. Whatever you do, concentrate on being number one – or near the top. It's a waste of time being an also-ran."

"Once I came fourth in my class," Jacquie remembers. "It wasn't good. I was expected to come top. 'We're not like other people,' Daddy used to say."

*

Micky parks the car by the railings of Ruskin Park, and this time I put some money in a nearby meter. Micky has not been inside the park for more than fifty years, and he seems surprised by how pleasant it is. I think he was half-expecting drug-takers' needles in the grass and unsavoury characters lurking at every turn. Instead, there are young mothers with buggies arriving for a One O'Clock Club and an air of care about everything. The old wooden bandstand has been restored, and the bowling green, where Micky and his scruffy playmates used to peer through the Rose Arch, watching with fascination the strange curve of the woods, has been converted into an attractive wild flower labyrinth.

We stand beside the tree where he and his friends gathered. On summer days they would be there before nine in the morning, and they would still be there as the light faded in the evening. A run home for lunch and for tea, an occasional trip to the shop outside where they could buy a pennyworth of sweets out of a large jar, but mostly it was cricket. And football in winter. All day long.

"If there had been television in those days, I'd probably have been at home watching that. Or a computer. But there wasn't. So I played all day in the street and in the park."

Their cricket on the rough grass was fairly basic. "We were only supposed to use a tennis ball. The park keepers were afraid a hard ball might injure people out walking. But when they weren't looking, we'd use a composite cricket ball. At first we didn't have any stumps so we draped a coat over a stick stuck in the ground. Of course, this caused a lot of argument whether you were out or not. We also played a rule that two hits into the adjoining gardens and you were out – so I learned to play the ball down."

Boating on the lake at Dulwich Park
The boy next door is rowing

Then they moved onto the asphalt football pitch, and they acquired a cork ball and a set of stumps that they pushed awkwardly into the surface. The games grew a little more structured and, despite often being the smallest boy there, Micky more than held his own. "You didn't give the bat up till you were out, and one time I batted for a whole week."

At the top of the park was a cricket pitch where he watched carefully the adult matches, copying in his own play the way they batted and bowled. So by playing and imitating, he developed his own game. No coaching, nothing organised. Just enjoying hitting the ball and learning how to stay at the wicket. Also, as a small boy, learning to stick up for himself. "You got trodden all over if you showed any sign of real weakness. And if they were bigger than you, you had to make sure you were quick."

On Friday 1 September 1939, fifteen days short of Micky's seventh birthday and two days before the declaration of war, all the local children were assembled in the park. They were issued with gas masks in cardboard boxes and identity labels that were hung about their necks. Jacquie remembers spotting their father watching from behind a tree as they were marched away to Denmark Hill railway station. From there they travelled to Sevenoaks where they were herded into sheep pens in the market square before being allocated to local families. Some days later their mother joined them.

There followed two years of coming and going. They were back in Oakbank Grove by Christmas, staying through most of the Blitz before evacuating a second time to Oxford where they were put up first in the village of Kennington, then in Cowley. But by the autumn of 1941 they were back home once more. "We always seemed to be in London when the bombs were falling," Micky says.

His memories are flickering. There was the day in Sevenoaks when his father turned up with a pair of football boots and a brand new football: "a proper one, tanned leather that you had to dubbin. And the boots had leather studs and toe-caps that were as hard as iron." Back in London his father only allowed him to use the ball in matches after he had demonstrated that he could strike it equally well with both right foot and left.

There was the evening in Oxford when his mother gave him her last threepenny bit and sent him out in the blackout to buy a loaf of bread: "It was a little silver coin. I dropped it, and I couldn't find it anywhere in the dark. It was the last money we had till my father came back."

In Cowley he remembers the unpleasant waft of incense at the school's religious services, the regular fights between the local boys and the evacuees, and the long hours rummaging at a dump for pieces of shrapnel.

The games in Ruskin Park resumed, though often they were interrupted by air raid sirens, causing them all to run home. "I suppose I was too young to understand. Lots of houses were destroyed, but other parts of the war were exciting: seeing the searchlights picking up the German bombers, watching the dogfights in the sky."

And the mark it left on Micky? "It made me prouder to be English. There was a spirit that got people through those years. Everybody pulled together. They were Londoners. They dealt with the war by retaining their humour." He pauses. "Where's that typical London character gone? Has it disappeared altogether?"

There is a man working on the cricket square, and we decide to walk up there. "Do you remember Freddie Mills the light-heavyweight champion boxer?" Micky asks on the way up. "His manager, Ted Broadribb, had a house in that road there. When I walked up Herne Hill Road to school, I'd often see Freddie Mills out running."

Boxing was another important part of Micky's south London childhood. His father bought him two pairs of gloves, even before he had a football or a cricket bat. A friend of the family trained Al Delaney, the Canadian light-heavyweight champion, and Micky sometimes went with his father to watch him at Jack Solomon's gym in Great Windmill Street. He was also introduced to Ted 'Kid' Lewis, the welterweight champion.

"This bit of grass here," he says, pausing on an incline, "is where I played cricket with Harold Anfam."

Anfam was a wealthy Indian boy, several years older than Micky, and he had a set of stumps of his own. He was a fast bowler and a hard-hitting batsman, and one day he persuaded Micky to play with him on this slope. "I batted first, and inside six balls he'd knocked two stumps out of the ground. Then for the rest of the morning I bowled at him, uphill, and I had to fetch the ball every time he hit it." For several mornings the same ritual was enacted. Some weeks later, at ten o'clock at night, Anfam turned up at Oakbank Grove, wanting to take Micky for a ride on his brand-new motorbike. "I was in my pyjamas, and my mother refused to let me out."

The cricket pitch, when we reach it, is a synthetic one, and the outfield is decidedly bumpy.

"Who plays here?" I ask the groundsman, a Rastafarian with a weather-beaten face and greying dreadlocks.

"I haven't got a clue, man," he replies cheerfully. "They said to me a couple of weeks ago, 'Can you go out and mark the lines for the cricket?' Now they've asked me to do it again."

After the restored bandstand, the paddling pool, the tennis courts and the wild garden labyrinth, this is a disappointment.

"The pitch doesn't look too clever," Micky says, inspecting the pockmarks on it. "It looks as if people have been playing football all over it, with studs."

"What can you do?" the groundsman says with good-humoured fatalism. "In the old days there was a chestnut fence. But people used to pull it down and let their dogs in. That's life today, isn't it?"

I have only played cricket at a moderate club level, and there is a part of me that looks at this scene and thinks, "No changing facilities. A rough outfield. An artificial pitch. I wouldn't want to play here."

Micky, however, has opened for England at Lord's, and he does not view it like that. It's cricket, and for all its shabbiness he's glad that it's still being played in the park of his childhood. For five years in the 1990s, after he finished as England's team manager, he was Director of Coaching and Excellence for the England and Wales Cricket Board, responsible for what is often called the recreational, as opposed to the professional, game.

"I don't know what recreational cricket is," he says, "unless it means you don't get paid to play. But that's not right, anyway. Lots of people playing club cricket do get paid. Recreational, professional, first-class, it's all the same game. The game in this country is far too fragmented."

*

Micky drives up Herne Hill Road, pointing out on the left his first school, St Saviour's. It was not the beginning of his formal education, however. That had been in the front room at Oakbank Grove where his sister Jacquie had sat him down in front of a blackboard, between a teddy bear and a large doll called Janet, and taught him reading, writing and basic arithmetic. "I was a real bossyboots," she admits now. "But, when he got to school, he was a year ahead of all the others."

As a result, at the end of his first year at St Saviour's, Micky was transferred over the hill, away into the leafy streets beyond, to the elementary school at Dulwich Hamlet. At first his father accompanied him each morning, but in time he came to make the two-mile walk each way on his own.

On the right we drive past the grandly ornate Carnegie Library. "I read pretty well every cricket book they had in there," Micky says. "I suppose it was those books that hardened my ambition. By the age of seven or eight I wanted to play for England. By and large, that's all I thought about, really. When we played cricket, I'd say 'I'm Jack Hobbs' and, if I bowled, it would be 'I'm Harold Larwood.' It was all from the books I'd read in the library."

Micky had never seen Hobbs or Larwood. In fact, Hobbs had played his last day of first-class cricket before Micky's second birthday. But he could picture him clearly in the books. "I remember one day in the street this boy was holding the bat with his hands apart, and he said, 'That's how Jack Hobbs held it.' I said, 'He didn't. He had his hands together.' And it turned into a bit of a scrap."

Micky was born on Friday 16 September 1932, on the day when England's cricketers assembled in north London in readiness to sail the next morning to Australia, for what would come to be known as the Bodyline tour. Micky read all about it in Douglas Jardine's *In Quest of the Ashes*, and he also read Percy Fender's *Kissing the Rod* about the return series in England in 1934. According to Fender, England would have won that series if the powers at Lord's – in the aftermath of the Bodyline furore – had not cast Jardine and Larwood aside. Jardine was, in Fender's opinion, 'the best captain in England'.

Such politics would have been way beyond the comprehension of the wide-eyed, cricket-mad boy from Oakbank Grove, though in time he would come to understand them all too keenly, as he battled in vain with the men at Lord's to restore his victorious Ashes captain of 1986/87, Mike Gatting, for the return series of 1989.

At Carnegie Library he also devoured John Finnemore's turn-of-the-century books about boarding-school life: *Teddy Lester in the Fifth*, *Teddy Lester's Chums* and, best of all, *Teddy Lester, Captain of Cricket*.

"I remember thinking how terrific it would be to go to a school like that. Little did I know that I was going to."

*

On Good Friday 1939 his father took him to the Den to his first professional football match: Millwall versus Sheffield Wednesday. "All I can remember is that at half-time the St John's Ambulance came round, collecting money in a blanket, and I threw in this penny. I was pleased because it landed in the blanket. 'What was that?' Dad said. Then I realised it was the half crown he'd given me as an Easter present."

On August Bank Holiday 1942 Micky went for the first time to Lord's, taken by his father to see 'Middlesex and Essex' play 'Kent and Surrey'. "We were sitting in the Mound Stand, and I remember being excited before the start of play, seeing the figures through the windows of the Long Room before they came out. Then I remember being aware that they wore creams, not whites."

There were several top players in action – Denis Compton and Bill Edrich, Gubby Allen and Alf Gover – but they were all upstaged in mid-morning when an 18-year-old Dulwich schoolboy, Trevor Bailey, bowling at a lively pace, dismissed three batsmen, one lbw and two bowled, in his first over.

The following year Micky took the junior county scholarship, the forerunner of the eleven-plus, and he did well enough to be sent for interview to Dulwich College. He might have dreamed of following in the footsteps of Bailey – but no. "I didn't want to go there because they played rugby. When I took their test, I deliberately put down wrong answers."

At the interview the headmaster asked how he spent his time.

"What did you do on Monday?" … "We played cricket in the park."

"And Tuesday?" … "We played cricket in the park."

"What about in the evening?" … "We played till it was dark."

"I don't know why. I thought that was the way not to get in."

Dulwich duly rejected him, but on the strength of his original junior scholarship performance he was offered a free place at its sister school, Alleyn's, where they played soccer. Even better, the main body of the school had been evacuated to Rossall School in Lancashire, and he was able to experience the boarding-school life he had dreamt of with such longing in the Carnegie Library.

He was a shy boy, slight and short, and he had not been to prep school. But he had acquired from his parents and his sister a strong sense of right and wrong, he had already learned to look after himself, he had encountered a wide range of people and worlds, and he had a quiet determination to succeed.

It was not his intention to be an also-ran.

3

SECOND TO COWDREY

"Alleyn's had very strong sports and very strong arts: theatre and music," Micky tells me with evident pride as we make our way towards the gatehouse. Indeed, Micky is just as keen to tell me about the boy who became an opera singer in Italy as the one who represented Britain in the 1948 Olympics.

Micky spent his first five terms in Lancashire, in the magnificent splendour of Rossall School with its large quadrangle and its imposing, twin-towered entrance arch, and it seems he loved every minute of it. He was one of the smallest boys in the school when he arrived, and such was his performance in the junior county scholarship that he was put in a form with boys most of whom were a year or more older. Yet it did not overawe him. He was living his *Teddy Lester* dream, and he threw himself into a wide range of activities: from the school choir, in which he was a talented boy soprano singing in Verdi's *Requiem*, to the boxing ring where the school captain led the instructional sessions. "He used to pick me out because I knew what he was talking about. I could do the right thing to help him with the demonstration. Unfortunately on one occasion I had a lapse of concentration and he busted my nose. The first of six times in my life it was busted."

Most important, however, were the football and the cricket. Micky had only ever played one game of cricket on a proper grass pitch: in his last term at Dulwich Hamlet, when they had gone across to the Griffin Sports Ground behind the school. "Yet at Alleyn's, without having had any coaching, I was the best player in my year. And I knew that. It was the same with football."

Above all, he loved the sense of community that came with boarding-school life, the way the whole school turned out to support the football team and to listen to the orchestral concerts. Back in London after the war, when they all reverted to being day boys, he felt a great disappointment that this spirit was evaporating. In particular, he became frustrated that too many boys, especially those who had not gone up to Rossall, were going home as soon as the last lesson ended.

"My best friend Bob Bedford and I took to standing at the gate, asking them why they weren't staying to do something. 'You should support the school,' we said. 'If you don't want to play games, why don't you do something else? Play in the orchestra? Or join the Know London Society?'"

Even at the age of 13 he was preaching the virtues of team work and community above personal choice and individualism, just as he would be doing forty years later as manager of the England cricket team. Pride in his country, pride in his school.

The school is proud of Micky, too, and Susie Schofield, in charge of alumni, greets us with great warmth. They have had a rich line of old boys achieving distinction in the theatre – from Leslie Howard through John Stride, Julian Glover and Simon Ward to Samuel West and Jude Law – but there have only been two sporting greats: Henry Cotton, three-time winner of the British Open Golf Championship, and Micky.

"Henry Cotton was often at the Oval," Micky says. "He was very knowledgeable about cricket. He used to sit and talk to the Bedsers."

In fact, Cotton might have become a cricketer, had events followed a different course in the summer of 1923. At the end of a first eleven game at Marlow the prefects in the team went off to meet some girls, leaving Cotton and the other juniors to lug the shared kitbag and all their cricket clothes back to school on public transport. Cotton organised a letter of protest, then refused to be beaten for his insolence. His father weighed in, denouncing the headmaster at a fiery parents' meeting, and the young Henry was withdrawn from the school. His promising cricket career over, he took an appointment as a junior professional at Fulwell Golf Club.

Micky had no such rebel tendencies. At Alleyn's he played for four years in the first eleven, the last two as captain, and today he makes his way purposefully out onto the square where he tasted so much success. "The pavilion is much improved," he says, "but this outfield …"

Diplomacy prevents him from completing the sentence. Instead, he starts to reminisce about his first match as captain. "We had a tall, good-looking lad who was also into the arts – singing and acting – and he opened the bowling. David Palastanga. He was taken up by J. Arthur Rank Films. He married the German actress Hildegarde Knef.

"The girls all used to swoon over him. He would come in to bowl off a long run, and his knees used to click. He could bowl 4.2 overs of an opening spell, then at 4.3 he was knackered. I remember that first match I was captain. I was fielding at cover, somewhere about here, concentrating, and he started a fifth over. I thought, 'What's he bowling another one for?' And I suddenly realised, 'It's up to me to take him off.'"

"So what was your greatest achievement on this square, Micky? Any centuries?"

"I bowled out an England batsman once."

Alas, the story on telling turns out to be not quite as impressive as it sounds. The batsman in question was not Denis Compton or Len Hutton, not even Jack Robertson or Laurie Fishlock, but the Honourable Luke White, the Old Etonian who in 1945 at the age of 18 played an unofficial 'Victory Test' against an Australian Services side. The idea had been to look to the future by giving a chance to three of the best schoolboy batsmen of the previous summer – John Dewes, Donald Carr and White – but the jump in standard proved far too sudden for all of them. White played just three games for Middlesex before becoming a stockbroker.

"He was playing for the MCC. I think he'd scored a century for them the previous year. We had no one to open the bowling. David Palastanga was unfit and, as I could always swing the ball, I decided to do it myself. I ran in from the rifle range end, and I don't know how it happened. I bowled this ball that swung, pitched on the seam, went through his gate and knocked the lot over. As far as I was concerned, he was an England cricketer, and I'd bowled him out."

Susie Schofield has children to pick up so she takes us across to the school archivist, Neil French, a retired engineer who is a few years younger than Micky.

"Nice to see you again, Micky. Come on up."

We clamber up a narrow staircase to reach a cramped office where he has prepared for us by pulling out the school magazines for 1943 to 1950 and also Micky's Leaver's Card.

> *Michael James Stewart, born 16 September 1932.*
> *Father's occupation: Clerk.*

"That would be what my mother would have told me to tell them," Micky explains. "She used to say he was a clerk, or a commission agent. In those days saying he had a job in the racing business wouldn't have sounded so respectable."

The two of them talk about mutual friends and, while they do, I turn the pages of the magazines, looking for mentions of Micky. I don't have to search for long:

> *CRICKET*
> M.J. STEWART: *His experienced knowledge of the art of captaincy has made all the difference to many of our matches, whilst in practice his untiring help and constructive criticism have done much for every member of the side. Always his freshness of outlook and great enthusiasm have inspired his team.*

FOOTBALL

STEWART (Inside-Left): The chief schemer and potential goal-scorer. Possessing brilliant ball control, a good shot with both feet and a deceptive swerve, he is a vital factor in school football who will be sorely missed.

That small, shy boy, setting off on the train to Rossall in September 1943, not quite 11 years old and having little more experience of cricket and football than the makeshift games he had played in Ruskin Park, had become a self-confident young man, the best all-round sportsman the school has ever had. He was the first boy at Alleyn's to play for the Public Schools at Lord's, and he also represented the Public Schools at football. He even found time to be a member of what was arguably the best fives team the school has produced.

Whether he found time to do himself justice in his academic studies is not so clear. In his last years at school he was going out with Sheila MacCormick from the sister school James Allen's, a girl who in time would become his wife. She still possesses two letters written to her by Micky while he was sitting in the school exam hall, in those closing minutes when he had run out of things to put in his answers.

Still at school: Micky and Sheila

Well another exam is over a quarter of an hour before time ... It looks as though it is going to flipping well rain. If it stops the match against Rutlish B!*f.E.!! ... Michael Moorby can't understand how I can still be writing ... Master's said time. Oh! he nearly collected this up with my exam papers.

Despite the impression these letters give, the plan was for him to stay at school till the summer of 1951, sit the Higher School Certificate and go to Oxford University.

*

Neil French, Micky and I walk across to the brand new, multi-million pound Edward Alleyn

Building which includes the superbly equipped Michael Croft Theatre, named after the Alleyn's master who left in 1956 to set up the National Youth Theatre.

"He wrote a book *Spare The Rod*," Neil recounts. "Arguing against corporal punishment, and it was a great success. With the money he made from that, he could afford to take a sabbatical year, and that's how he set up the Youth Theatre."

"He was my English master one year," Micky says. "We had him period one on a Monday morning. The first 20 minutes of our 40-minute lesson were always taken up with Bob Bedford and me sorting out his football pools: how he'd got on the previous Saturday and what he was going to put down for the coming one."

Another who taught English during Micky's time was Edward Upward, a Thirties writer in the same set as Auden, Isherwood and Spender.

"Isherwood thought he was the best writer in the group," Neil says. "He used to send his manuscripts to Upward for his opinion. When he was teaching here, he got very concerned about the way the world had gone. In fact, he went Communist for a while, which didn't sit easily on his shoulders in a place like this."

"Sheila tells me sometimes I'm a Communist," Micky jokes. "But I'm not. I'm all for people making their own way in life. It's just that I don't think it's right that some people should have such an abundance when others are struggling for a crust."

Back outside, Micky looks across the quadrangle. "I think the woodwork hut was over there, wasn't it? With Wally Walters. Then there was the physics and chemistry lab. Mr Taylor, do you remember him? You always had to lower the scales before putting on an extra weight. I got fed up with that one day. I was putting on a weight, and suddenly there was a great whack. I was knocked off my stool, finished up in the gangway. 'Will you do that again, boy?' 'No, sir.'"

*

Home and school were different worlds: the regimentation of boarding life at Rossall and the rough-and-ready games in Ruskin Park. Yet Micky seems not to have felt ill at ease in either environment. Together with his father's life in the world of dogs and horses, Micky was experiencing the full range of English society. "That was a huge benefit to me in later life," he says.

He would never prove easy to pigeon-hole in the English class system. "Doesn't Michael speak nicely now?" his mother said when he returned home after his first term away. Yet, four or five years later, when he rang his new girl friend Sheila, he heard her brother calling to her: "There's a young cockney on the phone for you."

In the north he was allowed out twice a month to watch the wartime football matches at Blackpool, where he saw Stanley Matthews play. Then back in London in the summer holiday he would go to Lord's. He was in the crowd on the day in July 1944 when a flying bomb passed over.

"They were like little aeroplanes. As they came down, the engine cut out and they started to glide. Jack Robertson was at the wicket, and he threw himself down. All the players went flat on the ground, and we all did in the stand, too. Then it went over and exploded in Regent's Park, and the players got back up. The bowler ran up, Jack Robertson went whack and the ball went for six. And the whole crowd started singing."

There'll always be an England,
And England shall be free
If England means as much to you
As England means to me.

"I was relating this in the England dressing room at Lord's when I was manager, telling Allan Lamb. 'Get out of it,' he said. 'I can't believe that.' And, blow me, within five minutes, there was a knock on the door and the attendant came in. 'Excuse me, Mr Stewart,' he said. 'Is it possible for you to sign this book?' He gave me the book, with a picture to sign, and, when I turned over the pages, I saw this photo of that game in 1944, with all the players lying flat on the ground. Within five minutes of my telling the story. It was extraordinary."

That summer he also saw the great West Indian Learie Constantine. "He was the one who first inspired me with fielding. I went up with a group of lads to Lord's, and we used to come back on the tube to the Elephant and Castle, catch the 35 bus, walk up the hill to Ruskin Park and try to imitate all the things Learie Constantine had done. He was brilliant. He fielded at cover, and that's where I wanted to field. And I'd read that Jack Hobbs had always fielded at cover."

By the summer of 1946 Micky was making his own debut at Lord's, as captain of a London Schools Under-14 eleven against a team from the provinces captained by Brian Taylor, the future Essex captain. Micky was still a tiny figure, even among boys of his own age, a point not lost on his assembled family.

"When's he coming in?" asked his Aunt Tressie.

"Number three," her husband Jack said.

"Number three?"

"Yes. He's got to get in early before the grass grows."

The first wicket fell. "We'd arrived the day before and been put in the away dressing room, but for the match we were in the home one. When it was my turn to bat, I was full of nerves. I went down the stairs and, thinking we were in the away dressing room, I turned right to go through the Long Room. I finished up in the MCC Committee Room where there was a meeting in progress, chaired by Sir Pelham Warner. 'I think you'd do better with that bat out there, young man,' he said."

Away from school Micky took his first steps into adult cricket and football. It resulted from his friendship with the oldest boy in their group in Ruskin Park, John Mansfield, an apprentice compositor in the printing business. He lived in Cambria Road, beside the park, where in his front room he had a miniature snooker table on which the two of them would play. In the summer of 1945 he took Micky with him to play a few matches, alongside older men, for the cricket team of the 18th London Home Guard.

In the winter the boys of the park formed a football club called Parkside Rovers, who played on the asphalt at Brockwell Park. Fixtures were arranged for Sundays, but there was no booking system for the pitch; it was first-come, first-served. "For a two o'clock kick-off we'd get there by half past eight or nine in the morning and do shifts to make sure we kept the pitch till kick-off. Occasionally, when another team came along, there'd be a bit of a scrap."

Micky became their Secretary, applying for the grass-pitch permits which cost three shillings and sixpence a match. If they played at Blackheath or Clapham Common or Brockwell Park, he would make sure they arrived early to collect the goalposts from a shed. Even at this stage, a small boy among men – 'Weenie', they called him – he was a star player, a quick-footed inside forward with great ball control, and it was not long before he was snapped up by another team of local boys, Minden United from the streets around Loughborough Junction. "In the little off-licence beside the Cambria pub in Cambria Road. That's where I was transferred from Parkside Rovers to Minden: for a sixpenny piece and a bottle of fizzy grapefruit juice."

In the summer of 1946, when he won the Alleyn's Under-14 Cricket Prize and played at Lord's, he played a few Sunday games for the newly formed Parkside Cricket Club, on Clapham Common and in Dulwich Park, but shortly before the end of the season his father's friend Bill Burroughs took him to play for West Surrey, a wandering club with fixtures against many of the best clubs in the south-east.

"My first game was an all-day match against Barclays Bank. I was caught at the wicket for nought. The following week we played against East Grinstead; Jim Parks was playing for them. I went in at number four on a fiery wicket and had to face a fast bowler who was in the Sussex second eleven. I found out later that there had been a discussion about whether I should go in so high up. I was a midget, and the first ball went straight through my hair. But I got 15 or 16."

In those days club cricket in the south of England was very different from how it is now. There were no leagues and, though teams played to win, winning was not everything. "It was more about testing your individual skills. The enjoyment of scoring runs and taking wickets, and the way that was achieved, was what mattered most. Some of the individual statistics were tremendous."

At Alexandra Park Cricket Club, in North London, Len Newman played for fifty years, scoring 80,000 runs, with 250 centuries, while his opening partner Con Davies scored 64,000 as well as taking more than 5,000 wickets. "They couldn't do that now. Those figures, they would be impossible to achieve in the modern club game."

At West Surrey Saturday games started at two o'clock, but the big day was always Sunday, an all-day match which families would attend. The top clubs maintained an elite among themselves, and the upholding of high standards was a vital part of that. "If a club went away for a Sunday game and the dressing rooms weren't too clever, or the outfield hadn't been properly cut, they would send a letter afterwards, saying how very disappointed they were. 'I'm sure you'll put it right by next year. Otherwise we may have to reconsider our fixture.'"

The founder and president of West Surrey was William Comben Longstaff, who would later become chairman of the English Hockey Association. He ran a coastal shipping business and he pressed Micky, in his last year at school, to join his company. He wanted him to go to university and to play cricket as an amateur. "He even asked Sheila to try to persuade me."

West Surrey put out two sides each Saturday and Sunday, and the following summer, 1947, when Micky was only 14 years old, he started on the lesser side, scoring a century against the Metropolitan Police in the first game. Soon afterwards he was promoted to the first team, where he remained. "They were brilliant to me there. From the age of 13 I never batted outside the first four. The club had a huge effect on my progress."

From the start of that summer Micky was a regular in the Alleyn's first eleven, for whom he topped the batting averages and took enough wickets to be described by the school magazine as 'an extremely useful slow off-break bowler'. Also in the Alleyn's team that summer, breaking into it towards the end of term, was another 14-year-old: John Pretlove, a slow left-arm bowler who would later play for Kent.

The new master in charge of cricket was Geoffrey Charnley, a Cambridge geography graduate who had played club cricket in Liverpool. He was excited by the young Micky's talent and fascinated by his father's occupation. "They were from very different backgrounds, but they struck up quite a friendship. He used to come over and ask him all about the betting, how it worked, but my father would never take a bet off him."

Charnley's cricket coaching left a deep mark on his young protégé. "He was excellent at all the etiquette of the game: the way you turned out, the way you conducted yourself. He protected the qualities of the game. And he showed me how to go about things sensibly, not to throw my wicket away, and how in schools cricket you could always get wickets if you bowled straight. Fielding was crucial, too. In the summer term, in every break he had the whole first team outside for fielding practice."

Yet, more than this school cricket, Micky owed his rapid advance to the matches he played at West Surrey: "playing against the top adults in club cricket, mature cricketers, where at school we played against other youngsters." There was John Cracknell, an electrician and friend of the family, and Jim and Albert Plummer, brothers who ran an engineering firm. They took the young Micky under their wing, and they drilled into him some of the finer points of the adult game. All three of them, in time, would become godfathers to his two boys.

In winter there was no footballing equivalent of West Surrey for his Sundays. Clubs within the jurisdiction of the Football Association were banned from playing on the Sabbath so he continued, as he did through his last three winters at school, to play for Minden and, when they folded up, again for Parkside Rovers. "The gap I had to bridge if I was to play professional football was far, far greater than it was with my cricket."

An outstanding season's cricket in 1948 led to his selection for the Young Amateurs of Surrey. The previous summer he had 'played hooky' from school to watch Surrey play Old England at the Oval, now he was stepping out onto the great field to play a two-day match against the Young Amateurs of Middlesex. It was his first encounter with the irascible and somewhat eccentric Surrey Secretary Brian Castor.

"We were in the field, getting smashed all over the place. After one over had gone for about twelve runs, there was a click on the tannoy and a voice said, 'Stop the game. I'm coming out.' We waited, and out came Brian Castor with his monocle, calling our captain over. 'I shall place the field,' he said and proceeded to move us all around. Then he turned to the umpire. 'I'm going to stand out here beside you. Do you have any objections?' As the umpire was getting his expenses signed off by him, he couldn't say much. 'Right,' Brian Castor said at the end of the over. 'Keep it like that.' And off he walked."

Towards the end of the summer Micky made some runs for West Surrey against Malden Wanderers, whose captain Vic Ransom played occasionally as an amateur for Hampshire. "Would you like a game of cricket next week?" he asked Micky. "Hampshire second eleven are playing Sussex."

"I went down to Bournemouth with him and stayed at the Station Hotel. I'd never stayed in a hotel in my life before. And I played in the match. On the Hampshire side there was Neil McCorkell, Arthur Holt, Tom Dean. Sussex were captained by Patsy Hendren, he was their coach, and they had a young Alan Oakman and David Sheppard. I got 0 and 5, I think, and we lost the match."

As he packed his bag in the dressing room the Hampshire Secretary, Desmond Eagar, approached him. "I've heard all about you from Vic. We'd like you to join our staff."

"What do you mean, Mr Eagar?"

"Vic said you were looking to play."

Micky was taken aback. He had scored 0 and 5 and had no idea that he was on trial. "No, no," he said. "I just came down for a game of cricket."

"They had to pay my train fare and my hotel. I don't think Desmond Eagar was very pleased."

In the winter there was more glory on the football field, the highlight the school's 7-2 victory in January over a side put out by the prestigious amateur club Corinthian-Casuals. The Casuals were full of praise for the Alleyn's team, voting them 'The Best Soccer School'.

In the summer term of 1949 Micky became captain of cricket, and in August he was back at Lord's, playing for Southern Schools against the Rest. "Geoffrey Charnley never stopped trying to get me opportunities." In the two-day game he and a boy from Tonbridge, Colin Cowdrey, put on more than 100 for the third wicket, as a result of which they were both selected to represent the Public Schools against the Combined Services.

"Colin didn't possess the most athletic figure, but he was a fine player, a perfect example of how you can play the ball with very little effort, just on timing. Very nice to watch."

A school match at Alleyn's
Micky runs in to score, but the cross from his friend Bob Bedford is too long

In the winter of 1949/50 Micky was captain of football, and the school had an outstanding season. Micky was the principal goal-scorer, and he was selected to represent the Public Schools against Corinthian-Casuals.

"Once a week that winter we had some FA coaches at school. One was Ted Gaskell, the Brentford goalkeeper, a lovely fellow who finished up later as manager at Hendon. He was always ringing me, trying to get me to play for them. We worked on some of the basic skills such as screening the ball or striking it in the middle or the lower half. Technically I had a bit more coaching at football than I did at cricket."

Another of the coaches was Johnny Paton, a Scottish winger who also played at Brentford. He took Micky's father aside after one match: "You don't want to worry about his not making the grade at cricket," he said, "because he'll always make it at football."

One morning, as Micky walked uphill to school, a man on a bicycle appeared at his side. It was Bill 'Robbie' Roberts, trainer at Wimbledon, one of the top amateur clubs, and after several such meetings he persuaded

Micky to join them. At first he played on the 'A' team, then the reserves, but within a year or so he was in their first eleven.

In spring 1950 Micky played on a midweek afternoon for the London Schools Representative XI against the Provinces at Highbury, and he had a good game. Among those watching were Tom Whittaker, the Arsenal manager, and Jimmy Logie, the club's inside-right, a Scottish international in the same mould as Micky: short of stature and quick-footed. Logie was impressed by what he saw, and after the game a message came to Micky: "Tom Whittaker would like to see you." He went up to his office through the marbled hall and, with his father also present, he agreed to go onto Arsenal's books as an amateur.

Should he look to become a professional footballer in due course? Or should he aim to play his football as an amateur, as some still did in the immediate post-war years? One at Arsenal was Kevin O'Flanagan, a general practitioner in Ruislip, who remained an amateur so that he could also play rugby union for London Irish. Another was Bernard Joy, a schoolteacher who became a journalist, the last amateur footballer to play for the full England team.

At home the discussions grew intense. Micky had visited Oxford University, where a place at Worcester College was on offer if he stayed at school for a further year and passed the Higher School Certificate. An Alleyn's Old Boy Jimmy Crisp, a football blue, was at Worcester College, as was Donald Carr, also a football blue and that summer's captain of cricket.

Micky's parents wanted him to go to university, as did Geoffrey Charnley, his cricket master, who worked out all the pros and cons of the professional and amateur routes into cricket and football. Then there was William Comben Longstaff and his offer of a job post-university in shipping. So the decision was made. He would apply for deferral of his National Service, spend an extra year at school and go to Oxford.

His father was a confident man in company, always at ease when he talked to the masters at Alleyn's, but he had no direct experience of universities. Nevertheless he knew that they offered a path to a successful life. He also knew what he thought about 'shamateur' sportsmen, cricketers and footballers who enjoyed the kudos of amateur status but were given surreptitious payments or set up with phoney jobs. "If you play as a pro, Mick," he said emphatically, "I shall give you every support. But if you take a penny as an amateur, I'll sling you out of the house."

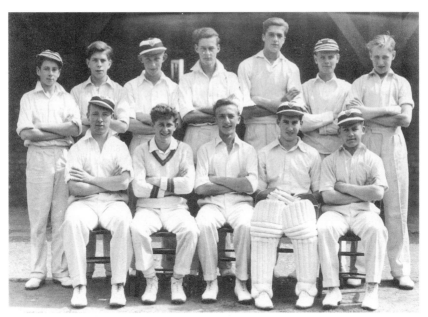

Alleyn's 1st XI, 1949
Micky (captain) is sitting in the centre
John Pretlove is sitting, second from left
David Palastanga is standing, third from right

Parkside Rovers football team
Micky is kneeling, front left
John Mansfield is standing, fourth from right

Several times in the Easter holiday Micky went up to Highbury to train. He remembers the full back John Chenhall borrowing his training shirt. "You train in this?" the professional said to him. "This is better than the best shirt I wear on Sundays." He also remembers Alex Forbes, the red-haired Scottish international who was recovering from injury, building up his stamina by running round and round the pitch. "That really impressed me. I was never much of a one for long-distance running, not unless there was a ball at the end of it. But after that I went back to school and three times the following week I did twenty laps round the pitch."

The summer term of 1950 brought more cricketing success, with Micky topping the school batting averages for the fourth successive year. They won 13 and lost only two matches, though there was no opportunity to take on Dulwich College. "With John Pretlove and David Palastanga, and some of the others, we'd have beaten them easily in my last two years. But they didn't play us. They didn't think we were good enough."

Again he was selected for the Southern Schools against the Rest, scoring 79 and 24 not out, then for the Public Schools against Combined Services where he was outshone by Colin Cowdrey, who made 126 not out and 55. They were, in the judgement of EM Wellings in *Wisden*, the two outstanding schoolboy cricketers of 1950. Stewart, he wrote, 'revealed good strokes in all directions, and in several seasons would have been considered the leading batsman of the year. Stewart should regard being second to such a batsman as Cowdrey a more honourable position than number one in a lean year.'

Micky only discovered this passage recently, and his response to it was immediate. "Second to Cowdrey? It's a good job my Dad didn't read that. That wouldn't have satisfied him at all."

Micky returned to school for the Christmas term, embarking on a year's study that would lead him to Oxford, but by this stage he was having doubts. His cricket had made such a leap forward – at Alleyn's, at West Surrey and with the Surrey Young Amateurs – and he was starting to think he might prefer to take the more direct route into the county game: to forget university and start his two years of National Service.

He captained the football team again. They wanted to have 'an attack like the Spurs and a defence like the Arsenal', and in the first three matches they scored 30 goals and conceded only four. Such was their reputation that they received the rare accolade of having a *Times* reporter attend their home match on 30 November against Brentwood, their arch rivals.

A disjointed first-half performance left them 1-0 down, but they were a different side after the interval :

For the second half Alleyn's had buckled the armour and sounded the trumpet for within ten minutes they had scored three goals ... Individualism gave way to team work, and results were soon forthcoming. Pater and Pretlove, particularly, made the right wing a force to be reckoned with, and Stewart, at inside-left, played as well and unobtrusively as ever, his positioning and unselfishness making him a joy to watch.

They won 6-4, and Pater, Pretlove and Micky were all selected for a Public Schools XI that played at the Oval, on a pitch that ran across the outfield in front of the Vauxhall Stand. Their captain was Charterhouse's John May, younger brother of Peter, and they surprised everybody by drawing 2-2 with a strong FA Youth XI that featured a 15-year-old Johnny Haynes, the future England captain. Once more the *Times* reporter was impressed by Micky, his footwork and his positional sense.

Micky decided not to go to Oxford but to play his cricket as a professional, a decision that his father accepted. "If you do play as a professional," he told Micky, "you'll know for sure that you're worth a place in the side."

He left school at Christmas, returning in January for one last game of football. "We won 2-1, and I scored the winner."

*

Our afternoon at Alleyn's is over. The pupils are streaming out of their classes, and I have a train to catch.

"This is where the quadrangle was," Micky says. "I can still picture myself after we won that game 2-1. I was captain of football, and I'd scored the winner in my last game. I swaggered across this quad, with all the youngsters watching, and inside 48 hours I was climbing out of an army lorry to start my National Service. We got to the camp, and I put all my gear on my bed, including a little holdall with my football boots in it. They were still damp from the match at school."

As he pulled his boots out of the bag, a voice behind him spoke.

"What have you got there, Sapper?"

He turned to face a big man with three stripes on his arm.

"Football boots."

"That's 'Football boots, *Sergeant*' to you, Sapper. What are they?"

"Football boots, Sergeant."

"Well, let me tell you this, son. When I get you to Korea, I want you to stick a bleeding great bayonet in, not kick 'em to death with football boots. Do you understand me, Sapper?"

"Yes, Sergeant."

4

I NEVER THOUGHT ABOUT FAILING

Micky's intention had been to undergo his National Service in the Royal Air Force, but a chance encounter on the cricket field changed his thinking.

It was late in the summer of 1950, just as he was starting to change his mind about staying at school and going to Oxford. He scored a century in a Club Cricket Conference trial match at the Barclays Bank ground in Norbury, an innings that impressed his captain, R.T. Bryan, a 52-year-old banker who had skippered Kent before the war.

"What are you going to do when you leave school?" he asked.

Micky outlined the two options he was considering.

"And what about National Service?"

"I thought I might go into the RAF."

"Well, if you join the Royal Engineers, I can get you some cricket."

The banker's younger brother, Colonel G.J. Bryan, was captain of the Army side, and it was all arranged. In January 1951, at the age of 18, Micky arrived for 14 weeks of basic training at the Royal Engineers' Guillemont Barracks in the village of Cove, near Farnborough, on the Surrey/Hampshire border.

He had made his choice. He would do his two years of National Service, then become a professional sportsman.

Or had he? Within a fortnight of arriving at barracks, after a round of tests and interviews, he was being told that the War Office Selection Board had identified him as potential officer material. So a fresh dilemma presented itself: if he signed up for officer training, he was advised, there was no way that he would be given time off to play cricket. The training of officers was far too expensive a business.

He wrote to Sheila: 'What do you reckon I ought to do?' Then a week later, in a letter full of moans – an arm stiff from inoculations, a stomach still hungry after a miserable tea ('spaghetti on dry toast, which I detest') and a long day of shooting practice in 'wind that cut through you' and 'rain that was thrashing down' – he told her the outcome of his deliberations:

> I've decided to stay in the R.E.s and give up the idea of a commission. I hope I've decided correctly.

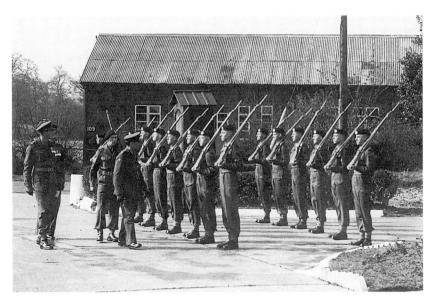

On parade at Cove

Already, however, he was discovering the perks that came with being a talented sportsman. His mornings started with training with the regiment's football squad; this allowed him to get up half an hour later than the others, to enjoy a larger breakfast and to miss the first drill period.

In March came a letter from Brian Castor, inviting him to play in Surrey's first trial match of the summer, a two-day game spread across a Saturday and Monday. He expressed his delight in a letter to Sheila:

> *Cor! Was I pleased. Just think, batting against Alec Bedser or fielding while Laurie Fishlock or Jack Parker were batting.*

Full of excitement, he applied to his Party Officer for leave, but he did not get the reply he was expecting. Only in exceptional circumstances could recruits on training be granted extra leave, and he did not think the Commanding Officer would see this request as exceptional.

> *To top it all he asked if the Saturday alone would do. As though you could play in half of a two-day match. One of those people who know nothing about cricket whatsoever. What flippin' luck – to have him as a Party Officer.*

Despite this, the Commanding Officer did grant him leave, and on the Saturday evening of the match Micky found himself at the wicket with Jack Parker, the veteran all-rounder who had started out in the early 1930s when Hobbs and Sandham were still opening the Surrey batting.

"I went in at four or five. There were only a couple of overs till the end of the day, and I called him for a quick run to get off the mark. Arthur McIntyre, who was keeping wicket for the other team, used to be brilliant at kidding batsmen that the ball was coming in. 'Yes, we've got him,' he shouted, and Jack had to take off and dive into the crease. Mac was laughing his socks off. Jack was covered in dirt, and he came down to me: 'Here, do you think I'm one of those greyhounds your dad backs at Wimbledon?'"

Services cricket took priority over Surrey second eleven, and Micky soon found himself playing for the Army against Oxford University at The Parks. His captain, Colonel Bryan, had set up this life of cricket for him, but he was not so happy with his young charge at teatime on the first day.

"In the last over before the break I played back to this left-arm spinner. It was a rain-affected wicket, and the ball came up and just flicked my glove. Frank Chester was the umpire, and he said 'Not out'. Five minutes later I'm taking my pads off for tea, and in comes Godfrey Bryan."

"Wait here a minute, will you, Stewart? I've just come from the Oxford dressing room. Did you hit that ball?"

"No, sir. It just flicked my glove."

"Well, why didn't you walk?"

"But the umpire said 'Not out'."

"But you knew it had gloved you."

It was a black mark in his first game for the Army. "In spite of all the teaching I'd had from Geoffrey Charnley at school, I'd never heard of walking. But I soon found out. All the pros in the Army and Combined Services sides were walkers. If somebody didn't walk, there was hell to pay."

A second black mark followed when they went into the field. "I was running down to the boundary to stop this ball. There was nobody watching hardly, but they had seats close to the line. If I'd run straight at the ball, I'd have finished up in the seats. So I came at the ball at an angle and kicked it along the line, then picked it up and threw it in."

This time the rebuke came from the second officer in the side, Major Howard-Jones: "You don't field a ball with a boot, young man," he barked.

Shortly afterwards Micky was at the Gover/Sandham cricket school. "You'd better brush up on your fielding, old boy," Alf Gover told him. "You've had a bad report."

The star of the Army side that summer was Signalman Brian Close, home from a winter in which he had toured Australia with the full England side. He scored an unbeaten 96 at The Parks, 135 for the Combined Services against the touring South Africans at Portsmouth and 134 against the Royal Navy at Lord's.

"The Secretary of the Army Cricket Association, Lieutenant-Colonel Kilgour, used to hand out the money. A lovely man. He gave us the expenses forms on the first day, then at the end of the match he would pay us out of a kitty."

The team all soon realised that there would be no kitty to be paid from if they did not get in ahead of their Yorkshire team-mate.

"Now, Brian," Kilgour would protest. "You are claiming a first-class train fare from Sandhurst to London. I've told you it's only command officers who have a first-class train fare."

"But I did get a hundred, didn't I?"

"And why on earth have you gone via Leeds?"

"Well, I didn't have any clean shirts."

Another contemporary was M.J.K. Smith, who played with Micky for Aldershot Services. Surprisingly, in light of his later success in first-class and Test cricket, he was never selected for the Army side.

For Micky the summer of 1951 was one that was filled with cricket – for the regiment, the Royal Engineers, the Aldershot Services, the Army and the Combined Services. There was only one match that he involuntarily missed.

"We played Cambridge University at Sandhurst, and the next game was against the British Army of the Rhine at the Officers' Club at Aldershot. I used to play there regularly. Colonel Kilgour read out the side, and I wasn't included. I said, 'Why aren't I playing?' He said, 'You're not released.' The CO of the regiment loved me playing, but he was away and the second-in-command hated it. He said it was the annual admin inspection and nobody was allowed off."

Back at base the second-in-command sent for him. "I want you to know, Stewart, that I expect you and all your equipment to be in tip-top condition, the same as everybody else's. Don't think that just because you're playing cricket all the time you're going to get special treatment. Do you understand?"

"Yes, sir."

Frantically Micky dug out all his equipment, kit that had not seen the light of day all summer. "I had to lob out two-bobs and half-crowns to all my mates to get it cleaned in time."

Come the day he stood on parade, with everything immaculately laid out on a blanket in front of him. "And who should be inspecting us but the chairman of the Aldershot Services Club? He walked past me, then stopped, came back and looked at me. 'Why aren't you at the club, Michael?' 'Annual admin inspection, sir.' He turned round to the second-in-command. 'We need to have a word about this.'"

Aldershot Services Cricket XI
Micky, front left; Keith Andrew, front right
Standing, third from left, is Maurice Reeves, whose furniture store
in Croydon was burnt down during the riots of summer 2011

The following summer presented more cricketing opportunities. Micky scored 94 against Cambridge University at Fenner's, facing the fast but erratic bowling of the South African Cuan McCarthy, whose quickest ball was the subject of mutterings on the circuit. "During that innings at Fenner's I remember thinking, 'He threw that.' That was the first time anything had ever come into my mind about throwing."

At this stage Micky had been promoted to Lance-Corporal: Acting Unpaid Lance-Corporal, to be precise. It was the only way he could be allowed into the mess when he played at Catterick. But later in the month, in the *Wisden* scorecard for a match at Gillingham between the Combined Services and the touring Indians, he was back to Sapper Stewart.

Five of that eleven at Gillingham – Fred Trueman, Ray Illingworth, Jim Parks, Keith Andrew and Micky – would go on to play Test cricket, though the one to make the greatest mark on this match, in more ways than one, was the young Gloucestershire off-spinner 'Bomber' Wells. With his one-pace run-up and quicker-than-expected delivery he bemused the Indian batsmen on the first day, taking five wickets, but as always he found time for a joke.

"He was stationed in the company stores, and a consignment of new army blankets had gone missing. They thought some guy had shovelled them onto a lorry out the back. So there was an investigation, and the military police turned up during the match to interview Bomber. Alan Shirreff was captain. Bomber was bowling at one end and, while Fred was bowling his over at the other, the police spoke to Bomber down on the fine leg boundary. 'Can we have a word with you at tea?' And Bomber said to them, 'I'll tell you what. We can do better than that. I'll bowl this over, then you come on and march me off.'"

In front of a large crowd the arrest was enacted, all behind the back of Alan Shirreff at slip. Eventually, hearing the noise, he turned round. "Where's he gone? Come back."

Bomber's clowning was also to the fore when they went on a cricket trip to Germany. On the way out he and two others bought large water pistols and, as the coach pulled into the base, they crouched down behind the door. The door swung open, and immediately they opened fire, drenching a welcoming party which had at the front, in a double-breasted blazer, the Head of the British Army of the Rhine.

"Fortunately," Micky said, "he had a sense of humour."

Towards the end of Micky's second summer of National Service, still stationed at Cove, he played a two-day game for the Royal Engineers against the Yellowhammers, a Kent team comprised mainly of old boys of Tonbridge School. He scored a century in each innings, and this immediately interested the Yellowhammers captain, Bryan Valentine, a former Kent captain who had heard that Micky was wanting to play as a professional.

"Where do you live?" he asked Micky.

"Between Dulwich and Herne Hill."

"Herne Hill? That's in Kent."

"No, it's in Surrey."

"Well, have Surrey said they want you to play for them?"

"No, they haven't said anything."

"Well, if Surrey aren't interested, would you be interested in playing for Kent?"

"I haven't thought about it. Yes, if Surrey aren't interested, I suppose, well, yes."

Later that week, he was padding up to bat for the Army against the Royal Navy at Lord's, and bursting into the room, ignoring the notice on the door 'Entry only allowed with the permission of the captain', came Brian Castor, the Surrey Secretary.

"Michael, what's all this I hear about you wanting to play for Kent?"

"I don't, Mr Castor, I'd like to play for Surrey."

"I've had Mr Valentine on. He says you want to play for Kent. And what's this about your wanting to play as a professional?"

"That's right, Mr Castor."

"But you went to a public school … Anyway, I've brought the contract. You can sign it now."

"I'm going out to bat soon. And, before I do anything, I'd like to show it to my father."

"Well, don't take too long over it."

As Brian Castor handed it over, Micky, glancing down, spotted the words 'six pounds'. He remembered what he had been told: "If you've played first-class cricket in the services, you get eight pounds a week."

"Shouldn't that be eight pounds, Mr Castor? I've played first-class cricket."

In fact, he had not. Unusually the Combined Services game against the Indians, though three-day, had not been classified as first-class. But Castor did not know this, and he was in no mood to deal with such a detail.

"I hope we're not signing a barrack-room lawyer," he said as he left.

*

It was early April of the following year, 1953, a week before the Surrey players reported for pre-season training, when Micky finally arrived at Brian Castor's office with the contract.

He had left the army in January and was spending the rest of the winter working for the engineering firm in Wimbledon run by the Plummer brothers of West Surrey Cricket Club. "They made tools for the car industry. I used to do all sorts: dipping the tools into particular solutions, putting them in the van and driving them to the finishing company. A lot of general office work. On one occasion I had to drive a lathe worker to hospital with part of his finger in a matchbox. They used to stitch them back on."

He stood in the Surrey Secretary's office, ready to sign the contract, when Peter May appeared. May, who played as an amateur and was already established in the England team, was three years older than Micky, but by this time the two of them knew each other quite well.

"Welcome to the Oval, Micky. Good luck in your career."

"Thank you, Peter."

Then Micky signed his contract and handed it to the Surrey Secretary.

"I won't be here tomorrow, Brian," Peter May said. "I've got to go up to the office in the City."

"Right you are, Peter."

"All the best to you, Micky. See you next week."

"Cheerio, Peter."

"You mean Mr May," Brian Castor interjected. "You're a professional cricketer now."

It was the other way round when he reported for training the next week. The first time he addressed Alec Bedser he called him Mr Bedser. Back came the gruff reply: "Call me Alec, same as everybody else."

Micky was 20 years old, setting out on the career that he had dreamed of since the age of seven or eight, and he had no internal doubts – though such was the strength of that Surrey side that he knew it would be harder to gain a place than if he had gone to Kent.

"I never thought about failing. When I signed I said to Brian Castor, 'I'm giving myself three years to get into the first team. If by then I'm not in, I'll want to go and play elsewhere – because I want to play for England.'"

"You do realise," Castor replied, "that Patsy Hendren didn't play for England till he was 31."

Micky's was confident talk – but, if the words of former Surrey captain Monty Garland-Wells are to be taken seriously, he came within one ball of having his contract ended after only three weeks, not three years.

Garland-Wells was a larger-than-life character who had captained Surrey with some success before the war. By this time his cricket was confined to social games at high-class venues, at one of which – at Sir Humphrey de Trafford's estate near Newmarket – Micky found himself making up numbers.

"Brian Castor summoned me to his office. He told me to report to Monty Garland-Wells' flat in Knightsbridge early on Sunday morning. We got driven up by a chauffeur and, when we arrived, everybody was in this ornate marquee. Eventually the match started, we fielded and wickets fell. Then with an over or two to go to lunch Monty Garland-Wells called across to me: 'Come and have a bowl, Stewart.' I came up, bowled straight, and this bloke missed it. And in came this fairly aged fellow, with these old pads with struts. Monty Garland-Wells came across. 'This is our host, Sir Humphrey de Trafford,' he said. 'If you get him out before lunch, I'm telling you now, your contract will be the shortest there's ever been in the history of the Surrey County Cricket Club.'"

At pre-season nets at the Oval the first-teamers practised on the side of the ground beside the Archbishop Tenison School, the second-teamers by the gasometer. The 62-year-old Andrew Sandham, scorer of 107 first-class centuries, was the coach, always wearing his England sweater, and he moved back and forth between the two nets.

"On the first day I remember watching Alan Brazier and Ronnie Pratt batting in the second-team net, and I was thinking, 'Am I as good as them?' Then suddenly someone said, 'Watch it, the Little Man's on his way over.' And, as soon as Andrew Sandham arrived, instead of continuing to bat fluently, they were nervously playing and missing."

Sandham had a great influence on Micky's early development, turning him immediately into an opening batsman. "He was very good on how you put runs together, how you summed up the pitch conditions, how you went about your batting. He was a little man, and he'd been a good puller and hooker, a good cutter as well. So was I. So he knew my game. But I'd always read that Don Bradman hooked the ball down so I was trying to do the same. In my first innings for the second eleven, against Middlesex, I got to 90, and I holed out at mid-wicket. The ball got a bit high on my bat, and I was trying to keep it down. He said to me, 'Why didn't you hit that over his head? There's nothing wrong with clearing him.' Another time he said, 'Wait until you've got 100 before you make room to cut – or you'll drag it on. And don't cut balls coming into you.' They were things I'd never heard before."

In a Club and Ground game at Epsom Micky faced an in-swing bowler Fred Monroe who, with no restrictions at that time, packed his legside field. When the ball swung down leg, Micky repeatedly left it. He had reached a score of about 70 when Andrew Sandham arrived.

"He was down at the sight screen, as always with his brown trilby hat, raincoat over his arm and the *Daily Telegraph*. He used to do the crossword. A couple of times I let the ball go, and he started waving his arm at me. At lunch he came in: 'Why are you ignoring all these boundary opportunities on the legside? … Forget about the fielders. You should play them.' I got another 30 or 40, and I got caught down at deep square leg. I was taking my pads off, and I heard him coming down the corridor. 'I suppose you blame that on me, Michael,' he said, 'and you'd be right.' Then he walked out."

Sandham was a hard man from an older school. He had a good sense of humour, but it never interfered with the discipline he instilled. "He quite liked me. He thought I could play – though you'd never know it."

In most weeks there were three or four Club and Ground games, held around the clubs in Surrey, but there were so many players on the staff, over thirty if you included the amateurs, that people had to take it in turns to play.

"The first time I dropped out I had to score. It was against Wimbledon. I had to go to the Oval to pick up the scorebook, the flag and the expenses to be paid to the amateurs. Then I had to get down to Wimbledon Cricket Club, all on public transport. I got home about half past nine in the evening, and I'd no sooner sat down than the doorbell rang. My mother went to the door, and there was a telegram: FLAG STILL UP POLE AT WIMBLEDON. GET IT. CASTOR."

By August the runs were flowing from his bat: 143 against Wiltshire at Swindon, 126 against Devon at Guildford. "I got 3,000 runs that summer – for the second eleven, for the Club and Ground and for West Surrey."

Did somebody add them up then? "Yes, I did."

In the Minor Counties Championship Micky scored 659 runs at an average of 41.18, though such was the depth of talent at the Oval that this only placed him fourth in their batting averages behind Dennis Cox, Ronnie Pratt and Ken Barrington.

The first eleven had won the championship the previous year and, despite the retirement of Jack Parker and Laurie Fishlock, they retained it in 1953, becoming the first county to win in two successive years since the war. Much of their success stemmed from an outstanding bowling attack – Jim Laker and Tony Lock, Alec Bedser, Peter Loader and the skipper Stuart Surridge – but they also had batsmen who could score the necessary runs: pre-eminently Peter May but also Bernie Constable, Tom Clark, David Fletcher, Eric Bedser and, after the end of his university term, Raman Subba Row. With Arthur McIntyre behind the stumps, it was a fairly settled side. Ronnie Pratt and Ken Barrington had brief runs in the first eleven, but there was no such promotion for Micky. Not yet.

In late June Surrey had a week away from championship cricket, playing Oxford and Cambridge Universities, and a rumour circulated that John Pretlove, Micky's former team-mate at Alleyn's, was going to be drafted in. "It was purely because he was an amateur. Maybe a potential captain of Surrey. I was not at all happy. I knew I'd always been a better player than him. So I let it be known that, if he played, I'd be off."

The step from second to first eleven, particularly at Surrey, was a great one. "If somebody had asked me after I'd been playing for a bit, 'What's first-class cricket like?' I'd have said, 'You do the same things as in school and club cricket, but the pace bowlers are quicker, the ball swings more and the control of swing is greater; the spin bowlers spin it more and, although they have flight, they are quicker, too. And when you've got used to all that, you still don't have as many scoring opportunities.' With the bowlers, accuracy was absolutely key. You wouldn't get into the Surrey side unless you were capable of bowling a maiden over."

Derek Pratt, Ronnie's brother, bowled leg-breaks, playing one of his first games for the first eleven at Hastings when Laker and Lock were on Test duty. "His first ball, against Jim Parks, was fractionally over-pitched, and Jim got down and timed it through the gap between extra cover and mid-off, all the way for four. Stuey Surridge went mad. 'This is not the f---ing second eleven now,' he shouted at him. If you were at all delicate or sensitive, you'd had it. But if you could get through all that, it stood you in good stead."

Geoff Kirby, the reserve keeper in Micky's first summer on the staff, employed the tactic of humour on his rare appearances in the first team. A brilliant mimic, he kept relaxed by impersonating his team-mates. "It was before my time," Micky says, "but after one game when he'd had a nightmare session behind the stumps Stan Squires sat him down. 'I've got a suggestion you might consider, Kirbs,' he said. 'Next time why don't you try impersonating a wicket-keeper?'"

"It was a tough environment. If somebody was nervous and didn't produce, they'd just say, 'He's got all the ability in the world but his heart's like a pea.' He was just written off. There was never any discussion about how you could bring out his ability, his self-belief."

*

On Wednesday 14 July 1954 Micky's turn finally came. An overcast morning at the Oval, with grass on the pitch. Batting first against Gloucestershire, Surrey were soon 5 for two – Subba Row, caught Wilson bowled McHugh 0, Clark caught Cook bowled McHugh 1 – and the fair-haired newcomer found himself walking to the wicket. Now he had to show that he had the heart, that he could produce.

"I had been absolutely wrapped in the game since I was a kid. I knew all the Surrey players, knew the history. So, come the moment, it was very emotional – but I had to make sure that the emotion did not affect me physically."

The Surrey batting that summer had been a disappointment, so much so that they had slipped to eighth place in the championship table and seemed too far behind the leaders to complete a hat-trick of titles. With over half the county programme completed, Yorkshire had won ten games, Warwickshire nine and Surrey just five. So, with Peter May playing for the Gentlemen against the Players at Lord's, the county shuffled the pack, bringing in Micky alongside a returning Ken Barrington.

Waiting to bowl was Frank McHugh, a Yorkshireman who had just won his county cap for Gloucestershire. "He was tall and bouncy, and in conditions like that he could be quite fast. Early in my innings he dropped one short, I went to hook and I clipped the ball onto my head. And I hit the deck. It's the first time I'd ever been hit on the head by the ball."

Gloucestershire's George Emmett, another short man who liked to cut and hook, bent over the youngster. "Are you all right? Are you sure? … Well, don't stop playing the shot. People of our size have got to keep hooking."

Micky picked himself up and batted on, making 52 before being caught in the slips off McHugh. Then Ken Barrington hit his maiden century, and Jim Laker weighed in with his first and only championship hundred.

On the final morning, in the chase for quick runs, Micky was bowled by McHugh for 6: "I played loosely. I wasn't happy with the way I approached it mentally. I got bowled driving, and I was never a great driver from the crease." However, his part in the game was far from over. Gloucestershire were set a target of 224 in 145 minutes, and they were soon in trouble.

"It was the first time I'd ever been on the field in a competitive match with Stuey Surridge. I hadn't even done twelfth man duties. There was a fellow called Johnny Jones on the staff. He'd played football on the wing for Millwall and Fulham, and he was quick, an excellent outfielder, so he was always doing it. Ronnie and Derek Pratt and Alan Brazier used to moan about it, because you got match money as twelfth man."

In the heat of battle Surridge was an enormous presence, loud, demonstrative and intolerant of his own team's failings, and there was chatter all round the wicket.

Michael Stewart will remember his first-team début for Surrey. You see him, above, knocked out in trying to hook Gloucestershire pace-bowler McHugh. But he recovered, to reach 52.

*Two scenes from Micky's debut innings
(top) Felled by Frank McHugh
(bottom) A stroke to leg
Andy Wilson is the keeper, George Emmett at slip*

"What you got him over here for?" would come the Cockney chirp of Bernie Constable in the covers, querying the skipper's field placings. "You don't need as many as this on the off-side."

"Be quiet, Bernie."

"Better give him a pack of cards for something to do. Nothing will go there."

Then, when Alec Bedser was bowling, his twin Eric would start up at mid-on. "You want to get another in there, square."

"No, I don't."

"You do. Go on."

"Who's f---ing bowling, you or me?"

If it intimidated some second-teamers coming up, it did not have that effect on Micky – "It suited me all right" – and he was soon in the action, dismissing both Gloucestershire openers with turn-and-throw run-outs from square leg. Then, with Jim Laker bowling, he held two sharp catches at short leg – 'dazzling', *Wisden* called them. Laker took six for 20 in 15 overs, Gloucestershire were all out for 78, and Surrey's little run of failure was over.

"Everything turned to gold for me. As far as Stuey was concerned, right from the start I was the blue-eyed boy."

The next game, against the touring Pakistanis, brought even greater success. Rain washed out most of Saturday, and the Pakistanis batted through Monday, from which Micky's only memory is of fielding in the covers next to Bernie Constable. Three balls in a row were hit to the side of Micky, and he dived and stopped each one.

"What are you doing?" came the Cockney chirp. "What's all this diving business?"

"I'm stopping the ball."

"You can't afford to do that. I know how much you earn. It costs three and six to get your flannels cleaned."

"I was brought up," Micky remembers, "that if you grassed your flannels you weren't allowed to go out in them for the next session. You were supposed to put on a clean pair. But you learned to wet a cloth and put on talcum powder."

Surrey did not bat till Tuesday morning, when Micky was promoted to open the innings with Tom Clark, a former Aston Villa footballer who took the youngster under his wing. "He was very helpful to me. He'd tell me about all the bowlers. If we were playing Derbyshire, he'd say to me,

'Now you haven't played Jackson before. He's a bit different. He's got a low arm, and he nips the ball back like crazy."'

It did not always prove good advice, however, as Micky discovered when he faced Statham for the first time at Old Trafford. "Tom had told me he brought it in. I took strike. The first ball went away like a rocket, and I edged it to the keeper."

On the final day of each match, wherever they were playing, Clark could be relied upon to tell them from memory the departure times of the next trains, as if he were a walking *Bradshaw's Railway Guide*. He was also a constant source of facts from cricket's history, earning himself the name of Thomas Henry Wisden Bradshaw Clark. "He was a cricketer through and through," Micky says. "He liked his jazz, too. When we walked out to bat, he used to whistle this number *Lemon Drop*. And I tried to join in."

Against Pakistan they put on 82 before Clark fell for 33. Then came Ken Barrington, and the two newcomers to the side were soon at ease. "It was a good batting pitch. The pitches for the tourists, they generally prepared them differently from what they did for the county matches. And I played exactly the same way I would have played for West Surrey or the second eleven. There was quite a bit of spin bowled, and I was a good player of spin."

In mid-afternoon he was in his 90s, and Ken Barrington came down to him, with all the experience of his one first-class century. "Don't do anything silly," he said.

The significance of their performances was not lost on the correspondent who reported the game for *The Times*:

> *Surrey, in a drawn match against Pakistan, at last found the missing link in their early batting when yesterday at the Oval, too late for this year as many will think, two young players, Stewart and Barrington, each made a century. Each had been struggling for a place in the championship county side, Stewart with an innings of 50 in his only previous trial to suggest more to come, and Barrington with much success in minor county affairs behind him. … Stewart is already accomplished. He has supple wrists and he uses his feet, so that in this way would-be spinners were made into full pitches. His on drives brought him many runs, and several shorter balls were square cut beyond the range of fieldsmen.*

The next morning Micky was again opening the innings with Tom Clark, this time at Colchester. "A green wicket. A lot of wickets were green in Essex in those days. You had to play the ball late because it swung, and you didn't have to go at the ball too hard. Most of the Essex team hadn't seen me play before so they didn't defend the areas where I scored strongly."

Micky and Tom Clark open the innings

Tom Clark made 21 in a first-wicket stand of 34. Then came Bernie Constable, and shortly after his arrival at the wicket Doug Insole the Essex skipper, someone Micky knew well from his amateur football in the winter, surprised everybody by bringing himself on to bowl.

"I didn't know he bowled," Micky said to Bernie Constable. "What does he bowl?"

"Bugger all. You don't want to worry about him. He can't bowl."

Wisden records the outcome:

B. Constable   ct Dodds b Insole, 6   ct Preston b Insole, 6

Fletcher, Subba Row and Barrington all went for single-figure scores but, at 123 for five, when Arthur McIntyre arrived at the wicket, Micky was into his 80s. In no time he was closing on his hundred, his first in the championship, and Arthur Mac came down the wicket to him. "Now don't be nervous," he counselled. "Just play normally and the hundred will come."

In the next over there was a "yes-no-yes" from Mac, and Micky was diving for his ground in panic. "He nearly ran me out twice. I think he was more nervous for me than I was for myself. In the end I chipped a ball wide of mid-on. A more agile fielder than Jack Bailey would probably have caught it. And we scampered the single."

Alas, in Essex's reply, Micky blotted his copybook. When a chance flew into the slips, both he and Ken Barrington left it to the other to catch. "Stuey Surridge was bowling, and his reaction was still going on half an hour later."

In the second innings he was bowled by an in-swinging yorker from Ken Preston for 21. Then on the Saturday, against Kent at Blackheath, he hit a free-scoring 66 before being caught at mid-wicket. "If I'd listened to Andrew Sandham, it would have been six. I was batting so well. I could have got 100 before lunch."

He had been a county cricketer for just ten days, from 14 to 24 July, and in six innings he had scored 388 runs, with two centuries and two fifties.

That weekend the England selectors sat down to finalise the party for the winter's tour of Australia, and only recently Micky has learned that his name was mentioned briefly in the discussion.

Late on Tuesday afternoon, as the players were packing their bags to leave Blackheath, the tour party was announced on the radio, and there were several ripples of shock in the pavilion, none perhaps greater than the inclusion of a young batsman just leaving the Kent dressing room, Micky's fellow 21-year-old from the Public Schools side of 1950: Colin Cowdrey.

Stewart again: Vital 134

ANOTHER splendid century by 21-year-old Michael Stewart, his second in successive innings, saved Surrey at Colchester.

On an easy-paced pitch Essex took half the champions' wickets for 123 runs, but all the time Stewart stood firm, and in all he stayed 230 minutes for his 134 contribution to Surrey's 229 total.

Most of his 16 fours came from drives; and he used his feet cleverly. His one chance came with the stroke that took him to three figures. Jack Bailey, at mid-on, allowed a ball hit hard and high to pass between his hands.

Two scenes from those triumphant first weeks
(top) Returning to the pavilion at Colchester
(bottom) Hitting out at Blackheath
Maurice Fenner is the Kent keeper

What different paths the two of them had followed in the four years since 1950. Micky had undergone his National Service and had spent a summer and a half as a professional at the Oval, accumulating plentiful runs in the second eleven to force his way into an outstanding Surrey side, a side under Stuart Surridge that had a singular focus: to win the championship.

Colin Cowdrey, by contrast, had stayed at school for a further year and had gone straight into the Kent eleven at the start of the 1951 season. The county was accustomed to bumping along in the lower reaches of the championship, they had a stronger amateur tradition than Surrey, and they stuck by the youngster, even though his first nine matches produced six ducks and a top score of 54.

Cowdrey then had three years at Oxford. When he did finally report for National Service, he was discharged on the grounds that he had stiff joints in his two big toes.

When the selectors sat down in late July 1954 to pick the party for Australia, Micky was playing in only his fourth first-class match, Colin Cowdrey in his 97th. Yet Micky had already scored a championship century, and Cowdrey, in 76 championship innings for Kent, had not. It would be June of the following summer before he would do so, by which time he would have scored a glorious match-winning hundred for England at Melbourne.

Micky is under no illusion. He accepts that Colin Cowdrey was a better player, but the different routes they took into the first-class game did much to shape their later lives in cricket. Yet Micky had come so close to following the same path as Cowdrey. He could have gone to Oxford, he could have played as an amateur; he might even have signed for Kent.

"My life would have been hugely different if I'd gone to Kent to play," he reflects now. "Their cricket was much more of an extension of the school and club cricket that I'd experienced. There wouldn't have been the same intensity as there was at Surrey: the intensity of having to win every session of every match, having to score at the right rate to leave the bowlers the maximum time to take twenty wickets. But I loved the Surrey way; it was a team game. We didn't play for our individual performances; we played to win matches. That's how I was introduced to first-class cricket by Stuey Surridge. I've never looked at the game in any other way."

5

TWINKLE, TWINKLE, LITTLE STAR

At Alleyn's Micky enjoyed his football every bit as much as he enjoyed his cricket, and in time he would play both games professionally. Yet his path into the world of professional football followed a quite different route from that by which he became a professional cricketer.

Both sports had amateurs and professionals. In cricket they played alongside each other in the county teams, though there were certain respects in which they were differentiated. The amateurs changed in a separate dressing room, they had their initials printed ahead of their surnames on the scorecard, and at some counties, for away games, they travelled first-class on the railway and stayed at a different hotel. There was an expectation that Oxbridge graduates would be amateurs, also those who had been to public school, though there were a few exceptions to this including Micky.

It was a legacy of a pre-war world in which amateurism was perceived as an ideal way of life for gentlemen of means, but so much of that had been destroyed by the war and by the long years of austerity that followed. By the 1950s suitable amateurs were not available to captain all the counties, some of which were, with some reluctance, appointing professionals to lead their sides. In other cases a pretence of amateurism was maintained, with non-existent jobs created for university graduates so that they could appear to be playing cricket without any financial reward.

The set-up in football was quite different. It was possible for an amateur footballer to have a full-time job and still to play each Saturday, fitting in two evenings of training during the week. A small number of these amateurs played for top Football League clubs, though they were few in number by the 1950s. For the most part the amateurs played their football in separate leagues, such as the Isthmian and the Athenian in the south-east. The senior amateur clubs all entered the qualifying rounds of the FA Cup, but they also had their own trophy, the FA Amateur Cup. Unlike in cricket, there was a separate England Amateur XI as well as a team that represented Great Britain in the strictly amateur Olympic Games.

In the professional game, where the players were employed full-time, training each day, there was a maximum weekly wage. By 1956 it was £15, with the possibility of small bonuses for winning. In the amateur game it was against the rules to pay anything more than basic expenses. In time, though, Micky would discover that things were not always as they appeared.

*

Throughout his National Service Micky left camp each Saturday in winter to play for Wimbledon. He also played many games at his camp and for the regiment, though he did not progress to the full Army side which was dominated by lads who from the age of 15 had been on the books of the top professional clubs, training every day. As footballers they were physically more advanced than Micky.

As National Service drew to a close, Micky made fresh contact with Tom Whittaker, who was both Secretary and manager at Arsenal. This led to an invitation to him to appear for their London Mid-Week League XI on the afternoon of Monday 13 April 1953.

A letter from Whittaker – 'Dear Michael' – outlined the drill:

> *I wonder if it is possible for you to report at the Stadium at about 12 noon on this date, so that you can have a pre-match meal with other members of the team before departing by coach to Crystal Palace.*
> *The only equipment you will require will be your football boots, so please remember to bring them with you.*

Almost sixty years on, he reads the letter with amazement: 'I wonder if it is possible for you …' "I find that incredible, that he wrote to me like that." But then Micky was a young amateur at this stage. At the Oval, as a professional, it would have been 'Dear Stewart, You will report …'

Micky appeared in three or four such mid-week games for Arsenal, but he was 21 when he played for the last time, nearly four years on from when he had first caught their eye. "I got the dreaded letter," he says. "Well played, they said, but we've got players of similar ability who are three years younger than you."

He continued with Wimbledon, enjoying the happy ambience of the amateur side. 'Doc' Dowden was the manager, an honest, down-to-earth character whose full-time job involved supplying equipment to professional golfers at all the clubs. There was also a trainer, Johnny Price, a friend of the Bedsers from Woking, who led their sessions on Monday and Thursday evenings. There were no floodlights so it was all running and body exercises.

Micky stayed there till the latter end of the winter of 1953/54 when Ted Gaskell, who had coached him once a week at Alleyn's, finally persuaded him to join Hendon in the Athenian League. The main attraction for Micky was that, while Wimbledon played a long-ball game, there was a better quality of passing football at Hendon, with several amateur internationals in the side. As an inside-forward it suited him better.

During Micky's time at Wimbledon, though not for much longer, only bare expenses were paid, and even they were carefully policed. "One time I had to get off at a different railway station, and the fare was sixpence more. 'What's this extra sixpence?' they said. I had to explain it."

That was the way it was supposed to be. It was said that back in the 1930s, when Dulwich Hamlet played an Amateur Cup semi-final match at the Crystal Palace ground, one of their players, Cecil Murray, was detained at work on Saturday morning and consequently missed the team coach. He arrived by taxi shortly before kick-off, playing a key role in their victory, but the club refused to pay his fare.

At Hendon, as at many amateur clubs by the 1950s, the attitude to expenses was quite different. Micky played the final games of the 1953/54 winter, travelling from his work in Wimbledon to all the training sessions and never discussing payment. Then early the following winter the Hendon Secretary came up to him.

"We do appreciate the way you've attended training regularly," he said. "We'll be showing our appreciation by recompensing you."

"If you take a penny as an amateur," his father had told him repeatedly, "I'll sling you out of the house." So Micky, sensing that they were not talking about a few bus fares, had no intention of accepting the money.

That summer he had broken into the Surrey side, performing so well that already the talk was of his playing for England soon. He was a golden prospect, to be nurtured with care, and there were several on the Surrey committee who were uneasy about his winters playing football. Jim Laker, one who worried more than most about injuries, had become a kindly mentor to Micky, and he too suggested that he give up football.

It was a hard decision for Micky. "All through my career I played my football and cricket for the enjoyment of playing, just as I had as a kid. At the end of the cricket season I was looking forward to playing football. At the end of the football I looked forward to the cricket."

A few games into the winter programme, he reached a decision. He would heed Surrey's advice and give up his football. However, expecting that week to receive Hendon's 'recompense' and curious to discover how much it was going to amount to, he delayed telling them till the end of the week.

"Unfortunately it didn't arrive in time. So I never did find out."

*

He missed the football so much that in the latter half of the winter he volunteered to play for the Alleyn Old Boys, who for the first time won the cup competition for old boy sides. Then the next summer Surrey changed their tune.

The Oval ground was hired in winter by the Isthmian League side, the famous Corinthian-Casuals, who played in front of the Vauxhall Stand, contributing half their gate money to the cricket club. It was an arrangement that had been set up by the Surrey Secretary, Brian Castor, who took Micky aside one day.

"The Casuals are very interested in your playing for them."

"But I understood the club weren't happy with my playing football."

"Oh, that's just certain people on the committee. Don't worry about that. It's not official."

So in October 1955 he joined the Corinthian-Casuals – for what would turn out to be the best season of his amateur football career. Indeed, it could be argued that the club also had its best season, reaching for the only time the final of the FA Amateur Cup.

Micky joined two cricketers in the line-up. One was Doug Insole, the Essex captain, who for fifteen winters would play on the right wing for the Casuals. "Doug wasn't the quickest," Micky says. "You had to pass the ball to his feet. But he had a great vision of the pitch; he always knew where I was. And he was a superb crosser of the ball. Bill Nicholson, the Spurs manager, said he hadn't seen a better striker of a football outside the professional game."

Doug Insole, a grammar school boy from East London, had spent the latter part of the war at Arkley, the army station which intercepted the messages that Bletchley Park decoded, and from there he went up to Cambridge University. He was employed all the year round by George Wimpey, the property developers, who continued to pay him during his summer-long absences on the cricket field – though they did not allow him to accept the offer from MCC to captain the six-month tour of India in the winter of 1951/52, an offer that if accepted would have placed him in the pantheon of England cricket captains. His chairman, who was not a sporting type, made his views clear: "We let him go all summer. If he misses the winter as well, what bloody use is he to us?"

Doug Insole did tour South Africa in 1956/57 as vice-captain to Peter May. His release from work came about as a direct result of an approach from the MCC President, Lord Monckton, to the Wimpey board of directors, an approach that fortuitously occurred while the chairman was on holiday in Italy. "He picked up the *Financial Times* somewhere and got on the blower: 'What the bloody hell is this?' But the deed was done." Wimpey paid his salary through the winter, with MCC adding expenses of £150 or, as Doug puts it, "a pound a day".

He fitted in his winter football around his work, often unable to attend training, which mostly consisted of running and physical exercises. In the amateur game training had not moved on much from the days of the 1920s when Graham Doggart, a leading Corinthian, had been a good enough footballer to captain the full England side. In later life he was asked by Doug what he had done to keep fit. "I ran round Edwardes Square twice on a Thursday night," was his reply.

The other cricketer at Corinthian-Casuals was the West Indian Gerry Alexander at right back, also a Cambridge graduate, who was training to be a vet. On his return to Jamaica in early 1957, to much surprise, he was selected for the forthcoming West Indies tour of England. Then the following winter, at a time when being white was a great advantage in the Caribbean, he was appointed captain.

"He was a competent, workmanlike keeper," Doug says. "No more. He struggled badly with the spin of Ramadhin and Valentine. But he improved and improved, with the bat as well. He made a remarkable transformation as a cricketer."

Times moved on. The captaincy passed to Frank Worrell, but Alexander stayed in the West Indies team, completing the final run-out in the famous tied Test at Brisbane. In the five Tests of that series he took 16 catches and, batting at number eight, scored 484 runs, his average of 60.50 the highest on either side. Then, at the end of the tour, in his prime as a cricketer, he retired to build up his veterinary practice.

He played his sport alongside his working life – a true Corinthian.

"He could have made the best living there was in pro football," Doug reckons, thinking back to the football Gerry Alexander played before his Test cricket began. "He was strong and very skilful. In fact, at that time, he was a much better footballer than he was a cricketer."

*

The Corinthian-Casuals were the truest of all the amateur sides. They might have paid travelling expenses, but that was all. Far from surreptitiously 'recompensing' their players, as the great majority of the amateur sides were now doing, the club charged an annual subscription.

The club was founded in 1939 from an amalgamation of the Corinthians and the Casuals. By this time the Casuals were the club in greater health, but it was the Corinthians who had the more prestigious history. In 1894 they provided all eleven members of the full England side, amateur and professional, that beat Wales 5-1, and in 1904 they inflicted on Manchester United what remains the worst defeat, 11-3, in the club's history.

They also had high ideals about the playing of the game, as their founder 'Pa' Jackson explained in 1932:

> *A sportsman is one who has not merely braced his muscles and developed his endurance by the exercise of some great sport, but he has, in pursuit of this exercise, learnt to control his anger, to be considerate to his fellow men, to take no mean advantage, to resent as dishonour the very suspicion of trickery, to bear aloft a cheerful countenance under disappointment, and never to own himself defeated until the last breath is out of his body.*

Not for them the abuse of the referee or the employment of the professional foul. Indeed, when the penalty kick was introduced into the rules of football in 1891, a prominent Corinthian, CB Fry, called it 'a standing insult to sportsmen to have to play under a rule which assumes that players intend to trip, hack and push opponents and to behave like cads of the first kidney'.

For some years, if a penalty kick was awarded against the Corinthians, it was their practice to withdraw their keeper. There were even occasions when, on being awarded such a kick, they elected to shoot the ball wide.

This had died out by the time Doug and Micky were playing, but to this day they run a side which, like MCC, fulfils a fixture list of school matches, spreading like missionaries the cause of skilful play and good sportsmanship.

There were other amateur sides with high ideals. In 1946, when Arthur Phebey signed as a professional cricketer for Kent, he was told by Dulwich Hamlet that, under their strict interpretation of the word 'amateur', this now prevented him from playing football for them. By the mid-1950s, however, such attitudes were dying out fast.

In many ways the idealism was admirable, championing the playing of sport for its own joys and not for money, but it also served a less lofty purpose: to sustain the distinctions of the English class system.

Micky, in this respect, was of a rather indeterminate background: a professional gambler's son who had been to public school. His friend from Alleyn's, John Pretlove, was another whose position in the system was not clear cut: a shopkeeper's son who attended Cambridge University and consequently played his cricket as an amateur for Kent, an arrangement based on his being given the nebulous position of Assistant Secretary. Even this, however, did not open all doors to him. Shortly after his arrival at Canterbury he was invited to join the Band of Brothers, the county's exclusive wandering club, for whom he duly completed the application form. For five or six weeks he waited in vain for a reply. "I filled in the form for the BB," he said finally, "but I haven't heard a thing." There followed a long, embarrassed pause. Then: "I'm sorry, John, but your father's in trade."

Also at Kent, as a professional, was Derek Ufton, who recalls a match at Worcester when, on the Sunday, four of them including Colin Cowdrey played golf at a local club. "At the end of the round we went to the clubhouse, and only Colin was allowed in. We were professionals in another sport. To be fair to Colin, he stayed with us, but we couldn't have a wash or a beer or anything. And that applied to the club professional as well. Even the top golfers in the country, they couldn't go into their clubs unless one of the members invited them in."

Such was the backdrop to this amateur/professional divide.

*

Micky scored in his first league game for the Corinthian-Casuals, a 3-1 victory over his old side Wimbledon at the Oval in October 1955. In all, that winter he scored 12 goals in 23 appearances, and in early February he was selected to play for England against Wales at Swansea. The side represented something of a shake-up, with the dropping of the veteran Bishop Auckland wing-half Bob Hardisty, for many years the England captain.

'One of the most interesting new faces,' *The Times* wrote, 'is Stewart, the Surrey opening batsman. He is a natural games player of intelligence and balance, and his constructive inside forward play has had no little say in the revival of the Corinthian-Casuals this season.'

In the event Micky did not play, nor did Gerry Alexander. Their Amateur Cup second-round tie against Wimbledon had been postponed from the previous Saturday, and after much soul-searching they decided to give that priority. "It was at the Oval, at the Vauxhall end. The snow was still on the ground, but we played. Early in the game you could retain your feet, and I laid on the first goal. After that, though, the football skills went down and down. By the end I didn't figure too much."

They won 3-2, beat St Albans 1-0 in the next round and were drawn at home to Hitchin Town in the quarter-finals. With half an hour to play

Micky headed home to give the Casuals a 3-1 lead, but two late goals by Hitchin took the game to a replay the following Saturday.

Micky missed the replay. The Casuals won 5-0, securing their first ever appearance in the semi-final stage of the Cup, but by then Micky was far away, having on Monday evening flown out of Heathrow for a cricket tour of Barbados and Trinidad, organised by Jim Swanton of the *Daily Telegraph*. Micky had now played a second summer in the Surrey first team, and the invitation from Swanton suggested that he was being seen as a future England cricketer, one whose prospects would be advanced by the Caribbean trip.

The tour was intended to heal some of the diplomatic wounds opened by the Test series two years earlier when the behaviour of several of Len Hutton's side had caused offence. Colin Cowdrey was tour captain, and his deputy was Hubert Doggart, himself a former Corinthian-Casual, son of the great Corinthian footballer Graham Doggart. He and Micky celebrated the Casuals' 5-0 victory in the quarter-final. Then the following week they were celebrating again, with news of a 3-1 semi-final victory over Dulwich Hamlet at Stamford Bridge. The Casuals were in the final.

The member of Swanton's tour party to attract most interest was Frank Tyson, the fast-bowling sensation of the previous winter in Australia. He would be bowling for the first time to the great hero of Barbados, the powerfully built Clyde Walcott who twelve months earlier had scored 827 runs, with five centuries, in a series against Australia. Tyson versus Walcott, the local newspapers were full of it.

In the first match at the Kensington Oval in Bridgetown Walcott batted only once, bowled for 2 by Tyson. The following week, still at the Kensington Oval, he fared even worse. "When he came in," Micky recalls, "there was this great buzz all around the stadium. Tyson pushed off, bowled the perfect yorker, and first ball he knocked two stumps out of the ground. Walcott nought, first ball."

Tyson was bowling when Walcott came to the middle in the second innings. "The same situation. Tyson pushed off, and up he came. It wasn't quite the yorker, but it was straight. Walcott was still on the back foot, and down came his bat – whoosh! – and the ball went like a rocket for four." This time Walcott hit 130, punishing the off-spin of Sussex's Robin Marlar and the leg-breaks of Nottinghamshire's Gamini Goonesena.

"When Gamini was bowling," Micky remembers, "I was fielding at cover. And the outfield wasn't the greatest, not once the ball was off the cut. Clyde hit five consecutive balls out of the middle of the bat at me.

I think I stopped three of them with my chest. After the third one, the crowd started calling out. 'Clyde, 'it 'im again. 'It 'im again, Clyde.'"

Marlar was combining the tour with his honeymoon, and the crowd, cottoning onto this, took to calling out to their hero: "Clyde, 'im 'oneymoon bowler, give 'im licks." And Walcott duly obliged.

The second match at the Kensington Oval marked the first-class debut of a young local, a motorcycle messenger for Cable and Wireless, Wesley Hall. Seven years later he and Micky would be pitted against each other at Lord's in one of the greatest Test matches of the era, but at this stage the 18-year-old Hall, though very quick, was wayward. "I think I might have faced his first ball in first-class cricket," Micky says. "I clipped it down to fine leg for four." Micky scored 63, and later in the innings Tom Graveney made a remorseless 154. Hall, in his autobiography, admitted to feeling out of his depth.

> *Tom Graveney was pounding away at our bowlers, and I was beginning to feel like a wet rag. In desperation I put every ounce of strength into one delivery, only to see Graveney lift it straight out of the ground.*

"It was my first overseas tour," Micky says, "and I couldn't believe how different batting was. The ball hardly went sideways at all so you didn't have to delay your stroke. You could go onto the back foot and hit it on the up through the line. Clyde Walcott was a great mate of Jim Laker, and I got very friendly with him as the tour progressed. He was very affable; he'd help anybody with their game. He was standing in the slips when Wes Hall was bowling at me. I played one shot, and I said to him, 'Is that how you hit it on the up off the back foot?' 'Yes,' he said. 'Good shot. For your size. My size, I'd be hitting it on the drop.'"

It was a happy tour, and Micky did no harm to his rising reputation, as the vice-captain Hubert Doggart's report in *The Cricketer* magazine suggested: 'Stewart, whose fielding earned him much praise, batted well enough for one to hope that he will one day soon open for England.'

Jim Swanton himself, writing in the *Daily Telegraph*, was of the same view:

> *Stewart takes the eye whether batting or fielding, always full of energy and initiative ... He may conceivably win his chance this summer against Australia. Certainly he is an ideal member of a touring side.*

The party travelled from Barbados to Trinidad where the climax of the tour was a game against a West Indies XI that included Walcott, Weekes and Ramadhin as well as such promising youngsters as Hunte, Kanhai and Sobers.

*Opening the innings
with Colin Cowdrey
in Trinidad*

It was Micky's first taste of five-day cricket, and he found himself taking guard to the first ball of the match. He was in good form and, as his letter home to Sheila makes clear, he knew that it was a golden opportunity to make a mark.

> *We lost a wicket with no runs on the board and with five days' play in front of us I decided to take no chances. This I did with moderate success especially as the wicket was damp and the ball turning. Then attempting to sweep Ramadhin I middled the ball, hit Everton Weekes on the left shoulder standing at short leg from whence it rebounded about twenty yards to be caught at square leg. It seems impossible for me to get a hundred.*

By the close of the second day, Saturday, the West Indians were well on top, but Micky's mood was brightened immediately by the arrival of a telegram from Hubert Doggart's mother in England, reporting the result of the final of the FA Amateur Cup. In front of 80,000 spectators at Wembley Stadium, Corinthian-Casuals had held the mighty Bishop Auckland, holders of the trophy, to a 1-1 draw.

It was a major event in the nation's sporting calendar. Both television channels, BBC and the new ITV, provided live coverage of the second half, there was radio commentary on the BBC's Light Programme, and the following week in cinemas *Pathé News* included two minutes of highlights from the game.

The surviving film opens a window on another world. Amid shots of an orderly crowd – an elderly, half-toothed man in a cap biting at a sandwich, a schoolboy with glasses chewing on a banana, a fresh-faced young woman excitedly waving a rattle – the well-spoken commentator conveys the fast-moving excitement of the contest:

> *This is Corinthians' first appearance in a final, and they are putting up a magnificent fight. Right-half Guy Shuttleworth passes to winger Doug Insole who beats his man, but Bishops send it over the line and it's a corner. Doug Insole takes the kick, Kerruish nods it in, Hardisty stops it, but it's a goal, a goal for Corinthians.*

Bishop Auckland soon equalise, and the game goes into extra time, thirty minutes in which the Corinthians' Danish keeper Paul Ahm is repeatedly in action, defying the northerners.

> *Time and again Bishops reach the goalmouth but cannot press it home. So it ends in a draw, a result well earned by plucky Corinthian-Casuals.*

The replay was set for the following Saturday, at Ayresome Park, Middlesbrough, and this opened up a fresh possibility, as Micky reported in his Sunday letter to Sheila:

> *This morning a cable came from the Casuals asking me to play next Saturday, and that's what I intend doing if it's at all possible. Jim Swanton is busy working out routes and time checks to get back. … I'll start training tomorrow morning!! What a terrible thought. I haven't a clue how the climate will affect me for football in England but I have my fingers crossed !!*

Swanton came up trumps. Micky could complete the five-day game in progress, then catch a seven o'clock flight on Thursday morning. It would refuel at Caracas in Venezuela, then fly on to New York, arriving at 4.45 in the afternoon. That would allow him to board a plane that would land at Heathrow airport at 1 p.m. on Friday. From there he would travel to Darlington where his team-mates would be staying. According to *The Times*, it would be 'the longest journey ever made by a player to take part in a Cup tie in these islands'.

Micky outlined the plan in a telegram to the Casuals that ended: 'HAVE LEARNED LATEST CALYPSO TO BOOST CASUALS MORALE AND COUNTER BLAYDON RACES STOP STEWART'.

On Monday morning he got up at six o'clock and went across to the racecourse next to the hotel for a session of running and ball work. Clyde Walcott, always happy to be of help, joined him, feeding him the ball so that Micky could reacquaint himself with his skills. Then back at the hotel Micky showered, had breakfast and spent a long day under a tropical sun fielding while Weekes, Kanhai and Sobers piled on the runs. Tuesday and Wednesday morning brought further early-morning practice, then on Thursday he was seen off by Jim Swanton, who supplied him with a sleeping pill for his long night flight across the Atlantic. The capsule was a novelty to Micky, and in his naïveté, when the time came to take it, he broke it open, losing half the powder in the process.

The journey did not go to plan. At Caracas there was a lengthy delay. "We had to stay in our seats for ages and, when we were finally allowed off the plane, we were greeted by half a dozen Venezuelan soldiers pointing their guns up the steps." Whether it was an attempted revolution, or an excessive display of security, Micky never discovered, but the consequence was that he did not reach New York till 6 p.m., by which time his plane to Heathrow was taking off.

He was forced to spend the night in a New York hotel. "I can remember thinking, 'This may be the only night I ever spend in New York. Do I go out and see the sights?' But I had a steak in a nearby restaurant and went to bed."

Eventually, after much sending of cables, he left New York the next day on a KLM flight that would stop for refuelling at Ganda in Newfoundland, arriving at Edinburgh at dawn on Saturday morning. Time was getting tight, and the situation was made worse by dense fog which prevented the plane from landing at Ganda. The pilot, a football fan who was desperate to do his best for Micky, arranged to refuel at a military airport in Stephenville and eventually they were in the sky once more. The kick-off in Middlesbrough was set for three o'clock, and it was well past mid-day when they landed in Edinburgh, more than 150 miles away.

"When I came down the stairs of the plane, there were all these photographers at the bottom. I thought, 'Blimey, there's some film star on the plane.' But all the cameras were pointed at me. Grace Kelly was about to marry Prince Rainier of Monaco, and the newspapers were full of that and of me coming back for the Cup Final. Will I make it? They were the two main stories.

"By then I was thinking, 'Oh well, I'm not going to play; that's it.' But there was a guy waiting for me. He shepherded me across the tarmac to something that looked like a Tiger Moth biplane and flew me down to a military airfield near Middlesbrough. Then I was bundled into a police car and driven at high speed to the ground. All the time I was looking at my watch."

From seven a.m. Thursday in Trinidad to three p.m. Saturday in Middlesbrough. It was a two-and-a-half-day journey, covering 4,500 miles, and it was all to no avail. "The policeman opened the door of his car and, as he did, the referee was blowing his whistle for the start of the match. I was too late."

"Micky was a class performer," Doug Insole says. "We were very disappointed when he didn't make it."

The Times called it 'a fabulous sub-chapter to the main story, which will always live as a curiosity in the history of the competition'. Micky's view of it was not so romantic, especially when he settled into a seat and saw the first effort of his replacement, the Old Reptonian Gerry Citron.

"It was almost the first thing in the game I saw. Somebody knocked the ball over to him, and he missed the thing. It went straight under his foot and into touch. 'Bloody hell,' I said to myself. And this girl sitting next to me, a very attractive girl, she turned to me. 'Excuse me,' she said. 'I know you're Micky Stewart, but you don't know who I am. I'm Gerry's girl friend.'"

After 34 minutes Citron picked up the ball on the left side, swept past the Bishop Auckland full back and from outside the box fired a left-foot rocket past an astonished goalkeeper and into the net. In the words of *The Times*, 'it was a goal to bring a glow to all Reptonians', and it brought a glow to Micky, too. "Gerry's girl friend was so delighted, she gave me a great big kiss."

The fairy tale soon ended. Auckland equalised before half-time. Then in the second half, with BBC television once more showing play, the veteran Bishop Auckland captain Bob Hardisty took control of the game from the midfield, scoring their second goal and leading them to a 5-1 victory.

Would the presence of a travel-weary Micky have made any difference? It was a full seventeen years later when he discovered the answer – during a Gillette Cup match at Chester-le-Street against Durham, a game in which he scored a century on an awkward pitch and won his only Man of the Match award.

"Bob Hardisty was there, and he came up to me after the game. I'd never really met him before, but I'd always admired him as an outstanding footballer. He was a schools PE inspector, a really first-class fellow, and he started talking about that final."

"You know, don't you, that if you'd got there in time I wasn't going to play."

"How was that then?"

"I was a more attacking midfielder. If you'd been playing, we'd have needed a more defensive tactic."

"Go on. You're flattering me."

But it was true, as Micky found out in blunter terms soon afterwards. In the bar at the annual dinner of the Barnes Cricket Club a stocky man with a thick Geordie accent tugged at his arm.

"Here," he said. "You cost me a f---ing Cup Winners' medal."

"What are you talking about?"

"When you didn't make it to the final. I was all stripped, ready to play."

*

Micky stayed with football for one week before returning to Surrey. On Tuesday he scored for Corinthian-Casuals against Leytonstone. Then on Saturday he finally made his amateur international debut for England against France at the Dulwich Hamlet ground at Champion Hill. He remembers a training session at Paddington Recreation Ground, during which it was decided that he would be the penalty taker, though this did not arise in the match.

"I had a good first half, but we lost our left half and there were no subs in those days. I had to go back and play in a more defensive role."

Despite playing much of the game with ten men they won 3-1, all three goals coming from the Corinthians' centre-forward Jackie Laybourne, and Micky's first-half performance was noted. Reflecting on an indifferent England performance in their previous game against Scotland, *The Times* celebrated the newcomer's impact:

> *The inclusion of Stewart provided the creative mind that had been lacking against the Scots, for here is the thoughtful ball player, capable of drawing the defence and fashioning the unexpected direction of attack.*

The 1956 Olympic Games were to be held in November in Melbourne and, when the Great Britain side was announced, Micky's name was on the list, along with his fellow Casuals Jackie Laybourne and Gerry Alexander.

It was a requirement of the Games that the players be amateurs, which strictly most of the Great Britain squad, apart from the three Casuals, were not. Certainly none of those who played for Hungary and Yugoslavia in

England

(White shirts and dark blue shorts)

RIGHT   LEFT

M. Pinner
(Cambridge University)

2   3
G. Alexander   **L. T. Farrer**
(Corinthian-Casuals)   *(Walthamstow Avenue)*

4   5   6
L. Topp   **S. Prince**   **H. E. Dodkins**
(Hendon)   *(Walthamstow Avenue)*   *(Ilford)*

7   8   9   10   11
F. McKenna **M. Stewart** **J. S. Laybourne** **G. Bromilow** **G. Twissel**
(Bishop   *(Corinthian-*   *(Corinthian-*   *(Southport)* *(Plymouth Arg.*
Auckland)   *Casuals)*   *Casuals)*   *& R.N.)*

O

Marino   **Theo**   **Giamarchi**   **Mouchel**   **Moreau**
(Draguignan) *(Lens)*   *(Annecy)*   *(Cherbourg)*   *(Rheims)*
11   10   9   8   7

Durecu   **Tylenski (R.)**   **Ferrier**
(Quevilly)   *(St. Etienne)*   *(St. Etienne)*
6   5   4

Schollhammer   **Tylenski (M.)**
(Rheims)   *(St. Etienne)*
3   2

Dantheny
(Rheims)

LEFT   RIGHT

France

(Blue shirts, white shorts, red stockings)

Referee	..	..	..	..	..	Mr. A. ASMUSSEN
						(Denmark)
Linesmen	..	..	Messrs. L. ROCKMAN	&	R. W. SPENCER	
			(London)		*(Surrey)*	
			(Cerise flag)		*(Orange flag)*	

Reserves :

FRANCE   ENGLAND

Brandon (Caen) *goalkeeper.*   **D. Darvill** (Dulwich Hamlet) *goalkeeper*
Grossans (Stirin) *centre half.*   **T. Robinson** (Brentford) *half back*
Jacquet (Rheims) *forward.*   **D. Lewin** (Bishop Auckland) *forward.*

The Band is that of the London Fire Brigade.

77

the Helsinki final four years earlier were; they were full-time sportsmen masquerading as members of their countries' armed forces – and so it would be in Melbourne where the three medals were won by the Soviet Union, Yugoslavia and Bulgaria.

"I was ready to get measured up for the uniform," Micky recalls. "The white panama and the blazer. Then in July Surrey were playing down at Hastings and, when we came off the field at lunchtime, there was a message for me to see the Secretary. He told me I had to ring Stanley Rous, the Secretary of the FA."

"I've got sad news," Rous told him. "The Olympic Committee won't accept you as a member of our side as you're a professional cricketer.'"

Such was his disappointment that at the end of the day, back at the Castle Hotel, he allowed Alec Bedser to buy him a half pint of mild beer. "I'd had a sip of champagne at my sister's wedding, but I'd never touched beer. I hadn't been brought up with it. I didn't even like the smell of it."

Many years later, on an international tour with the veteran Australian opener Arthur Morris, he recalled the story of this first drink. "Alec bought you a drink?" Morris repeated with surprise. "We should form a club. He bought me one once."

Micky's father was livid at the Olympic decision, and the hypocrisy of it still rankles with Micky, too. "There was all this shamateurism in the amateur game, but I'd never taken a penny to play football. Yet I was the one who couldn't go."

Doug Insole was so outraged that he wrote an article for the *News Chronicle*, proposing that everybody should just be footballers, not amateurs or professionals. He received in the post a congratulatory letter from Stan Cullis, manager of Wolverhampton Wanderers, then one of the very top clubs. He related to Doug how he had tried to sign a player at a leading amateur side, offering him the maximum wage of fifteen pounds a week. They had talked terms in a café, and it turned out that the man was earning more than that in money in brown envelopes slipped into his boots. Furthermore the money, under the counter as it were, was untaxed, and the man had a good full-time job in the civil service. Cullis could not match such an arrangement.

*

Already that summer a number of professional clubs had approached Micky and, dispirited by his exclusion from the Olympic Games, he decided finally to go down that road. His career as an amateur footballer clearly had no future.

He received offers from several clubs, among them Blackburn Rovers, Portsmouth and Leyton Orient. "I spent two hours with Ted Drake the Chelsea manager at a café in Streatham, and I had a meeting in Jimmy Hill's car about going to Fulham." There were also financial offers from amateur clubs, including one in which the chairman's proposed package involved a £40-a-week job with his company plus a further £30 for football which, with bonuses, took Micky's pay to almost five times the maximum wage for the professionals.

Then there was the business of hidden signing-on fees, with some professional clubs offering four-figure sums. At the end of it all, shocked by some of what he had discovered, Micky signed for the club he had supported as a boy: Charlton Athletic.

His attachment to Charlton came in a roundabout way. The nearest clubs to his childhood home were Millwall and Crystal Palace, but during the war he and his Ruskin Park friends took to walking up the hill to the Dulwich Hamlet ground. There they watched an amateur team called Charlton Rovers who had an outside-right called Leslie Fell who became their hero: "He was the quickest thing we'd ever seen." So, when the war ended and Fell started playing for Charlton Athletic, they followed him.

They were glory days for the south-east London side, reaching the FA Cup Final in each of the first two summers after the war. The Parkside Rovers gang gathered round the radio in Micky's front room to hear them lose 4-1 to Derby County in 1946, then the following year they celebrated when Burnley were beaten 1-0. In both matches play was suspended as a result of the ball bursting, an oddity that remained a mystery to Micky till he went to work for Slazenger in the 1970s. "There were rubber shortages after the war, and they used some bladders that had been sitting around in storage for too long."

The Charlton manager who signed the 23-year-old Micky was the legendary Jimmy Seed, in charge since 1933 when Micky was barely a year old. He joined Charlton when they were languishing in the middle reaches of the Third Division South, and in three successive winters in the mid-1930s he took them to two promotions and to the runners-up spot in Division One, the highest placed side in London.

It was not uncommon in the 1950s for county cricketers to play professional football in the winter. Cricket's County Championship, unlike today's sprawling programme, was tightly packed into the four months from May to August, starting after the finish of the Football League programme and ending when the next football season was only a fortnight old.

The last of the double internationals, Willie Watson and Arthur Milton, had both retired from soccer by this time, but in the winter of 1956/57 Hampshire's Mike Barnard played regularly for Portsmouth, Lancashire's Jack Dyson for Manchester City, Yorkshire's Ken Taylor for Huddersfield and Essex's Gordon Barker for Southend. Several Gloucestershire players turned out for the Bristol clubs, City and Rovers, and there was a similar link-up between Sussex and Brighton and Hove Albion.

Around this time Charlton had four Kent cricketers on their books: Derek Ufton, Stuart Leary, Syd O'Linn and Freddie Lucas. Unlike Micky, however, they all had contracts that put their football first. With Micky, it was the other way round. He discussed terms with Jimmy Seed at a dinner at the Café Royal in Regent Street, with Sheila sitting in the car outside, and it was agreed that he would miss the two ends of the football season.

Micky had not signed his contract when the 1956/57 season began. He was still with Surrey, completing Stuart Surridge's fifth successive championship title, while Charlton were losing their first five league games, the fifth a humiliating 8-1 to fellow strugglers Sunderland. As a result Jimmy Seed was sacked after 23 years as manager.

Seed, who was ill at the time, asked to be allowed to complete the negotiation with Micky, who drove down to Bromley and signed his contract at the ex-manager's bedside.

Seed was succeeded by his deputy Jimmy Trotter, and this was not good news for the new recruit. In the first place he had not been the one who had signed Micky, and secondly he was not at all impressed by his being away playing cricket.

"Sacking Jimmy Seed was a terrible mistake," says Derek Ufton, a man who has spent a lifetime involved in football, including many years on the board at Charlton. "He was one of the great managers of all time, up there with Alex Ferguson. Jimmy Trotter was a lovely bloke, but he had no experience, and that didn't help Micky. Micky was a very, very good player technically, but he didn't have the experience of first division football. We were a struggling side, and Jimmy Trotter was desperate for immediate success because he'd got to prove himself. He would have been loath to play an untried player like Micky."

Micky was 24 years old, joining the professional game at a time when some of his contemporaries had been on the books for nine years. "It's very rare that you can come into the game at that age," Derek says. "The body gets physically stronger from the everyday training, and not just the training but the practice matches where all the fellows not in the team are competing with each other, fighting tooth and nail to make it. You can say to me 'Ian Wright, he didn't start till he was 22', but he had a very different physique from Micky. Plus the fact that Micky was an inside forward, and that was the hardest place to play in those days. So much was expected: you had to contribute to defence, you had to make goals for the other guys, and you had to score a few yourself."

Micky, after a spell in the reserves, made his first-team debut on Saturday 15 December, in a home match against Aston Villa. It was a wild, wet day, the drainage was poor at The Valley, and a crowd of only 13,000 braved the elements. The newspapers were full of his appearance – CRICKET STAR MAKES CHARLTON DEBUT – which did not impress his opponents.

"Things had gone really well in the reserves. I thought, 'This is all right.' And I was always dying to see if I could play first-division football. But it's like coming into first-class cricket. Nothing prepares you for it. It was quicker, stronger, harder, a total world apart from the Corinthian-Casuals.

"Early in the game the ball was played out to me on the left-hand touchline. I pulled it back with the outside of my right foot, thinking no one was near me. And suddenly these six studs went flying past me, crashing into this freshly whitewashed wall on the other side of the track. The whitewash came trickling down, and I thought, 'Christ, that could have been my leg.' It was Stan Lynn, the Aston Villa full-back, a smashing fellow. He looked at me, and he said, 'Do that again, son, and you'll find you've got the wrong f---ing pads on. You'll need those big white ones you wear in the summer.'"

Their tussle continued. At one point Micky, "being a bit cocky", tried to push the ball through his legs. Then they chased the ball to the by-line, and they both fell down. It was muddy, and Lynn got himself up by pushing Micky's face further into the mud. The 'Cricket Star' was not at the Oval now.

"Twinkle, twinkle, little f---ing star," the Villa man whispered.

"So that was my debut. For the first hour I did more than well, but with the pace of the game and the mud I got knackered."

They lost 2-1, and the following Saturday he scored his first Charlton goal in a 4-2 defeat at Luton, a result which left them three points adrift at the foot of the table. This time the *Times* football correspondent was present, and he was not much impressed by what he saw of the Charlton side:

> They are not recognizable as the same side of last Christmas. All their old verve and skill have departed and so have most of the well known names … Yet if any sparks of hope remain for the future they lie in the fighting qualities of a new team trying to find its feet in a relentless, unsympathetic world, and in the general constructive ability of Stewart, the Surrey cricketer, at inside-left, a natural games player who less than a year ago was a member of the Corinthian-Casuals. This at least was visible on a damp, muddy, raw afternoon, clothed with a veil of fog which had a curious diaphanous quality about it. It was no day for enjoyable football.

Christmas brought four games in eight days: Saturday 22, Tuesday 25, Wednesday 26 and Saturday 29. Worse, the two games on Christmas and Boxing Day were home and away to Wolverhampton Wanderers.

Wolves were riding high in the table, but in an upset they lost 2-1 at The Valley. "I made the second one for Johnny Summers," Micky says proudly. "An assist, they call it today."

After the game Micky went into the away team's dressing room to pick up an autograph book, and there was the great Billy Wright, the England captain, banging his boots on the floor to remove the mud. In walked Stan Cullis. "Don't bother doing that," he barked. "If you're going to play like that, you won't play another game for me." Micky beat a hasty retreat.

The next day they took the train to the West Midlands. "As the train left London, it started snowing. It got thicker and thicker and, when we reached Wolverhampton, we were told the game was off. We didn't even go to the ground. We just turned round at the station and came back. I was glad we didn't have to play."

Back at The Valley on Saturday, they played relegation rivals Sunderland, in mud and slush that did not suit Micky's ball skills. To make matters worse, Charlton had just signed a new goalkeeper from Hearts, Willie Duff, who insisted that they played with an old-fashioned leather ball at a time when many clubs were starting to use plastic-coated leather.

Micky had a bad cold. "The trainer Alec Herd gave me this little tablet. I didn't know what was in it. It turned out it was benzadrine, an upper. I was everywhere, full of energy. I laid on the second goal. I think the first half of that game was the best I ever played for Charlton, but gradually the ball got wetter and wetter, heavier and heavier, and it didn't suit me at all."

At one point he found himself at the corner flag, trying to get the ball off their big centre-half Ray Daniel, captain of Wales. "Little me. He was shielding the ball, preventing me from getting near it. 'I don't give autographs till after the game, son,' he said."

The Sunderland side included Len Shackleton, the great ball-playing 'Clown Prince of Football'. "In summer he used to write on cricket for the *Sunday Express*. I'd met him at Sheffield. He'd written some nice things about my batting."

Well before half-time Shackleton was making known his feelings about the state of the ball. "Come on, ref, change the ball. This is hopeless." He turned to his opposite number. "Micky and I, we're artists. Look at all this crowd, they want to be entertained. We can't be entertaining with a ball like this, can we, Micky?"

It was Sunderland's turn to kick off the second half, and he started again. "Have you changed the ball, ref?"

"Get on with it, Shackleton."

"Ah, well, we'll have to keep it off the ground."

"The ball was knocked to him from the kick-off," Micky recalls. "He flicked it up, went pop-pop-pop and let go this forty-yard volley that went straight to the feet of their left-winger."

"That's it, Micky. We'll have to play it like that then."

Charlton won 3-2, bringing them level with Sunderland at the foot of the table, but, alas, it was Micky's last taste of victory in a Division One game.

The following week the FA Cup began with an away game at second-division Middlesbrough, whose centre-forward Brian Clough was knocking in more than a goal a game. "He was very quick," Micky recalls, "and very aware of where the goal was."

For Micky it was a return to Ayresome Park, the ground where he had failed to arrive in time nine months earlier, and it almost ended in glory. With the minutes ticking away and the score 1-1, Micky got to the by-line and pulled the ball back to Stuart Leary in front of goal, only to watch as the centre-forward's shot went wide. The following Thursday afternoon at The Valley they were 2-1 up when Clough scored a brilliant individual goal to level the scores. Then in a dismal second half they conceded a third time.

Brian Clough scores in the Cup replay at The Valley

Once more the *Times* correspondent was not impressed:

The Charlton defence at times provided an open triumphal arch through which sides like Manchester United and Tottenham could have marched at will. As for attack, only some life from Lawrie on the right wing and the ceaseless and courageous foraging of Stewart in midfield saved Charlton from complete extinction.

"I got some stick afterwards from Jimmy Trotter. I was fouled in the penalty area, and I staggered on and recovered. And my shot was saved by Peter Taylor. 'You should have gone down,' Jimmy Trotter said. 'You'd have got a penalty.'"

Such a thing would never have been said at the Corinthian-Casuals, but there were so many ways in which the professional game differed from the amateur one. Law 12(d) stated that 'A player shall be penalised if he intentionally holds or pushes an opponent with his hand, or with his arm extended from his body.' That was what they played in the amateur game but among professionals, Micky says, "you wouldn't live if you didn't push." After he had been at Charlton a season or two, he played a charity match at the amateur club Wealdstone, "and the referee was blowing me up every few minutes for pushing."

The game contained a great deal more physical contact than is now allowed. "Over ninety minutes, if the referees had applied the laws as they are today, you'd hardly have had a player left on the pitch."

Yet for the most part it was an honest game, and the sense of fair play was in the crowds, too, something that in Micky's opinion started to disappear out of the game a few years later.

"I remember watching a match in the early '50s at Stamford Bridge when the Chelsea full-back Stan Willemse kicked Stanley Matthews, and the crowd booed him. His own crowd. But twenty years later, when Ron Harris did the same thing to George Best, kicking him out of the game in the first twenty minutes, they cheered. Times had changed."

What had not changed, though, was the reputation of Chelsea's hard men. "The Gloucestershire boys once asked Arthur Milton how many goals he'd have scored if he'd played a full season."

"Well, 40 matches," he replied. "I'd have scored …"

"No, no," they said. "It's 42."

"No, 40. The other two were against Chelsea, and you wouldn't have seen me anywhere near the ball."

*

By that January Micky was suffering, undiagnosed, from tight hamstrings and shin splints, and he only played two more times that winter: a 3-1 defeat away to Sheffield Wednesday and a 4-0 thrashing at home to Blackpool, a game in which he found himself up against Stanley Matthews, a day after the maestro's 42nd birthday.

Charlton brought back Syd Ellis at right back, to mark the veteran winger. "Before the match Jimmy Trotter said to us how Syd had played him out of the game at Blackpool; he'd got him taped. Then early in the game we had a corner. George Farm, the Blackpool keeper, came out and caught the ball and threw it straightaway to Stanley Matthews who was out on the touchline, level with the front of their penalty area. I was on the edge of the penalty area, and I ran after him. He was known for his speed over the first few yards. I found he was quicker running with the ball at the age of 42 than I was at the age of 24, running after him. 'He's yours,' I shouted to Syd and, as Stanley Matthews approached the by-line, Syd advanced on him to block the cross. Stanley Matthews just pulled the ball away, left Syd behind and made the cross. And Syd was supposed to have got him taped. 'That was your f---ing fault,' he shouted at me."

By the Easter weekend, when they had to play Friday, Saturday and Monday, their relegation was a certainty. Micky was at the ground for the

1-1 home draw against Tottenham on Good Friday. "The first-team group at Charlton were all supposed to report to the dressing room after the game, to hear the team for the next day at Highbury. But I was already back pre-season at the Oval. That was the agreement; we had a practice match starting the next day. So I didn't go into the dressing room."

Trotter, not fully aware of the terms of Micky's contract, had included him in the side, but at lunchtime the next day, when they assembled at the coach, there was no sign of Micky, leading an early edition of one evening newspaper to provide curious reading. On one page was the headline: 'Stewart not out 50'. On another it was: 'Where's Micky Stewart?'

"Stuart Leary had to play in my place, and he wasn't expecting it. I think he'd had a bit of a night out on Friday. I was out of order really; I had to apologise. But it was in my contract that cricket came first."

"It wasn't a sensible move to wander off like that," Derek Ufton says. "It definitely upset Jimmy Trotter."

*

Micky played just three more games for Charlton: one in the winter of 1957/58, two in 1958/59. In Division Two the football was different; it was a more direct game with less emphasis on ball skills and passing, and Micky's style of play did not fit.

"We were always pleased when Micky was in the side," Derek recalls. "But the manager wanted somebody more direct than Micky was. Ronnie White came in. He was a terrific dribbler, a wizard with the ball, but that was where it ended. Micky was a far more all-round player, but the manager preferred Ronnie and it was his job to select the team. A lot of us would have preferred Micky."

Micky's one game in 1957/58 was in late December, seven days too late unfortunately for him to have taken part in the greatest match in the history of Charlton Athletic. He was with the reserves at Norwich, hearing that Derek Ufton had gone off early on and that the ten men of Charlton were losing 5-1 to Huddersfield. So, when the second team manager announced that they had come back to win 7-6, he didn't believe a word of it. "I'll bet you my win bonus it's not true," he rashly said, and it was not long before he was handing over a one-pound note.

In all, Micky made 11 first-team appearances for Charlton, nine in the league and two in the cup. He scored three goals, the last of them in his final game, a 3-2 victory over Lincoln City. By this time, as the manner of the goal makes clear, 'Weenie' Micky had grown accustomed to the ways of the professional game.

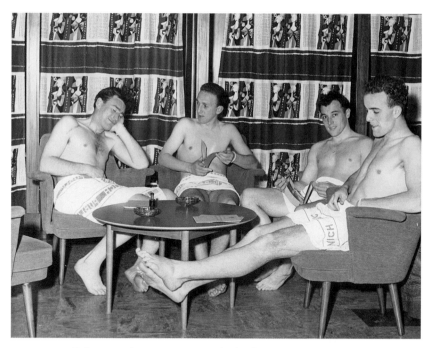

Relaxing after a sauna at Aylesford Paper Mills in Kent
left to right: Derek Ufton, Micky, Sammy Lawrie, Dennis Edwards

"In those days you were allowed to shoulder-charge the keeper. He caught the ball, and I came bundling in. Me, the Indian famine child. The ball bobbled loose out of his hands, it lodged between my forearm and my body, and I more or less carried it over the line."

Micky's goal sent Lincoln City into the Division Two relegation zone, and it was not forgotten by their long-serving manager Bill Anderson. "That bloody so-called goal," he would say to Micky whenever in later years he appeared at cricket, "it nearly got me the sack."

Shortly afterwards, in Friday morning training at The Valley, Micky was in a group of six, practising running with the ball at full speed at a defender, and he collided with Johnny Summers who was doing the same thing in the adjoining group. Micky's elbow caught Summers' jaw, and Summers' knee whacked into Micky's thigh. The blow disturbed the surface of his thigh bone, causing calcification at the site of the injured muscle, and for weeks he walked with a limp. It was not what Surrey wanted for one of their key players, not what he wanted either if he was to become an England cricketer.

When he recovered fitness, he played one second-team game against Fulham, marked by the former Scottish international Alex Forbes, then left the world of professional football behind. If he was to reach the top, it would have to be on the cricket field.

*

Micky played his remaining football in occasional games for the team that Corinthian-Casuals took out to schools, once more alongside Doug Insole.

Derek Ufton, meanwhile, left Charlton in 1960 to coach at Tooting and Mitcham, an amateur club in the Isthmian League. "I'll never ever forget the first day I walked into their ground at Sandy Lane. I couldn't believe what I was seeing. All the facilities. It was like a palace compared with Charlton. I had nothing to do with the finances, but in the end the players started to tell me what they were being paid. It was incredible."

Perhaps surprisingly cricket was the first major sport to lance the boil of the hypocrisy, abolishing the amateur/professional distinction in the winter of 1962/63. On the committee that recommended the change was Doug Insole, whose struggle to make the same change in football would take another ten years.

*

"I'd liked to have had one full season in Division One," Micky says now. "Just to see what I could have achieved."

Perhaps Micky was unlucky: unlucky to pick up injuries at the wrong times, unlucky that Jimmy Seed had gone by the time he arrived at The Valley, unlucky that Charlton had become a struggling side. Perhaps he would have enjoyed the modern game more: the lighter ball, the billiard-table surfaces, the greater protection from hard tackling, the faster pace of the game. "Like Martin Peters," he says with a laugh, recalling Alf Ramsey's famous remark, "I was ten years ahead of my time."

"I thought he had a lot of the attributes that would take him on," Derek Ufton says. "He was very unfortunate at the way it worked out. If he'd gone to another club, a more stable one, or he'd come to Charlton three years before, when he was that much younger and we were going well, his career in soccer might have been totally different."

Micky is not one to seek excuses, though. "I thought I was good enough to play more. But in the end it's down to you. You've got to play to the level where there's no way anybody could leave you out. And I didn't do that."

6

THE GREATEST COUNTY SIDE

Micky had made his first-team debut for Surrey in 1954, when for a second successive summer the championship pennant was fluttering above the pavilion at the Oval. Yet by July, when Micky joined the side, the prospect of a third success was remote, with Surrey marooned in mid-table. In their previous three games they had lost at home to Yorkshire and Glamorgan; then at Sheffield rain had saved them from a second defeat by Yorkshire. Even Peter May, for the first time in his career, was struggling for runs.

The arrival of Micky, along with Ken Barrington, brought a welcome freshness to the batting, but the games at Colchester and Blackheath both ended in draws. So, as the month of July drew to a close, they were so far behind the leaders Yorkshire that most observers had written off their chances of a hat-trick of championships.

County cricket was not then as it is now: not four-day matches, with breaks between games, played on surfaces scrupulously protected from rain, with pitch inspectors hovering whenever wickets fall too fast. They were three-day matches, two of them each week, played in a hectic round that took in frequent visits to out-grounds. Furthermore, there was no covering of the pitch once the game was in play. From match to match the surfaces and the elements varied, and adapting to that variation was a great part of the challenge.

It was never more so than in 1954, a summer that in the year 2000 was declared by statisticians to be, by some distance, the worst of the twentieth century: cold, gloomy and wet. In the final five weeks of the cricket season Surrey had ten matches to play, and in almost every one of them the elements played a part as scudding, rain-bearing clouds came one upon another off the Atlantic.

From Blackheath they returned to the Oval, where rain on the first day gave them much the better of conditions against Essex, and they won a low-scoring match by ten wickets. Jim Laker was the prime bowler in the victory, taking five wickets in each innings, but the next day, in the Bank Holiday fixture against Nottinghamshire, it was Alec Bedser and Peter Loader who exploited the still damp turf, skittling out the visitors for 77 and winning by mid-afternoon on the second day. The two victories lifted them to fourth place, only three wins behind Yorkshire and with two games in hand. The task of retaining their title no longer seemed quite so unlikely.

They travelled to Kettering to play the team that would give them more trouble through the 1950s than any other, Northamptonshire. It was the first time Micky had set eyes on Frank Tyson. "I can't imagine anybody bowling it faster than him, though that was only for a short period of time."

Micky and Tom Clark both liked to face the first ball of the innings so they took it in turns. But not at Kettering. "This guy's a little bit quicker," said the kindly Clark to his young partner. "If you want to see him run up, get used to his rhythm as he comes in, I'll take first ball."

Tyson ran in, pushing off from the sight screen, and Micky watched from the non-striker's end. The ball was a straight one, just short of a length, and Clark went back. "He used to use Slazenger Gradidge bats, and in those days the oiling instructions were on a little disc stuck to the back. He played this ball right in the middle of the bat, just below the splice … 'BOMP' … and the oiling instructions fluttered to the ground."

It was another low-scoring game, and on the evening of the second day Surrey's number eleven Peter Loader left the dressing room with seven runs still needed for victory. It was not a sight to inspire confidence among Surrey supporters, certainly not with Tyson about. As a bowler Loader could be mean and menacing, particularly with his bouncer, but with a bat in his hand, at the first sign of danger he was quick to retreat.

As Loader emerged from the pavilion his path was blocked by an animated Bernie Constable, who had earlier taken a few body blows from Tyson and was now waving his bat about and gesticulating repeatedly.

"What was all that about?" the others asked when Constable returned to the dressing room.

"I told him, if he takes one step to leg, he'll have this bloody bat round his head when he gets back. And it will hurt a lot more than a cricket ball."

Somehow Loader survived, and the victory was theirs. Down at Hove Yorkshire were on the verge of victory, too, but their game ran into the third day – and on the third day it rained.

It rained and rained, so heavily that on that Friday evening flooding caused havoc all over London. Railway lines were closed, trolley buses rerouted, houses and shops severely damaged. There were disruptions at West End theatres and greyhound stadiums, and work at the Mount Pleasant sorting office had to be suspended.

The next day at the Oval, against London neighbours Middlesex, the sun dried the square sufficiently to allow play to start at 3.30. Despite conditions 7,000 spectators waited patiently, and eventually they watched Micky and Tom Clark take the score patiently to 24 before the heavens opened once more. That was Saturday afternoon, and they did not resume till Tuesday, battling to a declaration of 193 for five at a quarter to four.

The game seemed to offer nothing for either side, yet the Surrey bowlers – the Bedser twins and Tony Lock – found greater venom in the pitch than their Middlesex counterparts had done. In 47.1 overs, with the support of superb close catching, they had the visitors all out for 51. It was in that innings that Micky, still discovering so much about county cricket, realised just how much more aggressively this Surrey side of Stuart Surridge was playing its cricket.

"Through our innings Bill Edrich and Denis Compton had been fielding close in on the leg side. When we went out to field, their footprints were still visible in the wet turf. And I could see clearly, we were standing three steps closer to the bat than they'd been."

No bowler could have made Micky feel safer in that leg trap than Alec Bedser. "He hit the wicket hard, and his control of length and line, particularly when it was swinging, was magnificent. I came into the side in 1954, fielding bat-pad, and the first time I recall a horizontal bat shot played past me was Reg Simpson at the Oval, August Bank Holiday, 1956."

Micky took to studying the close-catching positions taken up by opposing counties. "Glamorgan and Yorkshire were the two who stood closest, but not as close as we did."

Surrey's four points for first innings lead were more than the rain allowed Yorkshire to gain at Bradford, but the two teams both won their next fixtures: Yorkshire at Scarborough, Surrey at Leicester where yet more rain fell and it was Tony Lock's turn to be chief executioner, with match figures of ten for 50 in 57.3 overs.

Laker and Lock, Loader and Alec Bedser. It was a formidable county attack. Bedser was the leading wicket-taker of all time in Tests, Laker and Lock were supreme masters of their art, and Loader was a good enough fast bowler to be selected for England ahead of Fred Trueman. "They must be," Micky says, "the most talented and balanced all-round bowling attack that there's ever been in domestic cricket anywhere in the world."

Micky's form with the bat was starting to dip, and it did not improve in their next game at Cheltenham: caught Cook, bowled Lambert 3; bowled Mortimore 9. Fifty-seven years on, the latter dismissal still rankles with him: "He was bowling round the wicket, and I let the ball go. It pitched middle-and-leg and hit off stump. It was his arm ball. We'd played together in the army. I'd seen him bowl it umpteen times. What an idiot! Why can I remember that?"

Stuart Surridge, the ultimate competitor

It was in that game that the powers of Stuart Surridge started to assume mythical proportions in the eyes of his team. At lunch on the final day Gloucestershire, chasing 268, were 95 for two. Drizzle prevented an immediate resumption, but there was a wind rustling in the chestnut trees and Surridge, never one to give up the fight, kept striding out of the dressing room, glaring at the clouds as if to will them in another direction. Finally, though the light was dim and the air damp, he persuaded the umpires to resume, taking the ball himself and off a short run dismissing five batsmen. Within half an hour of the resumption Gloucestershire had lost their remaining eight wickets for 17 runs. Then minutes later the heavens opened, and the field turned into a lake.

"When we went out to field under Stuey," Micky says, "it was like going over the top out of the trenches. But he led by example. As a close fielder he set the standard for everybody. He'd stand there in the field bawling orders. I remember Keith Miller saying to him, 'I wouldn't talk to my dog the way you talk to Locky.'"

To Lock, yes, but not to Laker. 'I swore at Jim once,' Surridge later wrote, 'and he could not bowl for an hour.'

There were two-day victories at Worcester and Lord's, the latter proving all the more vital when on the third day, once more, rain prevented Yorkshire from completing an almost certain victory at Dover. 'It seems that Surrey are to be chosen by the weather as county champions of 1954,' *The Times* wrote, though it could just as easily be argued that it was their ability to win games quickly that set them apart from their rivals. Whichever explanation you prefer, the task for Surrey was now straightforward. Yorkshire had completed their programme, and Surrey had two games to play. For a share of the title, they needed first innings lead in one of those games. One victory would win it outright.

They were back at the Oval on Wednesday 25 August for what would turn out to be the most extraordinary game in which Micky ever took part. Heavy rain fell in the morning, and play did not get under way till two o'clock, with Stuart Surridge asking Worcestershire to bat first on a sodden pitch that was drying awkwardly under a hot sun. After 45 minutes the visitors had battled to 16 for one. Then, with Laker and Lock posing unanswerable questions on the lethal surface, they tumbled to 25 all out.

In reply Tom Clark was caught at slip for 10. Micky took the total past 25 for first innings points before being caught at mid-on for 11, the highest score of the match at this stage. Then after tea Peter May and Bernie Constable gained the ascendancy. According to *The Times*, May, driving superbly, 'played a little gem of an innings' and Constable 'waltzed along with nimble footwork and some fine hooks.'

"The Worcestershire bowling was nothing like as challenging as ours," Micky remembers. "Locky got so many revolutions on the ball, and Jim really spun it. All they had was Ashman, a left-armer who didn't really turn it, and Roly Jenkins bowling leg spin – and the pitch was too slow for him." Or, as Nottinghamshire's number six Freddie Stocks put it earlier in the month, twice coming in with hardly any runs on the board, "It's a different f---ing wicket when tha's bowling."

Constable fell for 29, to be replaced by Barrington. Then, at half past five, with the score on 92 for three, Stuart Surridge waved them in.

The story goes that Ken Barrington, seeing the signal from the balcony, went down the wicket to Peter May. "He's declared!" he said with astonishment.

"What are you talking about?" May replied. Then, seeing for himself Surridge's wave: "He didn't have a gin and tonic at tea, did he?"

May's autobiography records the general reaction in the team: 'In those days the amateurs still used the upstairs dressing room. Downstairs among the rest of the side the general verdict was that the captain must have gone mad. His explanation as he led us out was that it was going to rain, which did not entirely clear up the misgivings.'

'Fielders swarmed round the bat,' *The Times* reported, 'as Lock and Laker were whipping like rattle-snakes from the pitch, if anything more fiercely than before.' 'It is hard to imagine,' wrote the *Daily Telegraph*, 'any other bowlers in the world making more out of this wicket than they did.'

With grim defence the Worcestershire batsmen battled through fifty minutes to reach 13 for two, but it was all to no avail. The following morning, with the sun shining and the ball lifting viciously, wickets were soon falling. In a chapter of accidents one batsman hit his wicket, another retired with a fractured finger, and a third – the keeper Hugo Yarnold, who alone reached double figures – was hit on the head by a rearing off-break from Jim Laker. The only light relief came with the sight of the ever-jocular Roly Jenkins emerging from the pavilion waving a white handkerchief.

In barely an hour Worcestershire slumped from 13 for two to 40 all out, to leave Surrey, after declaring on 92, victors by an innings and 27 runs – and county champions once more. To this day the match total of 157 runs remains the lowest recorded in a completed first-class fixture since 1878. Surridge was walking on water, and the 3,000-strong crowd gathered in front of the pavilion to hear him make a celebratory speech.

Friday was now a free day, and Micky travelled up to Lord's where he paid an entrance fee and sat at the Nursery End watching the bowler he was due to face at the Oval the next day: Lancashire's Brian Statham. "He bowled a lot of overs. I remember thinking to myself, 'There's a fair chance he'll be stiff tomorrow.'"

Statham was indeed stiff the next morning, sending down a long hop that Micky pulled for four, but he soon found his customary control and Surrey were all out for 128. Yet once again the bowlers did their work, and the match was won. In those last five weeks, with rain never far away, they won nine out of their ten matches, gaining first innings points in the tenth when they bowled out Middlesex for 51. It was Micky's introduction to first-class cricket: an astonishing sequence of victories by the greatest county team there has ever been. Inevitably it shaped his future attitude to the game, and the triumphs did not end in 1954, either.

Micky, after scoring 388 runs in his first six innings, was out 14 times in those closing five weeks, scoring only 192 runs at an average of 13.71.

"It was a real education," he says, "to play on rain-affected or damaged pitches against bowlers who really spun or cut the ball. It was something quite different from anything I'd played previously in school, club or second eleven cricket."

An average of 13.71 sounds paltry, but in those last ten games the opposing batsmen did even worse, achieving a combined average of just 9.79. Seven times they were dismissed for totals under 100; not once did they reach 200.

"In years to come," Micky remembers Bernie Constable complaining, "when they talk about this Surrey team, it will be all about the bowlers and about Peter May. There won't be one mention of the rest of us poor buggers who've had to bat on these bloody pitches."

*

The elements of Surrey's success had been coming together in the years before Stuart Surridge was appointed captain. They might have been champions in 1948 under the joint captaincy of Errol Holmes and Michael Barton. In fact, they would have been champions had Jim Laker caught a simple return catch from Jim Sims when Middlesex were nine wickets down at the Oval.

"Jim was very upset," Michael Barton remembered many years later, "but no one said a thing. Then the next year he caught Jim Sims, a brilliant one-handed caught-and-bowled, and all he said was, 'One year too late.' It was the only time anybody ever mentioned it."

Two years later, in 1950, with the quietly spoken Barton in sole charge, Surrey shared the title with Lancashire, clinching the necessary victory on a tense last afternoon at the Oval. For a while it looked possible that the Leicestershire batsmen, Les Berry in particular, might thwart the Surrey bowling. Micky was not there, but the story of that day has been handed down to him.

"Locky was bowling, and Les Berry went to hit him over the top. The ball turned and stopped, and it went straight up in the air towards mid-off. Locky started going for the catch, and Michael Barton at first slip called out 'Yours, Laurie' to Laurie Fishlock. The older Locky would have taken no notice, but he was only young and he stopped as he was told, left it to Laurie. Only Laurie had gone off the field and the twelfth man's name wasn't Laurie. The ball fell to earth with a sickening thud. Jack Parker, who was very Surrey through and through, was standing next to Michael Barton in the slips. 'That's the first f---ing time you've opened your mouth all season,' he said, 'and you've just lost us the f---ing championship.'"

"The story is absolutely true," Barton confirmed to Micky, "but I did make Jack apologise to me in front of the side in the dressing room afterwards." Fortunately the miss, like several others that afternoon, did not prove fatal.

"Michael Barton was a very nice, popular person," Micky says. "But, when he was captain, there was still the amateur-pro divide. The amateurs stayed in a different hotel; sometimes they'd take a dinner jacket to wear for the evening meal. Stuey totally changed the environment. He still changed in the amateur dressing room, but he had grown up in Surrey, playing with so many of the team when they were all younger."

In the words of the great Australian Bill O'Reilly, written when the Surrey skipper retired, 'In 1952 Stuart Surridge inherited a group of fine cricket individuals. He welded them into a team; galvanised them with his keen enthusiasm; then showed them how to win an honour denied them for nearly 40 years, apart from sharing it with Lancashire in 1950 – The County Championship! And now they seem to have made a habit of it!'

The Essex opening batsman Dickie Dodds described superbly the effect of Surridge's captaincy in his book *Hit Hard and Enjoy It*:

> *At one time Surrey seemed to have eleven captains, but all this ended abruptly when Stuart Surridge took over. Stuart was a large man in every way. He had a large frame, a large heart, he bowled large swingers, and he cracked the whip. Without question he was the boss. He led from the front and gave his orders, reprimands, encouragement and praise in language as spoken in the Borough Market.*
>
> *This is not to say that the Surrey players stopped chuntering as they batted, bowled, and especially as they fielded; it was that they now had a skipper who understood their chuntering and could orchestrate it and blend it into a harmonious, constructive whole. Through it all Stuart Surridge remained himself, and his own man, and that was perhaps his secret.*

It was 'Win, Win, Win' with Surridge, and that appealed to the young Micky. "I'm the sort of person, I've got to be The Guv'nor. To play in a side where we were the governors of county cricket and knowing that I had to contribute to that situation, that suited me. Stuey Surridge would be bawling at people left, right and centre. I don't say I enjoyed it. But it was a challenge. And, after a couple of years, sometimes I did have a word back."

Twenty years later, when Surridge was in his late fifties, Micky played under his captaincy once more. It was Esher cricket week, and Surridge, leading out the President's XI, had not mellowed at all. "These poor old boys in his team, he was clapping his hands and shouting at them. 'Come on, come on.' He was still all keyed up."

*

The summer of 1955 was an altogether drier, warmer one than 1954, though the change of weather did nothing to impede the onward march of a Surrey side growing ever stronger in self-assurance. They ended the summer of 1954 with six straight victories, and they began in 1955 with twelve in a row, establishing a sequence of 18 successive victories that remains the record for any team in the history of first-class cricket. To have achieved this in the three-day game, where draws were so common, is remarkable.

Micky, however, had an unpleasant shock at the start of the season. "The team went up for the first game, and I wasn't in it."

With Surridge as captain, four front-line bowlers other than him and Arthur Mac as keeper, that left room for only five batsmen. Peter May, Tom Clark and Bernie Constable were automatic choices, and Ken Barrington had done well in the closing weeks of 1954. So, even with Raman Subba Row departing to Northamptonshire, that meant that there was room for only one of David Fletcher, Eric Bedser and Micky, and the county opted to give another chance to the experienced Fletcher. The policy was to start the summer with the senior, capped players.

"I said to Jim Laker, 'If I'm not in the side by the time this season ends, then I'm away.' I had never given it much thought before then, but I felt a bit emotional."

In late May, with Barrington and Loader selected to play for MCC against the touring South Africans, Micky finally got his chance – though, alas, things did not go to plan. At teatime on the first day at Leicester they were 42 for one, in reply to the home side's 114 all out, and he was looking forward to going in at number five. There then followed a period of play as remarkable as any in the whole history of cricket.

Charles Palmer, the Leicester captain, a gentle medium-pacer with a bad back, under doctor's orders not to bowl, gave himself a single over to switch the ends of the two spinners. With his second ball he bowled Peter May, kept himself on and at one stage had figures of 12 overs, 12 maidens, 0 runs, 8 wickets, seven of them bowled.

"I got a first-baller," Micky recalls. "I think it went straight along the ground. There was this wet patch that he kept hitting. It was just one of those things. It went on and on."

Jim Laker was in the middle when Palmer took his eighth wicket and, according to Micky, there was chat in the dressing room about Laker losing his world record figures of eight wickets for two runs, taken five years earlier in a Test trial at Bradford. Laker's response was to chance his arm. He got an inside edge that went between his pads and his leg stump, and they ran two. Then he hit the next ball in the air between two off-side fielders and ran another two. In the end Palmer came off with figures of eight for seven.

In the second innings Surrey won by seven wickets, and Micky had time only to score five not out. He had had his chance, and he returned to the second eleven. "You knew you had to produce. You could work as hard as you like on your game, but that sort of thing could happen. You could get a ball like that or a dodgy decision. You just had to accept it."

As Micky's progress faltered, Ken Barrington, two years his senior, moved forward in leaps and bounds. At Lord's, for MCC against the South Africans, he caught the eye with a hard-hitting and uninhibited 27. Then, taking back Micky's place in the Surrey eleven, he scored consecutive hundreds at the Oval and at Trent Bridge. In the former he scored at twice the pace of Peter May, occasioning a lengthy tribute from the *Times* cricket correspondent: 'One was struck by his judgment of length, his quickness of foot, and his power and timing, which made some of his strokes seem to travel at the speed of sound.'

Ken Barrington
between the Bedsers

The latter century, a second thrilling display of hard hitting, brought him his county cap, as well as calls from several newspapers for him to gain his England cap, calls that the next week the selectors answered. In his own view this was too rapid a promotion, and after Test scores of 0, 34 and 18 he was discarded. It would be four years before he would return, and by then a caution was starting to creep into his play.

"When he first went in the England side he was playing in a relatively free way," Micky says. "He was powerful, and he scored runs all round the wicket. But when he got left out, he started to cut out some of his shots."

The Trent Bridge square was a batsman's delight, and Surrey won the game there on the last afternoon, scoring 188 for two in just 28.2 overs. Such a rate of scoring was rare and, as the Surrey batsmen hit the ball to all parts, the Notts bowler Arthur Jepson grew increasingly frustrated, blowing his top several times. Micky was the unwitting beneficiary of Jepson's behaviour when in August they played the return game at the Oval.

"About the third ball of the innings he bowled at me. It must have pitched middle and leg, straightened and hit me below the right knee. It would have knocked out middle stump. He let out a great appeal. Alec Skelding was the umpire. 'Not out,' he said. 'NOT OU-U-UT.' And it ran off for a leg bye."

In conspiratorial tones Skelding explained his decision as the reprieved batsman arrived at his end. "Don't worry, Micky lad, there'll be one or two more like that today. He gave me a torrid time at Trent Bridge."

It was late June when Micky returned to the mix of the first team, travelling to Headingley as twelfth man. Yorkshire again were Surrey's main rivals in the championship, but after tea on the second day the game was flowing Surrey's way, with a first innings lead of 102. Then, with the large Yorkshire crowd in a state of high excitement, they had to face the fast bowling of Fred Trueman and Mick Cowan in light that Micky reckons was the darkest in which he has ever seen cricket played.

"I think it's getting a bit lighter," Kenny Barrington suggested at one point as he waited anxiously to bat.

"I should think so," Bernie Constable replied. "The bloody moon's out."

Surridge tried to protect Barrington by sending in first Tony Lock, then Alec Bedser, then himself, but it was all to no avail. Off the day's last ball Barrington was yorked by Trueman for nought, and the bright light on the scoreboard, shining in the words of Peter May 'like a beacon on the Eddystone lighthouse', illuminated a score of 27 for seven.

The next day Yorkshire were left to score 178 to win, and almost immediately Len Hutton was bowled by Alec Bedser for one. Hutton, troubled by a bad back, retired from cricket the following week, and this proved to be his last innings on Yorkshire soil. He and Denis Compton had been Micky's childhood heroes, and during the great man's brief innings that day Micky was on the field – "for the only time. I was very disappointed that I never got to play against him."

The next batsmen prospered, and Yorkshire won by six wickets. It brought to an end Surrey's long unbeaten sequence.

Thereafter, with Peter May often away with England and Tom Clark struggling with his hips, Micky was a regular in the side, scoring two centuries inside a week in early July and passing 1,000 runs for the first time. Once more the championship was won, this time with an extraordinary record of Played 28, Won 23, Lost 5, which put them ahead of Yorkshire who won 21, lost 5 and drew 2.

"You would never get those statistics on the pitches that are played on now," Micky says. "The surfaces then were part of the character of English cricket – and part of the character of the English cricketer. You judged a batsman by how he could play on a cross-section of different surfaces. You'd go to Leyton or Ilford where there was grass all over the place and the ball would deviate off the seam, then to Swansea where it turned square but didn't bounce hugely. Then to Bradford, where it was a sporty pitch and the crowd were all around you. If you did well, they might even spit on you as you came in. Then to a good batting pitch at, say, Blackheath, where it came on and was pacey. Then back to the Oval, where the pitches were prepared to turn by at least teatime on the second day. You had to apply your game differently each time."

At some counties, where winning the championship was never a serious ambition, batsmen could go about their business at whatever pace suited them, but at Surrey there was always a pressure to move the game forward. If the pitch was good, you had to put your runs on the board quickly, to give the bowlers time to do their work. On the other hand, if it was difficult and you managed to survive for a while, then it was vital that you went on.

"If you got to 30 or 40 on a dodgy track, then you played a couple of maidens and out of frustration had a whack and got out, there would be a huge reception for you in the dressing room. You'd be up against the wall, with Bernie Constable saying, 'What do you think you're doing? You've thrown it away. Now somebody else has got to start all over again.' Then

The Surrey and Sussex players look on as Stuart Surridge cuts the cake to celebrate the 1955 championship

Andrew Sandham (coach) third from left, Herbert Strudwick (scorer) ninth, Sandy Tait (masseur) sitting front left

the phone would go – Stuey upstairs. You'd go up to his room, and you'd get it all a second time."

Then there were the frantic last-innings run-chases when you had to play your shots straightaway. There were so many factors at work, and not all of them were reflected in the players' individual statistics.

"During the years when we won those championships, averages were never talked about. It was all about winning the games."

*

Of the thirteen men who played in the majority of Surrey's games in those seven golden years, only David Fletcher and Micky now survive. Fletcher is not in the best of health so Micky's memories of that great bowling attack have become extra special.

Alec Bedser *(medium-pace swing and cut)*

"He was a big, strong man with huge, strong hands and the heart of a lion. He wasn't the quickest, but he was quick enough to inflict plenty of bruises on batsmen.

"His stock delivery was the in-swinger, but he also bowled the leg-cutter. On receptive and rain-affected pitches he spun the leg-cutter with the seam almost at right angles, like a leg-spinner. At his pace it was close to unplayable. On firmer pitches he would hold it with the seam pointing to second slip, as if it were an away swinger, with his hand behind the ball.

"The discipline he showed in his bowling was one example of the discipline instilled in him by his mother, who was a great influence on both him and his brother Eric. Mrs Bedser, a tall, lovely lady, ruled the roost. She emphasised the importance of hard work, punctuality, good manners and respect for your fellow man. She always preached that success only came from hard work, and that is exactly what Alec put into his cricket, technically and physically."

Peter Loader *(fast)*

"At his best Peter was a devastatingly quick swing bowler with an armoury that contained out-swing, in-swing, a slowie and a bouncer, all delivered with great accuracy. He was of a slim, wiry build and very aggressive, with a smooth rhythmical approach to the wicket and a good leap in the delivery stride. If we batted first in a championship match, we would look to declare in time to give us half an hour to bowl with the new ball. This is when Peter came into his own, often claiming two or three wickets with his accurate, pacey swingers. In any other era he would have played many more Tests than he did."

Jim Laker *(off-spin)*

"To me Jim was an absolute artist. His control was immaculate, and the spin he imparted on the ball was incredible. I fielded at short leg, either at bat/pad or forward close in, and I could hear the snap of his fingers, followed by the zzzzzz of the ball coming down the pitch. My forward position was real 'Bomb Alley', but such was Jim's accuracy that I never felt in any danger.

"It irked him that he was overlooked for two tours of Australia. There was a theory that off-spinners couldn't operate there, but he knew that he could control what was going on. He used to reckon that he could bowl a maiden over on any surface against any batsman he'd bowled against, except Don Bradman. He was the number one finger-spinner that I've ever seen.

"His method took its toll, and he often missed matches through arthritis in his spinning finger, which was twice the size of the one on his other hand. Also, from time to time, the seam of the ball would split the finger to the bone, which he treated with friar's balsam.

"Although Jim came across as a cool and calm person, he was in fact quite emotional at times – although this was rarely seen on the cricket field. The image of him that people have is of him at Old Trafford, when he took 19 Australian wickets in the match, the cool way he collected his sweater and led the England team off the field.

"He told me once how he projected this calm image after talking to Bobby Locke, who was at the time the leading South African golfer. Locke told him that he had trained himself never to do anything in a hurry. He developed a slow tempo and rhythm when walking the fairway, addressing the ball and putting his swing into operation. 'By nature I'm quite excitable,' he told Jim, 'but I've schooled myself so that I've got total control, no matter what the situation.' Jim did the same. He never rushed about. This, of course, was fine when things were going well; people admired his control and mastery. But, when things were not going so well, the same people would say, 'Look at him, he's not trying' or 'He doesn't care.'

"Stuey would sometimes shout and bawl at Tony Lock, but never at Jim. Jim always bowled with a fielder at 'cow-shot corner' for the 'slog-sweep' as it's called today, and sometimes, when we got down to nine, ten and eleven, Stuey would want to bring this man in from the boundary. Jim wouldn't argue back. He'd just put the ball down. 'If you want him up,' he'd say, 'then get someone else to bowl.'

"After Jim died, his wife Lilly asked if I would scatter his ashes at the Oval. I agreed, of course; I was honoured to do it. But when I was leading his family down the pavilion steps I realised that I hadn't really thought about where on the playing area I was going to do the scattering. I couldn't put them on the square. Then I thought, 'There is only one place for them – cow-shot corner.' In front of where they have now sited the Laker/Lock Stand."

Jim Laker, the consummate artist

Tony Lock *(slow left-arm)*

"Locky's body language was the exact opposite of Jim's. He expressed every emotion physically and verbally, in both success and failure, and Stuart Surridge treated them very differently. If Jim came up and bowled short outside the off stump and the batsman cut him for four, there'd be nothing from Stuey. Not a word. But if Locky bowled the same ball, all hell would break loose. Locky would get all wound up, but then the more he got wound up the better he bowled.

"He was a real hundred-percenter. Not only was he an outstanding left-arm spinner and world-class fielder, but in addition he could make vital contributions, when required, with the bat.

"There were times on receptive surfaces when Locky was unplayable. In tandem with Jim Laker, they were the perfect duo. He had a strong, aggressive, physical presence on the field, never giving the opposing batsman a minute's rest. He was an incredible wicket-taker.

"In his early days, when coaching in the winter of 1951/52 at Alders department store in Croydon, he changed his delivery. Because the ceiling was low, he had to push the ball through with a lower trajectory. He returned to the Oval for pre-season nets and, when he bowled out Jack Parker first ball, he received a volley of abuse from Jack, suggesting Locky's delivery was a throw. Yet, in the seven summers we won the championship, he was only called for throwing in one game – by Fred Price, against the Indians in 1952.

"It was when he saw a film of himself in a cinema in New Zealand in 1959 that he realised. So he decided to change his action. In the summer of 1959 his bowling arm came in from behind his back in a long sweep, something akin to the way Johnny Wardle bowled. Then the next summer he changed to the more orthodox method of his bowling hand coming up in front of his chin and then over in a complete arc. I don't know of any other bowler who has taken 100 wickets in three consecutive summers with three different actions. It was incredible.

"He was a world-class fielder in any position. He had a bullet-like throw from the deep, but his specialism was at backward short leg where he caught balls that were travelling at the speed of light. He was the best in the business, and he knew it. When I took a good catch off his bowling, he would come running over and put his arm round me. Sometimes he'd even kiss me. 'Mi-kell,' he'd say. 'You're the best catcher in the world ... in front of square.'

"During that fantastic run of success in the 1950s Surrey operated as a team. We had to win. But if I was compelled to name the one man in the side who contributed the most, it would have to be Tony Lock."

And if these four were not sufficient, there was:

Eric Bedser *(off-spin)*

"Like Alec he had huge hands and strong fingers. He was a big spinner of the ball, and he delivered it from a great height. He had to play second fiddle to Jim Laker but, when he was called on, more often than not he delivered the goods. If he had been playing in recent years, certainly up till the emergence of Graeme Swann, he'd have been the best off-spinner in the country, by some way.

"As a batsman he was a fine timer of the ball, but he should have been more aggressive, as he was in the nets."

And to support them all behind the stumps:

Arthur McIntyre *(wicket-keeper)*

"Up and down the country it was the general opinion that day in, day out Mac was the best wicket-keeper on the circuit. He was so consistent in his 'no-fuss' style. Godfrey Evans was brilliant in the Test matches, playing in front of capacity gates at places like Lord's, but he didn't find it easy to maintain the same high standard the next day in front of a sprinkling of spectators at a cold and dreary county ground.

"Mac was just brilliant: with his strong but soft hands and his smooth footwork. No matter whether he was standing up to the pace of Alec Bedser's swing and cut or the spin of Laker and Lock, the ball used to stay in his gloves. I used to marvel at the way he kept on some of the most responsive bowling wickets and all with no fuss. Of wicket-keepers since his day, he was more of the style of Bob Taylor than Alan Knott.

"He was also a very competitive person – very aggressive with the bat, with sweet timing, a fine player of spin.

"On the field he was relatively quiet. But if any opponent stepped out of line, like not walking, he would be the first in their face and be non-stop in their ear. Mac was a huge contributor to the success of that '50s side."

*

In the summer of 1956, Stuart Surridge's fifth and last in charge, Surrey won the championship for a fifth consecutive time, and Micky, despite missing six matches, passed 1,500 runs. It was Jim Laker's golden year, taking all ten Australian wickets when Surrey played them at the Oval in May, then at the end of July capping that with the greatest bowling feat in the whole history of the game: 19 Australian wickets out of 20 in the Old Trafford Test.

The previous weekend, however, Laker was not in action for Surrey, declaring himself unfit for the county's match in Sheffield. It was not the first time he had made himself unavailable for the trip back to his native Yorkshire, and it would not be the last, either. "We used to go by train," Micky says. "One time, I remember, Kenny and I were doing the bags, loading them into the taxi. 'What have you got Jim's bag for?' Bernie said. 'Hasn't he cried off yet?' A few minutes later we were taking his bag off the taxi. 'There you are,' Bernie said. 'What did I tell you?'"

The game was Micky's first appearance in Yorkshire, and it was all the more dramatic for being at Bramall Lane where the spectators were notoriously noisy. Three of the Surrey team survived from the famous game eight years earlier in 1948 when all of Yorkshire was in high dudgeon over the dropping from the Test team of their beloved Len Hutton. The chairman of selectors was Group-Captain Jack Holmes, and the crowd got it into their heads that he was the Surrey captain Errol Holmes, who was in any case just the sort of southern 'fancy cap' to get them going. He stepped out to bat on Monday morning amid non-stop abuse – ''Ere he comes ... Call thesel' a selector ... tha' couldn't pick a fine day' – and was bowled third ball for nought. Then, following on, he returned to the crease later in the day and hit his first ball over mid-off's head, only for the fielder to pull off a brilliant, one-handed catch. When the crowd realised the identity of the catcher, Hutton himself, there was utter pandemonium. "As I made the all too long walk back to the pavilion," Holmes later wrote, "taunts and abuse were hurled at my head. I felt as if I were being attacked by a swarm of angry bees, whose ignorance only added further pain to each stinging insult."

"The gates were closed on the Saturday morning," Micky recalls of the 1956 game, "and we were put in to bat. There was always a bit in the wicket there when it started, and not long after the start Tom Clark got rapped on the pads. There was a big appeal, the umpire's finger went up, and the crowd let out this great roar. I was non-striker, and I jumped. It was a tremendous atmosphere. I'd experienced it in football but never quite like that at cricket. I remember thinking, 'This is what it's all about.'"

On the third morning Yorkshire, needing 97 for victory, started out on 30 for two. "We arrived at the ground, and there was a huge crowd, all there to watch Yorkshire stuff Surrey. But Loader swung the ball beautifully, Locky got some turn, and wickets started falling. Billy Sutcliffe was captaining Yorkshire, and the crowd gave him huge stick when he came in to bat. 'Tha'll never be as good as tha' father.' It got to 15 to win, eight wickets down, and suddenly the ground was engulfed in smoke from a nearby factory chimney. My first thought was 'Somebody's set the place on fire. They want the game abandoned.' It was an incredible experience."

The last two wickets duly fell, leaving a despondent crowd to stream out into the street, delivering in the words of *The Times* 'many harsh and caustic comments' about their team.

"It was a quite different atmosphere at the Oval. They wanted us to win, but at the same time they wanted a good day's cricket. If we were playing Yorkshire, a large number of Surrey people would be hoping Len Hutton would get a hundred. The same with Middlesex and Denis Compton. That was their entertainment. During that run of success in the '50s, if we bowled the other team out and enforced the follow-on, we'd go down the steps and the members would say, 'Don't get them out too quickly. I've taken a day off work for this.'"

Another new experience for Micky that summer occurred in the August Bank Holiday match at home to Nottinghamshire. "It rained before the start, and Stuey asked everybody, 'What would you do if you won the toss?' He even asked Kenny and me. We all said 'Bat'. And back he came: 'Done it again, lads. Won the toss. All together.' That was what he always said when he was taking us into the field."

The pitch was slow to dry, Notts managed to reach 244 and, after a wet second day, Surrey were bowled out for 87 and had to follow on. As Micky prepared to go out a second time, he turned to his partner Tom Clark.

"What do you do when you follow on? Do you play the same?"

Clark turned to the rest of the team with a grin on his face. "Hey, did you hear that? Micky's never followed on before."

*

Before the war, according to Surrey's long-serving masseur Sandy Tait, when Lancashire visited the Oval, the first thing to appear in their dressing room at the start of a match was a barrel of beer. At the lunch table there were bottles of Pimm's Number One on offer. But nothing of that atmosphere was present when they were winning championship after championship in the 1950s.

"Some of the county sides on the circuit were big drinkers," Micky recalls, "but not Surrey. In fact, we weren't considered the most sociable of sides. Now and again Stuey would have a gin and tonic at lunch, so would Locky, but nobody ever went in the pub at the end of the day. It was explained to me that, if you went in there and got a nought the next day or took nought for plenty, people would say 'I saw him last night in the pub.' So, after the game, we'd go to the little bar in the ladies' pavilion, where the Bedser Stand is now. Not everybody came down – and, by and large, it was one drink, that's all. In those days people couldn't afford to drink that much, anyway."

There was plenty of humour, however, especially when the masseur Sandy Tait was about. His father had captained Tottenham Hotspur, playing in the team that won the FA Cup in 1901, but the young Sandy had contracted polio as a boy and walked with a pronounced limp, a wooden calliper attached to his leg. He had been at the Oval since 1929, spending his winters as a scenery shifter at the Penge Empire Music Hall and as a masseur at Dulwich Hamlet and Kingstonian football clubs.

His own sporting ambitions frustrated, Tait was not slow to tease the younger members of the Surrey team. "You think you're quick, son," he would say. "I could do you yards for years." It was a challenge that was finally taken up when one year Surrey beat Warwickshire before lunch on the final day at the Oval. In front of the pavilion, with the players of both teams on the balcony and a fair few spectators still in the ground, they measured out a hundred yards: Micky and Ken Barrington versus the ageing Tait. "He had a forty-yard start," Micky says, "and he won easily. To great cheers from the balcony and the crowd. I can see him now bobbing along in front of us."

The championship pennant went with them to all the away games, and 'Taity' took great delight in draping himself in it on the platform of York railway station, parading it in front of the success-starved northerners. He also helped out with the transporting of all the bags, insisting to whoever was on duty with him that they hired the old-fashioned London taxi cabs, the ones with a roof rack and a well next to the driver. "Unlike the newer ones we could get twelve bags into two of them. And he was given expenses for three."

When they went to Cambridge in early season Sandy Tait ran into his arch foe, the Fenner's groundsman Cyril Coote. "He would never light the coal fire in the dressing room, however freezing it was. Taity had umpteen rows about getting some coal. In the end we used to travel up on the train with a sack of coal in among the bags."

He was an old-fashioned, uncomplicated masseur: "I've never known anybody with stronger hands," Micky says. "If you asked him to rub harder, he'd say, 'I can really hurt you, son.'" But he was much more than that: "A huge help in those years, a very important part of the atmosphere in the dressing room."

Not all the fun revolved around Sandy Tait. Micky remembers a game at Cambridge when he and Ken Barrington, the youngsters in the side, arrived early at the hotel. As a prank they persuaded Arthur Mac to let

*Micky and
Sandy Tait*

them remove his room-mate Bernie Constable's bed and to set up a makeshift arrangement on the window seat behind the curtain.

"Where's my bed then?" Bernie asked when he arrived later after a meal on the way up.

"I think there's something behind there," Mac said innocently, sitting comfortably in bed in his pyjamas.

"Behind there? What do you mean 'Behind there'?"

"It's all laid out."

"That's ridiculous."

After much grumbling, Constable changed into his striped winceyette pyjamas. The window was right beside the flashing red light of the hotel sign and, as the Cambridge students spilled out of the bars, they spotted him, pointing up at the figure lying above them. "Look at him up there."

"In the morning," Micky says, still chuckling after fifty-odd years, "the maids came in to do the beds and they couldn't stop laughing."

*

*Two good days for Micky – for Surrey against the West Indians in 1957
(top) Coming off with 147 not out in June
(bottom) Pulling Roy Gilchrist for four in an innings of 78 in August
The keeper is fellow Corinthian-Casual Gerry Alexander*

The summer of 1957 was Peter May's first as captain. The field of play was not such a noisy place now, but any idea that his quietness represented a gentler, more amateur spirit is quickly dispelled by Micky.

"Stuey was obviously competitive because he was loud. But Peter was silently very aggressive. He'd give a steely look rather than shout. If a skier got dropped, he'd turn to the person next to him. 'How can you be a professional cricketer and drop a skier?' he'd say. He was a lovely man but he was a hard one, too. I admired him; he was a great influence on me – not always perhaps for the best. For example, I'd gone all through public school and National Service without ever swearing. And I'd stood in the leg trap, with Stuart Surridge next to me coming out with all sorts. But it was Peter's quiet language to himself, when he was captain, that got me started, I'm afraid."

Surrey were now providing as many as four to the England Test team – May, Laker, Lock and Loader – but their absence had little effect on their season-long domination of the county game. They won 21 of their 28 matches, ten of them by an innings and another four by ten wickets. Their victory margin over second-placed Northamptonshire, 94 points, remains the highest in the history of the competition. Also, to those who like to attribute so much of their success to the pitches on which they played at the Oval, they could point out that their 14 away matches produced 11 victories against 10 at home.

"The side was at its peak that year," Micky reckons. "The bowling was at its best, and the batting, which had been relatively inexperienced in the second part of Stuey's reign, was now considerably stronger."

Statistics can only tell part of the story, but that summer they were extraordinary. Micky turns to the page in *Wisden* that records each county's overall batting and bowling averages. With the bat Surrey scored 29.22 runs for each wicket they lost; with the ball, they conceded only 14.50. Never has one county so dominated the end-of-season bowling averages, with five of them finishing in the top ten.

There were many devastating bowling performances that summer, none perhaps more outstanding than against Hampshire in the week when Surrey took its cricket out to Guildford. "I loved playing there," Micky says. "The side boundaries were a bit narrow, and it was always packed – with several rows of seating. When you played at Guildford, you really did know that you were representing the county of Surrey."

The ball usually swung at Guildford, and that Wednesday morning it did swing for Alec Bedser and especially Peter Loader, as they shot out Hampshire for 66 in little more than an hour and a half. By three o'clock the next day, with Jim Laker extracting considerable turn, they had won by an innings.

Unfortunately this was not the outcome that the local dignitaries had wanted. It was the 700th anniversary of King Henry III's granting of a royal charter to Guildford, and the Queen and Prince Philip were scheduled to arrive shortly. "So we had to stage a beer match, to make sure some cricket was still going on." Soon enough the Hampshire wickets were falling again and, to slow down the collapse, Peter May turned to the part-time bowling of Ken Barrington and Micky, a move that did not, alas, meet with royal approval. "Prince Philip was quite a cricket enthusiast. He wanted to see some proper bowling."

The Queen and Prince Philip meet the teams, Guildford, 1957

The national batting averages did not display quite the same Surrey domination as the bowling did, though Peter May's 2,347 runs were at an average of 61.76, ten runs an innings higher than Colin Cowdrey in second place. His figures were all the more remarkable when you bear in mind what Micky says about him: "There was never any talk of averages in the Surrey team. It was all about what you could achieve in the conditions that prevailed. Peter was a very good team man. He never ever played for his statistics. He was always looking to win the match."

The key opponents each year were Yorkshire, and May showed his class in both games against them in 1957. At the Oval he hit a masterly 125, setting up a two-day innings victory. Then at Bradford, in a game reduced to a day and a half, his free-hitting 63 on a devilish track almost allowed the Surrey bowlers time to pull off an improbable victory. "Peter was very highly thought of in Yorkshire. Freddie Trueman, for example, was a great admirer of his. I don't know whether it was out of admiration or because he didn't want to be dropped from the Test team, but he hardly ever bowled him a bouncer."

The innings by Peter May that stands out most clearly in Micky's memory was played against Yorkshire the following summer. The Oval groundsman Bert Lock's attempt to prepare a track that would take spin by teatime on the second day went somewhat wrong. The pitch was dry and dusty, and within half an hour of the start Yorkshire's spinners Illingworth and Wardle were in action. Micky, batting at number three, was soon walking out. "The first ball Ray Illingworth bowled at me, I played forward and it hit me on the neck. It was only about a quarter past twelve." He soon departed for a duck, to be replaced by Peter May who then assumed complete control, hitting 155 while only Eric Bedser of the remaining batsmen, with 43, got beyond a score of 4.

"Johnny Wardle said he'd never seen a finer innings in those conditions. Peter kept hitting him over extra cover, at a time when very few batsmen did that. When you think about a match like that, how can you compare it with the present-day game? How can you compare the statistics?"

Then there was the fielding. Never in the history of the game, before or since, have there been three fielders, other than wicket-keepers, who have taken more than 200 catches between them in one summer. For all three to be playing for the same county is extraordinary. Tony Lock held 63, Ken Barrington 64 and Micky 77, one short of the all-time record set by the great Wally Hammond in 1928.

At Northampton in early June, on a rain-affected pitch, he held seven in one innings: six at short leg and one in the gully. It was a new world record for a fielder; it even equalled the world record for a wicket-keeper.

Surrey made certain of retaining the championship as early as August 16, when they beat Somerset at Weston-super-Mare. The match ended shortly before 5.30 on Friday afternoon, and the Surrey players celebrated with a drink in the little wooden pavilion.

Four catches

(top left) On the off side, catching Haydn Davies of Glamorgan
(bottom left) In the leg trap, with Tony Lock ready for the rebound
(top right) In the leg trap, catching the left-handed Ken Suttle of Sussex
(bottom right) On the off side, catching Martin Horton of Worcestershire

*(above) One that got away: Gamini Goonesena survives a diving effort at forward short leg
(top right) Catching Ray Illingworth – "off a full toss, one of the best catches I took"*

Brylcreem Fielder of July 1957, with 21 catches
Jimmy Hill presents a set of cuff links to Micky

Micky and Ken Barrington were still the two juniors of the side – Micky in his fourth summer in the first team and Barrington already a Test cricketer – so it still fell to them to pack the bags for the train. Back in London the two of them, with Sandy Tait, loaded them into taxis and took them down to the Oval, ready to collect before the game next morning at Lord's.

"It was all locked up when we got there. Taity made a call to the night-watchman, who said if we left them for him he'd put them in the office by the side of the Hobbs Gates. So we stood there on the pavement, lobbing all the bags over the top of the gates. That was our glorious homecoming, our welcome back to the Oval as champions."

Their championship programme ended at Hove on Friday 6 September. At that point Micky should have reported back to Charlton for the football season, but he had the small matter of his own wedding the following day. "My finest catch of the summer," he calls it.

On Friday evening he returned from Hove to Dulwich where he and Sheila met the vicar. Then back at Oakbank Grove a realisation dawned on him: "The honeymoon. Oh my god. Where's the AA book?"

The Surrey players at Micky's wedding
left to right: Eric Bedser, Alec Bedser, David Fletcher, Ken Barrington, Tom Clark, Micky and Sheila, Ronnie Pratt, Dennis Cox, Roy Swetman, Michael Willett, Jim Laker, Bernie Constable, Stuart Surridge

They finished up, after a reception in the ladies' pavilion at the Oval, at the Branksome Towers Hotel in Bournemouth, returning to London on the Monday morning. Then on Tuesday, not entirely to the pleasure of Charlton Athletic, he rejoined the Surrey team for a trip to Scarborough, to play for the Champion County against the Rest.

The idea was for Sheila and Micky to continue their honeymoon outside the hours of play, and with great consideration Peter May booked them into the Balmoral Hotel, away from everybody else. "The amateurs used to stay at the Grand and the pros at the Salisbury. But, after we booked in on the Tuesday afternoon, we went for a walk and met Peter Richardson."

"Where are you staying?" the England opener asked.

"The Balmoral."

"Oh, that's tremendous. Everybody goes back to the Balmoral after the bar closes at the Salisbury. There's a great pianist there. He plays till the early hours of the morning."

The match was special as it was the occasion of Denis Compton's last appearance as a professional cricketer. He and Len Hutton had been Micky's two heroes in the early years after the war, though their styles were in marked contrast. At Scarborough the *Times* reporter was in rhapsodic form:

> *It is difficult to be present on this occasion without a rush of clichés to the head … If Hutton might be called the Gielgud of cricket, withdrawn and cerebral, content to be a part of orthodox classical tradition, Compton remains an Olivier, original and flamboyant.*

In the Rest's first innings Micky took two catches which lifted his season's total to 77, one short of the record. Then, when the Rest followed on, Jim Laker and Godfrey Evans cooked up a plan, which was explained to Micky.

"When Godfrey comes in, he's going to give you a catch."

"No," Micky said, true to his father's hatred of anything not quite straight. "I don't want it unless it comes naturally."

He looks back now with a philosophical smile.

"Maybe I was a bit of a mug."

At the close of the Scarborough match on Friday they caught the overnight train to Aberdeen. It was the centenary of Aberdeenshire cricket, and MCC had promised that the champion county would play a three-day friendly match starting on Saturday morning. Fred Trueman was guesting for the local side, but still Surrey won by an innings, with Micky hitting the match's only fifty.

Standing (left to right): Herbert Strudwick (scorer), Ken Barrington, David Fletcher; Tom Clark, Peter Loader, Tony Lock, Micky Stewart, Bernie Constable, Sandy Tait (masseur) Sitting: Eric Bedser, Arthur McIntyre, Peter May, Alec Bedser, Jim Laker

Unusually for that time the second day of the game was played on the Sunday, a day that Micky remembers with a shiver.

"There was a huge gale. The coldest I've ever been on a cricket field. They went in to bat a second time, we went through them quickly but we couldn't get the last man out. Every so often there'd be a squall of rain, and every time we ran off the field our hosts would put out bottles of brandy and Scotch, which Arthur Mac and others would sample. After three or four squalls, Mac wasn't very tidy behind the wicket.

"Eventually, with nine wickets down, this chap whacked it miles up in the air and Bernie Constable got underneath it. The rain was getting heavier again, and we all ran off, leaving Bernie to the catch. And he dropped it. Mac took his gloves off, threw them down and called Bernie everything."

Finally the game was completed, and Micky telephoned Charlton. Their instructions were unequivocal: report back tomorrow morning. "So Sheila and I took the sleeper down to London, I dropped her at New Malden and went off to training."

*

For more than seven years, between the spring of 1951 and the winter of 1958/59, England did not lose a Test series. By 1957 their team was almost a roll-call of greats: Laker and Lock the spinners, Trueman and Statham the quicks, Evans behind the stumps, Bailey the all-rounder, and among the batsman May, Cowdrey and Graveney. If there was a weakness at all, it lay at the top of the order where there was no settled partner for Peter Richardson. Increasingly Micky's name was being mentioned in that context.

With 1,801 runs and 77 catches in 1957, he was named as the Cricket Writers' Young Player of the Year, winning the prestigious award with more than two-thirds of all the votes, and he was also chosen as one of *Wisden*'s five cricketers of the year.

"Keep pushing on next year," Peter May told him, "and you'll be on the boat to Australia."

Indeed, if the party had been selected at the end of 1957, he might well have been included, but in 1958, for the first time, his game went backwards. In a gloomy summer he was again the country's leading fielder, taking 61 catches, but with the bat he managed just 1,230 runs at an average of only 25.62. In those days, when performances in county cricket weighed more heavily in the selectors' scales, you needed to be in good form when a vacancy occurred. Mike Smith of Warwickshire was, emphatically so, but Micky was not. It would be another four years before his chance would come.

Surrey began the summer with a bang, winning all their five matches in May with great ease. The fifth, at Old Trafford, looked wide open at lunch on the final day when Peter May, himself batting with assurance during the morning session, declared to set Lancashire 205 to win in 185 minutes. Then David Gibson, a fast-medium bowler from the Streatham club, tore through the top order, Laker and Lock teased out the tail, and Lancashire were dismissed for 27, just two more than the lowest score in their history, made back in 1871.

Nine of the wickets fell to catches, mostly close to the wicket, but it is the other one that remains in Micky's memory: the fall of Lancashire's veteran captain, the somewhat stern Cyril Washbrook. "The young pros were all frightened to death of Cyril. He was facing Alec Bedser, with Geoff Pullar at the non-striker's end. I was fielding in the gully; he cut the ball to my right and Geoff called 'yes'. Well, it was damp, the ground slowed up the ball, and I stopped it. 'No, no, no,' Geoff goes, and Cyril's run out by half a pitch."

As wickets continued to fall, it was not long before Pullar was following his captain up the pavilion steps. "But, instead of going in the dressing room, he asked the attendant to get his car keys. Rather than face Cyril, he spent the rest of the innings sitting in his little Morris Minor, with his pads, bat and everything."

As the season progressed, Surrey found the going much harder than in 1957. The bowling relied more heavily on reserves, with Alec Bedser, turning 40 in early July, missing two months with pneumonia, and Test calls frequently depriving the side of Laker, Lock and Loader. With neither Ken Barrington nor Micky having good summers, and Peter May often on Test duty, the batting was also less effective than the previous summer, and the championship was not finally won till the end of August.

On the season's final afternoon, as if in warning that a golden age was drawing to a close, they were bowled out for 57 by Worcestershire. The only bright spark in their humiliation was an innings of 24 not out by a youngster making his debut in the county championship, John Edrich.

Micky remembers the first time they had all seen him in the nets.

"Who's that left-hander?" Eric Bedser asked.

"He's an Edrich."

"He plays in a funny way."

They fell silent for a while, then suddenly came the chirp of Bernie Constable. "I don't know about that. I'll tell you something. He hasn't missed a bloody ball yet."

"That was a typical Bernie observation," Micky says. "I learned more from him than from anybody else in cricket. He used to watch like a hawk when new players came in. Even the way they were holding their bat when they came out of the pavilion. They'd take guard, and he'd come in from cover, till he was only three or four yards away, looking at the way they were holding the bat. Staring."

Edrich played his next game for Surrey in the middle of May the following year. Drafted into the side when several batsmen were missing, he travelled to Trent Bridge and hit a century in each innings, adding another two hundreds before the month of May was out. Yet the team he joined in 1959 was not the same team Micky had joined in July 1954. Then there had been glory upon glory in store, a side which came only to know and to expect success. Now, with several key players ageing, they were in the first stages of decline.

It would be many years before John Edrich would enjoy the triumph of winning the championship. The captain by then would be the last one of that great 1950s side still playing, Micky Stewart.

*

Micky thinks himself lucky. There are not many, indeed hardly any, who have come into first-class cricket into a team so utterly dominant. For five years he only knew success, and it shaped his attitude and his expectations throughout his long career in cricket.

Furthermore, he played in the county game when it was rooted in the counties themselves. In those seven years Surrey had twenty players who appeared 20 or more times in the championship. Fourteen were born and brought up in the county. Of the other six, four were born in neighbouring Berkshire, including the Bedsers, Woking lads whose mother happened to be in Reading at the time of their birth, and Peter May, who attended Charterhouse School in Surrey. The only two from further afield were Tom Clark from Luton and Jim Laker from Yorkshire, though he was already working for Barclays Bank in Catford when he signed for Surrey.

That's the way Micky liked it, and it's the way he wishes it were today.

"I still feel strongly about it. The county game that I was introduced to, the majority of each side had played their early cricket within that county. They were representative of the type of cricket that was played there, from grass roots to the best weekend cricket. That was traditional county cricket. Now, with every year that passes, that is lost more and more. I really don't think it's too late to get it back."

7

FOR SURREY ... AND ENGLAND

The 1950s was for English cricket a rare time, a decade in which the structure of the county game remained almost entirely unaltered. There was one and only one competition, a championship in which the 17 counties each played 28 three-day games, starting in early May and concluding at the latest in the first week of September. There was one touring side, staying all summer and playing a series of four or, more usually, five Tests. And there was a clear-cut demarcation – on the surface, at any rate – between the amateurs and the professionals, with the two groups, Gentlemen and Players, contesting a showcase match each July at Lord's.

Through the decade the post-war boom in crowds gradually faded, with rising affluence giving access to alternative attractions, and this led to intermittent calls for 'Brighter Cricket'. Yet for the most part the English game maintained its annual rhythm, and part of that familiar rhythm came to be the winning of the championship by Surrey. Seven times in a row they were crowned champions and, when in early August 1959 they sat in first place once more, 14 points clear with two games in hand, few doubted that the natural order would prevail and that Surrey would make it eight in a row. *The Times* certainly thought so: 'The champions, it seems, are now almost home and dry,' it declared.

Yet, beneath that seemingly calm surface, much was changing, not least at Surrey.

The square at the Oval, for one thing. For several years the groundsman Bert Lock had prepared the pitches by rolling marl and manure into the natural surface, creating tracks that encouraged the bowlers. It was what Stuart Surridge and later Peter May expected. Indeed, Micky recalls one match when Surridge put the visitors in to bat and their openers survived unbeaten till lunchtime. "We were playing on the Archbishop Tenison side and, as we came off, Stuey headed across to the small scoreboard where Bert Lock used to be. 'Where are you going?' we asked. 'I'm going to sack Lock.'"

Undoubtedly it helped Surrey that they played on pitches at the Oval that produced results, but the advantage they gained was not as great as many on the circuit imagined. There were seasons when they won as many games away from the Oval as at home. In an attempt to counter 'discussion in the press and elsewhere', the Surrey yearbook for 1958 printed statistics that showed that during the previous three seasons Laker and Lock had taken considerably more wickets per game in away matches.

Nevertheless MCC were concerned about the standard of pitches up and down the country and, as a result, in 1959 Bert Lock altered his methods, reducing the marl and manure he rolled on top of the grass. Unfortunately, according to Micky, the grass had developed a thatched, deadening quality, taking some of the pace out of the square. Furthermore, through the seven summers of Surrey's dominance, several of them wet, the regulations prevented any covering of the pitch during the hours of play, even when the rain was pouring down. But for 1959 this was altered to allow covering once play had been abandoned for the day, and that, together with an exceptionally dry summer, created surfaces that provided a different challenge for the Surrey bowlers, not just at the Oval.

Alec Bedser was 41 in July, a great age for a hard-working pace bowler. Peter Loader, never the strongest in stamina, had spent the previous winter with England in Australia, where he had developed shoulder problems. Also in Australia were Jim Laker, 37 himself and struggling with his spinning finger, and Tony Lock, who was now in the process of remodelling his action. Two years earlier the Surrey bowlers had taken their opponents' wickets at 14.50 runs each; now the figure was 24.27.

The problems for Surrey did not end there.

In the seven and a half years from March 1951 to August 1958 England had played 14 Test series without losing one of them. In that time they had beaten Australia three times. So it was a great shock when in the winter of 1958/59, under the captaincy of Peter May, Australia crushed them 4-0.

Nothing seemed to go right on the tour. The manager Freddie Brown was not everybody's cup of tea; there was controversy over the bowling actions of several Australians and rumblings of discontent in the England camp over the relative payments to the amateurs and professionals. Jim Laker topped the bowling averages, but he caused an upset when he declared himself unfit for the vital fourth Test and there were further ructions when he refused to go on to New Zealand. Then, in a development that shocked and upset Peter May, several English newspapers broke with convention by creating a brouhaha over the arrival late in the tour of May's fiancée.

When the summer of 1959 started, May was absent from Surrey, on honeymoon in Cornwall. Whether the strain of the winter was a contributory factor cannot be known, but in July he was hospitalised with an internal abscess and did not reappear. Alec Bedser captained capably in his absence, and the newcomer John Edrich scored almost 1,800 runs. But, for all that, May was the best batsman in the world, and he was missed. They won six out of the seven games he played – and only six out of 21 when he did not.

The internal dynamic of the team was subtly altering. Arthur McIntyre, so long at the heart of it all, had given up his place to the young Roy Swetman, who was already England's reserve wicket-keeper. And Jim Laker in his last season was increasingly out of sorts with it all, expressing his views the following winter in a controversial book *Over to Me* that led to the withdrawal of his Surrey membership. Recognising Alec Bedser's difficulty in dropping his brother Eric, Laker stood down from the team for one game, but he was not at all happy the following week when Peter May left him out of the home game against Yorkshire – according to Laker, without explanation. As a result, wrote Laker, 'An atmosphere developed among the players in the Surrey dressing-room, an atmosphere which I couldn't ever remember before.'

Micky was a team player through and through, and he tried to take no notice of it all. Every cricket side has its points of friction, especially when matches are not being won. "But there were times," he says, "when you were aware that everybody wasn't going down the same road."

In Peter May's absence they lost their way in August, winning just six points in five games, but a good victory at Bath, where the ball turned helpfully for Laker and Lock, left them in the mix as the season reached its denouement.

	P	W	D	L	Points
Gloucestershire	26	12	4	9	186
Warwickshire	27	13	5	9	184
Yorkshire	26	12	7	7	178
Surrey	25	11	10	4	174

There was a maximum of 14 points for victory so their fate was still in their own hands, especially if they could win the next game: a top-of-the-table encounter at the Wagon Works ground in Gloucester.

Gloucestershire's great strength was their spin attack: off-spinners John Mortimore and David Allen and slow-left-armer Sam Cook who had all been taking wickets galore on a helpful pitch at Bristol. Nevertheless, it was a shock to the Surrey side when they arrived at the Wagon Works to find that they would be playing on a bare track, with a red dressing rolled into it that produced puffs of dust wherever the ball pitched. As the *Times* correspondent put it, 'To provide such a wicket for Surrey's visit might seem like playing with fire.'

Gloucestershire's only titles belonged in the 1870s, in the prime of WG Grace, before the championship was officially established. So the little Gloucester ground, with its cramped pavilion, was bursting with spectators as never before, and the roads all round were jammed with motor cars. Surrey, winning the toss, were all out for 130, and before close Laker and Lock had dismissed Gloucestershire for 101.

Ten minutes of play on that first day remained. Micky was down on the scorecard to bat at number four, behind John Edrich, Brian Parsons and Ken Barrington, and, with a night-watchman David Gibson padded up, he relaxed. "I'd been fielding at bat-pad. There was a bit of a breeze and, with the batsmen scuffing away at the crease, I'd got covered in red dust. So I stripped off and got in the shower."

Out in the middle Sam Cook took the new ball, rubbing it – as he was allowed to do – in the dust. Arthur Milton, at short leg, was standing almost in the popping crease, and he caught the first ball brilliantly off Parsons' bat. In the shower Micky heard the roar, and there was another roar next ball when Gibson was bowled. With Barrington marching out to bat, Micky was now next man in.

Without a stitch of clothing on, he did not waste time with a towel. "I was soaking wet, scrambling to put my whites on, and yet another roar went up." This time, fortunately for Micky, Barrie Meyer the Gloucestershire keeper had dropped Barrington off Cook, and the day ended with no further ado.

On the second morning Barrington opened proceedings with a straight six off Cook, scoring an attacking 49, and Micky chipped in with a 29 that *The Times* called 'a display of resource and judgement worth many a 60 or 70 on an easier pitch'. Gloucestershire were left 161 to win, which the home supporters, if not the pressmen, thought possible. But, with Laker and Lock unplayable, they were soon 26 for seven and by twenty-five past four had lost the match. Surrey were once more on top of the championship table.

The next day Yorkshire won a thrilling run chase at Worcester. Surrey, back at the Oval on Saturday morning, knew that if they did not beat Middlesex and Yorkshire did beat Sussex at Hove, their seven-year reign would be over. And that was what happened. On Tuesday afternoon Yorkshire, set an improbable 215 to win in 105 minutes, raced to a breathtaking five-wicket victory, while Surrey, hoping for a manageable run chase of their own, were held up on a placid pitch by obdurate Middlesex batting. For 78 overs they toiled while Middlesex made 175. "I can remember being in the field," Micky says, "sensing the time going by and knowing that they weren't going to give us a chance."

Eventually Surrey found themselves chasing 265 in 143 minutes. Micky was promoted to open in the hope of a brisk start, but he was immediately caught at the wicket for 0. Edrich and Barrington had both had golden summers, but they too were soon back in the pavilion. By the time the fourth wicket fell at 26, news had come through from Hove, where there was an earlier finish, that Yorkshire had won.

A funereal atmosphere filled the dressing room. "It hit me very hard," Micky says, "and Kenny Barrington. We had never known what it was like not to win the championship."

The next year, with Laker retired and May absent all summer with further health problems, they finished seventh. The following year there was no Alec Bedser and they fell to fifteenth. The summers of expecting success were over.

*

For Ken Barrington the summer of 1959 brought a silver lining. In the aftermath of defeat in Australia, England rebuilt their Test side and he regained the place he had lost after being picked prematurely in 1955. Against a weak Indian side he hit 357 runs in six innings, then the following winter in the Caribbean he hit his first two Test centuries. Naming him as one of its five Cricketers of the Year, *Wisden* described him not only as a prolific run-scorer but as an attractive entertainer:

> *Built on solid lines with a mop of black hair, Barrington has always possessed a powerful square cut and brilliant cover drives. Nowadays he is equipped with a very wide range of strokes and when he is master of the situation he provides plenty of entertainment for the onlookers.*

Then came the moment that changed the course of Barrington's career. He started 1960 in fine form, scoring 553 runs at an average of 69 in the first month. "I thought his game was tremendous at the beginning of that summer," Micky says. "He was full of confidence, playing an expansive game with so many shots. He was coming to the beginning of 'Ken Barrington – Tremendously Attractive Player'. If he'd gone on in that way, he'd have compared with the very best this country has ever seen."

"I'm really going to enjoy myself this season," he told Micky.

There then followed a seven-day spell in which he was out four times while scoring just 14 runs. In a frantic run chase against Somerset at the Oval he was out for 0, mistiming a drive. Then, on a green top at Hove, he was out twice more for 0, and he followed that with 1 and 13 not out at

Trent Bridge. By the time he arrived at Edgbaston for the first Test against South Africa, the word was that he was 'having a bad trot'.

'I don't honestly think I was in bad form,' he wrote later. 'My failures comprised only a few balls. Frankly, I felt due a big score.'

The selectors, together with captain Colin Cowdrey, saw things differently, causing great surprise on the morning of the match when they dropped Barrington in favour of newcomer Peter Walker of Glamorgan. Go back to Surrey and find your form, they said, leaving England to start their first home Test of 1960 as they had never done throughout the 1950s: taking the field without a Surrey man in the eleven.

Barrington did twelfth man duties at Edgbaston on Thursday and Friday, then returned to the Oval on Saturday for Surrey's game against Kent. "He had tears in his eyes," Micky recalls. "I remember him saying to me, 'They'll never leave me out again.' From that point on, he cut out all his more risky shots, building his game on consistency."

On that Saturday Barrington scored a resolute 126, with Micky at the other end making an unbeaten 169. He also hit good runs in the next two matches. Then, when Geoff Pullar dropped out of the second Test with a fractured wrist, Barrington was called back.

In all, Ken Barrington played 82 times for England. He retired from Test cricket eight years later with a batting average, 58.67, that puts him in sixth place in all Test cricket history, ahead of such greats as Hammond, Hobbs, Hutton, Tendulkar and Sobers. Among post-war batsmen only Graeme Pollock, in a shortened South African career, stands above him.

Yet for Micky such statistics do not tell the full story. "One of the saddest things I've known in my career is that the game of cricket never saw the best of Kenny Barrington, only in flashes. To me, without a doubt, he would have been one of the greatest all-round stroke makers, with power as well as timing, that there would have been in all English cricket."

Ken Barrington and Micky had come in to the Surrey side together. For several years they remained the two youngsters, both with bright futures predicted for them. They were close friends, rooming together, but they had quite different backgrounds and also different personalities.

Micky's father was a free spirit, an entrepreneur who mixed easily with all sorts, while Barrington's father was a regular soldier, a man who knew his station in life and was accustomed to the taking of orders. Micky had been to Alleyn's, at one stage planning to go to Oxford University, while Ken Barrington had left school at 14 to work in a garage for seven shillings and sixpence a week.

"Kenny was a typical product of the social set-up at that time. He came into the environment at the Oval, with the amateurs and the professionals, 'Mister May' and 'Mister Surridge' and all that, and he never lost that. Right to the day he died, he found it hard to call Stuey Surridge 'Stuey'."

Micky had a deep inner confidence, and he played his cricket in something of a Corinthian spirit. 'Micky Stewart was an utterly unselfish batsman,' Jim Laker wrote, 'and a brilliant close catcher who, more than any other cricketer I know, put the game of cricket far ahead of personal achievement.'

By contrast, Ken Barrington, for all his natural ability, was never sure of himself. "He was one of the biggest worriers," Micky says. "Before he went in to bat, he'd have two cigarettes going and he'd be reading the newspaper upside down. But what a player!"

In the nets, wearing a fancy cap with a pillow under his jersey and a tie around his waist, Barrington could do a fine impersonation of WG Grace playing all the shots but, after that dropping at Edgbaston, he always walked to the middle with a determination, above all else, not to give his wicket away. Once, against New Zealand in 1965, he was dropped by the England selectors for scoring a century too slowly, and twice the Surrey players, frustrated by his lack of adventure, sent him to Coventry.

In a game against Essex at the Oval in June 1962, when Micky was standing in as captain, the two of them shared a partnership of 316. It was a season in which the follow-on law had been suspended in county cricket, putting even greater pressure on the team batting first to score its runs at a good pace. Yet Barrington showed no sense of urgency. The off-spinner Paddy Phelan was bowling, and each of his overs seemed to follow the same pattern. Micky would work an early single, then watch in frustration as his partner blocked out the remaining balls.

Micky came down the wicket to remonstrate. "What's your game?"

"What do you mean?"

"Well, you must have played a dozen balls from him since you scored a run."

"Well, he's pitching them all on a length."

"What's that got to do with it? Come on. We've got to get to 350 by six o'clock."

"The next ball," Micky recalls, "up comes Paddy Phelan. Bang. Kenny hits it straight for six. The one after, bang again. This time it goes right up in the air and lands just between two fielders."

The mid-pitch conversation is resumed.

Ken Barrington, relaxing after a long innings

"What are you doing now?"

"That's what you wanted, isn't it? You wanted me to score some runs."

"Not like that."

"I don't know. I can never please you."

Micky shakes his head. "And he was an established England player."

For his own good, perhaps Micky went too far the other way. That was Jim Laker's view. Jim was an important figure in Micky's early years at the Oval, often offering sympathetic advice. For all the warmth of his tribute to Micky's unselfishness, though, he thought the young batsman should have played a little more for himself than he did.

"From a professional point of view," Micky says now, "maybe I was a bit thick. Why did I get out for 50s and 60s and not score more hundreds? Kenny Barrington had fourteen shots and, after he was dropped by England, most of the time he only played five. But I reached outside what I could do. Peter May was a fine driver. He would whack it back straight, and I would try to emulate him. But it wasn't part of my natural game."

At the start of 1958 Peter May thought Micky was one good season away from selection for the winter tour of Australia, but Micky had his first bad summer and dropped back in the line of young hopefuls. He regained his form in 1959, scoring 1,849 runs, but that was a hot, dry summer full of high-scoring batsmen. His performance in the indifferent summer of 1960, scoring 1,866 runs at an average of 41.46, was more outstanding, and it brought his name back into the frame when the selectors looked for an opening batsman to replace the injured Subba Row for the final Test.

The umpire Charlie Elliott was one whose opinions the selectors valued, so much so that in time he became a selector himself, and he was standing at the Oval on August Bank Holiday Saturday when Micky made a fluent 147 against Nottinghamshire. As the runs flowed on the easy-paced pitch, Elliott whispered to him: "You're in now, Micky." But, to Micky's disappointment, he was wrong. The selectors opted to ask Colin Cowdrey to open the innings, recalling Mike Smith to the middle order. It would be another two years before Micky would finally get called up.

In that game at the Oval in June 1962, when he and Ken Barrington put on 316 together, Micky hit an unbeaten 200, the first of two double centuries in his career. After a difficult summer in 1961, when he had often had to stand in as captain of a Surrey side in chronic decline, he was now in a rich vein of form. In the second innings he hit a rapid 67, and that took him to the top of the national averages. According to *The Times*, he was batting 'like a man tingling with confidence. His footwork was enterprising and his driving unusually effective.'

So, when on Tuesday Geoff Pullar dropped out of the team for that week's Test, Micky was the obvious replacement. He was in the field at the Oval, once more standing in as captain, when his movement between overs was broken by the crackling of the tannoy system and the sound of Surrey Secretary 'Bob' Babb's voice: "Ladies and gentlemen, I am pleased to announce that the England selectors …" In the words of *The Times*, 'The rest of the Surrey side looked as happy as Stewart himself, which was further evidence of the new spirit at the Oval.'

At the age of 29 he was finally to become an England cricketer.

8

A NERVOUS START AND A SICK ENDING

There was grass on the wicket at Lord's and a heavy atmosphere, leading the England captain Ted Dexter to invite the Pakistanis to bat first. The tourists were not a strong side, with their star Hanif Mohammad below his best all summer, and they had no answer to the bowling of Fred Trueman and Micky's fellow debutant, Len Coldwell of Worcestershire. At lunch they were 76 for six. At three o'clock, with Micky in the covers running backwards to dismiss the last man with a well-judged catch, they were all out for 100.

Micky stepped out to open the innings with Colin Cowdrey. Twelve years earlier *Wisden* had declared them to be the country's two most outstanding schoolboy cricketers. Now Cowdrey was about to play his 90th Test innings, thoroughly at home in the role, while Micky, preparing for his first, was all too aware of the enormity of the occasion. At last he was achieving what he had dreamed of as a boy when he sat in the Carnegie Library or played with his mates in Ruskin Park.

"I had practically every member of both sides of the family there at Lord's, and lots of people from Surrey club cricket, too, all come to see me. I remember going down the steps, thinking 'They're all here. I mustn't let them down.' It's the only time in my whole career when I let the nerves affect me physically. My feet didn't move properly. How I survived, I don't know. I scrambled 30-odd runs, but I didn't play anything like I'd played previously. Then I flashed at one and nicked it to the keeper. It wasn't me to play a shot like that; I wasn't a good driver. But I'd let the occasion affect me, and I knew that. I wasn't happy about it at all."

The Times put it bluntly: 'Stewart's timing never came to him. When he was nine he was dropped at leg slip off Farooq, and his 39, made out of 137, took him two hours and a quarter. It was not an innings that will have noticeably raised his stock.'

According to Jim Swanton in the *Daily Telegraph*, Micky 'even found himself chided by the talkative ones outside the Tavern.'

His second innings went somewhat better. At five o'clock on Saturday afternoon, with a 6.30 close and play scheduled to resume on Monday, he and Colin Cowdrey returned to the middle. There were 86 runs to be scored, and they began carefully. At ten past six, with the total on 36, Cowdrey was caught at the wicket. That brought Ted Dexter to the middle.

England team, versus Pakistan, Lord's, 1962
Standing (left to right): Geoff Millman, Ken Barrington, David Allen,
Len Coldwell, Peter Parfitt, Micky Stewart
Seated: Fred Trueman, Colin Cowdrey, Ted Dexter, Tom Graveney, Tony Lock

He marched up to Micky. "If we can finish this tonight, I can get to Longchamps for the races tomorrow. You carry on as you are. Don't take any notice of how I'm going to play." With that he set about the bowling – as *The Times* put it, 'demolishing like a bulldozer the last signs of resistance.'

"He was driving them back like rockets. I was standing at the non-striker's end, and I wasn't the slowest person around the crease. But it's the only time in my life when I've thought, 'If I don't watch out, I could get hit.'"

They scored the final 50 runs in 20 minutes, Dexter hitting 32 and Micky finishing on 34 not out. 'Stewart may have earned himself a second chance,' *The Times* judged. 'There will be a reluctance to discard so fine a fielder.'

In the third Test at Headingley, on the first morning, Micky walked to the middle once more with Colin Cowdrey, who was now being given a turn to captain the side. The pitch was another green one, and this time there were the added disadvantages of a grey, cloud-laden sky and a thickening drizzle that drove the players into the pavilion for much of the morning session. Micky got off the mark by hooking Farooq for six, but for the most part he played a cautious innings. Cowdrey, Dexter, Graveney and Barrington had all come and gone by teatime when England had reached 126 for four and Micky had brought up his fifty. "The ball was doing a lot," he says. "I played very well."

By six o'clock, after four hours at the crease, he had reached 86 and was facing once more the right-arm medium pace of Munir Malik, whose long spell had started three hours earlier. "He bowled out-swingers, and he sent this one down on middle-and-leg. I went onto the back foot and tried to play it through mid-wicket. Lbw. After being in all that time, it was a very poor shot. I should have got a hundred."

'Stewart,' wrote Swanton in the *Telegraph*, 'built up his innings without histrionics or splendour, but, for the most part, steadily and safely.'

The match turned into another three-day victory for England, this time with no second innings, and Micky, with 163 Test runs for only twice out, felt he was now in the frame to be selected for that winter's tour of Australia, the ultimate ambition of every English cricketer.

He might well have been selected, if it had not been for the return to cricket of the Reverend David Sheppard. Since his last Test five years earlier Sheppard had played in only ten county matches but, encouraged by the chairman of selectors Walter Robins, he had made himself available for the tour of Australia. Indeed, there was much talk that, if he could show some form with the bat, he would be appointed to lead the side, rather than Dexter or Cowdrey. The annual Gentlemen-Players match at Lord's was a major occasion, attended by all the selectors, and, when Sheppard scored a fine hundred on the first day, the newspapers all proclaimed him captain. They were wrong; the next day they had to report that Dexter was the chosen one.

Sheppard's re-emergence, along with the return of the injured Pullar, meant that, despite his 86 at Headingley, there was no room for Micky in the team for the fourth Test at Trent Bridge, a ground that favoured the batsmen much more than Lord's and Headingley. Doug Insole, his old footballing friend and now a selector, rang to break the news to Micky. When play began on Friday Pullar fell early, but Sheppard made a battling 83. Two days later, on the Sunday, the selectors released the names of the tour party for Australia.

"They were going to announce the team on the radio. Sheila and I were out somewhere, and I was very nervous. I thought I might get in ahead of 'Noddy' Pullar. He didn't contribute too much in the field. But he had a good record in Test cricket, and he was a left-hander. Ideally it's good to open with a left and a right-hander. When the names were read out, it took a while to sink in. I was very disappointed. Doug rang again; he said I'd missed out by a hair's breadth."

*

Consolation arrived in the form of an invitation to join Ron Roberts' International Cavaliers tour of Southern Africa in the spring. Richie Benaud, the former Australian captain, had recruited most of the side, and Micky was to be his vice-captain. For the Australians in the party, the preliminary match in Bombay was not a major detour, but for Micky the schedule proved quite an ordeal.

"The English winter of '62/3 was a terrible one. There was snow and ice on the roads from Boxing Day till the end of March. I'd never been so inactive. I couldn't run around the roads or parks; I couldn't get anywhere. And from that I had to fly out to the heat of Bombay, where we fielded first. I can remember chasing a ball and, when it reached the boundary, I was further from it than when I started. I got next to no runs in the first innings, and in the second I went down the pitch to a leg-spinner, played it into the gully and I was so knackered I was run out. I couldn't get back into my crease in time."

Nevertheless, in that second innings Micky was privileged to share a 100 partnership, scored in under an hour, with the former Australian opener Arthur Morris, whom Richie Benaud had persuaded to return to first-class cricket after a gap of eight years. "A lovely man. Even after all that time, he was real class. I can still see him now, hitting on the up off the back foot."

Five days after the Bombay game finished, they were in the field in Johannesburg, and the schedule caught up with Micky. "I never pulled muscles normally, but I chased a ball and my right thigh muscle went. The only time I was fit after that was in East Africa on the way back. It was very disappointing. It was brilliant to play under Richie."

In Nairobi Micky hit 77, and Morris, in his last international game, hit 70. Then they all went their separate ways – Micky back to Surrey where, three days after he reached home, Sheila gave birth to their second child, a brother for Neil who had been born almost three years earlier. They named him Alec.

*

Thursday 6 June 1963. Seven o'clock in the morning. The first day of the first Test at Old Trafford. In a twin-bedded hotel room in Lymm, the quiet Cheshire village fifteen miles from the ground, Micky and his Surrey team-mate John Edrich were still asleep.

David Sheppard had returned to his ministry; Geoff Pullar, after a poor tour of Australia, had played his last Test. So the selectors were looking to the Surrey pair to handle the fearsome new-ball attack of the West Indians Wes Hall and Charlie Griffith. It was Edrich's debut and Micky's third Test. "Just to let you know," Walter Robins had told them the previous day at practice, "that, whatever happens, you are going to be opening the innings for the first three Test matches."

"We were still asleep in our room," Micky recalls, "when the door burst open and there was Walter Robins standing in front of us in his pyjamas and dressing gown."

"I've got to tell you two," he said, "I've hardly slept a wink all night thinking about you poor buggers having to open the innings against those two today."

In fact it was the following evening before the two of them walked out to bat, by which time the West Indians had scored 501 for six declared. It had been a gruelling two days in the field, with vital catches dropped and the temperature rising on Friday to almost tropical heights. And on Micky's forehead, to add to the sense of drama, stitches were holding together a wound inflicted earlier in the week by the Nottinghamshire fast bowler Ian Davison.

Ian Wooldridge of the *Daily Mail* painted the picture vividly:

> *The day's drama was not done. Stewart and Edrich had to come in for fifty minutes and I would not have stood in their shoes at that moment for a year's salary.*
>
> *Worrell strolled out like Caesar with his favourite gladiators, Hall and Griffith, towering at either shoulder. Twenty yards behind came Surrey's opening batsmen, now the hopes of all England. Edrich took three steps to every two by Stewart. He looked as if he would have much preferred to be going to the pictures. Stewart, as always, looked as if he was going to the pictures. Nothing seems to worry him.*

Hall was quite a sight to watch from the batsman's end. "He had a long run-up, and he was quick from the start of it. It was best not to watch him from the end of his run-up; otherwise you're concentrating for too long a period. To people who bowled extra quick like Wes, you just had to move that little bit quicker."

Going out to face Hall and Griffith
John Edrich and Micky at Old Trafford, 1963
Stitches on Micky's forehead

Hall was at his very fastest in his first over, perhaps too much so as he sprayed the ball all over the place. "One delivery he came flying in, crucifix jumping about around his neck, and his studs got caught in the ground when he delivered the ball. He went sprawling headlong down the pitch towards me."

Griffith was a different proposition. "He bowled with a bent arm. Most of the time he was only quick-medium. But he had a quicker ball when he straightened it, and that was the danger. You always had to be looking for it. It's amazing how many good batsmen he bowled out or got lbw with his quicker yorker, when they'd got 50, 60 or 70. If the conditions are reasonable, good players don't normally get bowled out like that when they're in."

At number three in the England batting line-up was Ken Barrington, a worrier at the best of times. As the summer progressed he became more and more disconcerted by Griffith and his quicker ball, so much so that the following summer he refused to play in an end-of-season exhibition match against a West Indian XI that included Griffith. When the *Daily Mail* prised out of him the reason for his withdrawal, there was a furore which made the whole matter a great deal worse. "He hated controversy of any kind," Micky says.

In 1966 the West Indians toured again, and this time Barrington had let it all get to him so much that on the eve of the third Test he dropped out of the England eleven. He was suffering from nervous exhaustion, and at the height of the summer he went a full month without playing a single first-class game.

When the season ended, Micky tried to talk him into coming on a three-week tour of Bermuda, organised by the Cricketers' Club in London. "Go on. You can take it easy with Ann and get some sunshine. It will do you the world of good."

"No, I don't want to come. I need a break from cricket."

He agreed eventually, but unfortunately the tour did not do him quite 'the world of good' that Micky had anticipated. "In the first game we were playing on a matting pitch that was nailed down with pins, and the pins were covered by coca-cola bottle tops. I opened the batting with Roy Marshall, who got out just before lunch, and Kenny came in. There was a leg-spinner bowling. Second ball he dragged it wide and Kenny went to cut it. It hit one of the bottle tops, jumped up and smacked him on the side of his head. So off we went to lunch, with this trickle of blood coming down Kenny's face. 'I knew I shouldn't have come,' he kept saying."

They entered the pavilion, Micky going in first, and they made their way up a dark, winding staircase. On the first bend, bumping into Micky, who should be coming down the stairs but the last man on earth that Barrington wanted to set eyes on?

"Hallo, Charlie," Micky said. "What are you doing here?"

"I'm having a little holiday," replied Griffith, the most gentle of characters off the pitch. "And Kenny, how are you?"

Barrington, the blood oozing out of his wound, put his head down and marched on into the dressing room.

"Christ! Charlie bloody Griffith. That's all I need. This is all your fault, you know. I told you I didn't want to come."

At Old Trafford, in that first Test of the 1963 series, England's batting on the Saturday was a disaster – though it was not Griffith who did the damage. Hall had Edrich and Barrington caught at the wicket, then bowled Cowdrey. Then the off-spinner Lance Gibbs took five wickets, starting with Micky whose innings of 37 was ended by a bizarre catch. "The ball leapt up. I tried not to play it, but it skimmed my glove and flew to Gary Sobers at leg slip. He parried it, and somehow Deryck Murray got over in time to catch the ricochet."

His dismissal came just a few minutes before lunch but he was padding up again by teatime, when England were following on 296 runs behind. 'TUMBLE-DOWN BATTING PITIFUL TO SEE' was the *Times* headline.

Edrich departed shortly before the close for 38, but Micky survived with 44 not out. 'He has batted in this second innings with much character,' *The Times* judged, 'and character in Test cricket is half the battle.'

On Monday Micky took his score to 87 before edging a Gibbs off-break into the wicket-keeper's gloves. "I got a bit too cocky. I tried to run the ball down, and I caught it too fine. I threw away a Test hundred."

'It was sad,' wrote John Clarke in his book of the series, 'for his innings had about it, one felt, genuine Test-match quality and he deserved to reach three figures as some who do so do not.'

None of the remaining batsmen prospered, and by mid-afternoon the West Indians had won by ten wickets. It was a dismal display, though most of the press found some comfort in the performances of the two Surrey openers. 'Stewart,' *The Times* thought, 'has done his reputation a power of good.'

The selectors stuck with the same batting for the Lord's Test, though Dexter was promoted to number three ahead of Barrington, thus ending the curiosity of one county, Surrey, providing the first three positions in the England batting order. It had never happened before in a home Test, and it has only happened once since: against the West Indies at the Oval in 1995, when Lancashire provided Atherton, Gallian and Crawley.

They arrived at Lord's on the Wednesday, to find that after a short practice the Duke of Norfolk was taking the two teams for an afternoon's racing at Royal Ascot. It was a wet day, and there was still rain in the air when play was due to begin on Thursday. Yet the grey, spitting clouds did not dampen the pre-match anticipation. The 11,000 advance tickets had all been sold, and there were long queues at every gate. By the time the sun had broken through and play was under way, there were 25,000 spectators in the ground, at least a quarter of them West Indian supporters. The next day the number rose to 28,000, and on Saturday, for the first time since the Australian Test of 1956, the gates were shut – with nearly 33,000 admitted, more than the ground holds today. Such was the excitement that thousands more were turned away. In the free seats the spectators were squeezed tight onto benches, in some cases unable to see the full field of play.

England, having lost the toss, took the field just before midday. "Everything was wet," Micky recalls. "Early on, I chased the ball down to the boundary, and I thought I'd do a flashy pick-up-and-throw on the turn. But the ball was wet, and it flew out of my hands. So I had to chase after it a second time. Fred Trueman was bowling. 'What the bloody hell's going on with you, Micky?' he said."

West Indies made 301, their innings closing on the second morning, leaving Micky and John Edrich to resume their Old Trafford contest with Hall and Griffith. This time they were less successful. Charlie Griffith bowled from the pavilion end, where there was no sight screen, and Edrich, trying to glance his first ball to leg, got a thin edge and was caught behind. It was his 26th birthday and, according to John Clarke, he was 'a woebegone-looking figure' as he made his way back to the pavilion. It was not long before Micky followed him, caught at slip off Griffith for 2, off the last ball before lunch.

There followed an innings that has stayed firmly in the memory of those who saw it. The England captain Ted Dexter took the attack to Hall and Griffith, hitting ten fours in a thrilling 70 that *The Times* called 'the Test match innings of a millionaire':

> *He was only in for 80 minutes but what minutes they were! He batted not as though it was a Test match at Lord's so much as it was a benefit*

game at Henley-on-Thames, or a house match at Radley. His strokes were unstoppable, his style in the classical mould. No one, surely, ever hit the ball harder or more regally than Dexter.

It was 'the glimpse of an eagle in flight'.

"He played some incredible shots," Micky says. "He got hit a couple of times, and he really threw the bat. He was such a fine athlete, strong and well-built. As a man he could be shy at times, and he had to conquer that as captain. But with a bat or a ball in his hand he was a different man. Full of arrogance."

Dexter's brilliant stroke play overshadowed what for Micky, in the context of the match, was an innings of equal importance: a patient 80 by Ken Barrington. 'He quickens few pulses,' *The Times* wrote, 'but he drives many a bowler to distraction.'

The contest turned into one of the greatest Test matches, containing all the elements except fine weather. England were all out for just four runs fewer than West Indies, then struck back by taking five West Indian wickets for only 104, the fifth when Micky at backward short leg 'tumbled to his left to send back Solomon with a brilliant one-handed catch.'

The outstanding close fielder in the side, Micky had not been at short leg at Old Trafford, but "I'd had a moan about it so I went in close at Lord's."

The catch came shortly after tea on Saturday, silencing the large contingent of West Indian supporters, but they were in good voice by the close, thanks to a fighting century by Basil Butcher, with his captain Frank Worrell staying calm and steady at the other end. "That was a typical innings by Basil," Micky says. "Gutsy, and never missing an opportunity to score."

At close of play West Indies were 214 for five, a lead of 218. With the pitch showing signs of wear, it seemed that victory was slipping fast from England's grasp.

Nearly 30,000 spectators arrived on Monday morning, and they were still streaming into the ground when, off the third ball of the day, the partnership of Butcher and Worrell was finally broken. Ian Wooldridge described the moment:

Stewart, crouching like some persistent beggar demanding alms, was within three yards of Worrell's bat, hands cupped in readiness. Trueman tore in from the pavilion end, the ball whipped up waist-high, Worrell forced it hard down on the leg side and there was Stewart, legs kicking in the air, rolling backwards with the ball clasped to his heart.

Within half an hour the innings was over, with England needing 234 for victory. It was a much smaller chase than looked likely at the start of play but, as the historians were quick to point out, it was still a formidable one:

Not since 1902 had England scored more than 200 in a fourth innings to win a Test match in England. Only Australia, in fact, had done so. But nobody had done it at Lord's!

At five past twelve, with the ground abuzz with excitement, John Edrich and Micky emerged from the pavilion. Wes Hall took the first over, bowling downwind from the pavilion end, with its dark, screenless background, and he was a man inspired, bowling unchanged for 16 overs on either side of lunch. He had Edrich caught off the glove for 7, then he tormented Micky with a barrage of short-pitched deliveries. In the words of Alan Ross, 'Twice the ball, lifting from only just short of a length, whistled over his head, a third banged his gloves as he attempted a glance, another almost knocked him off his feet when he missed a hook.'

"I was black and blue afterwards," Micky says. "Then he whacked in this bouncer, and I didn't see it. It hit the handle of my bat and dollied up to Joe Solomon in the gully."

That was 27 for two, Micky out for 17, and four runs later Ted Dexter, who was suffering from a swollen knee and had not fielded the previous day, swung at a slow ball from Lance Gibbs and was bowled. Cowdrey and Barrington steadied the innings, taking the score towards 70, till Worrell, revealing a ruthless streak, changed tack. On an overcast afternoon, he surrounded the bat with close fielders and got Hall to bowl a succession of short-pitched deliveries, eight in a row, the eighth of which reared up viciously and fractured a bone in Cowdrey's left forearm. He was on the ground in agony for several minutes before walking disconsolately back to the pavilion, his arm held painfully against his chest.

Hall, a decent man, was distraught, and he bowled just one more over before giving way to Griffith at the pavilion end. Barrington, 'like a wild beast whose mate has been wounded', hit two sixes off Gibbs, but soon the game turned into a stop-start affair. They went off for bad light. They came back. They went off for tea. They were introduced to the Queen. Then, when rain arrived, they went off again. The score was 116 for three, and the crowd around the Tavern Bar, reluctant to go home, took to singing *Land of Hope and Glory* and the *Eton Boating Song*.

It was 2.20 on the final day when play resumed, bringing the clock firmly into the equation of the game. In all, there was time for 48 more overs, and Hall bowled all 24 from the pavilion end, helped by the break for tea and by an increasingly slow over rate as the game approached its climax. In an innings of 91 overs, spread across two days, the world's fastest bowler, coming off a long run, bowled 40 of them. By the end, he wrote later, 'My legs were like lumps of lead. Sweat stood out on my forehead and every movement was sheer agony, but I was determined to battle on until I dropped.'

The innings of the day was played by Brian Close, who with typical madcap bravery was content to let Hall's short-pitched balls hit him about the body. Thigh, hip, chest, shoulder, they all took a bruising, but he refused to flinch. Then, when the time came to counter-attack, he took to stepping down the wicket before Hall released the ball. It was theatre of the highest order and, with 20 minutes remaining, it took England to within 15 runs of victory. Then he tried charging Charlie Griffith and was caught behind for 70.

That left England eight down. At the wicket were David Allen and the number eleven Derek Shackleton. In the dressing room was Colin Cowdrey, with his arm in plaster, padding up. "He was going to bat left-handed," Micky says.

The last over, bowled inevitably by Hall, began with England still needing eight to win, and the instructions from the balcony were to go for it. But Shackleton swished and missed, then after two singles he was run out, leaving Cowdrey, 'cheered as only the brave are cheered', to appear for the final two balls, though only at the non-striker's end.

The match ended as a draw, the West Indian spectators pouring across the ground: 'They besieged the pavilion and called for Worrell as though it was election night.'

The nation had been gripped. If it had not been wet on the final morning, the attendance over five days would have set a new record at Lord's, greater than for any Australian match. The London telephone number UMP, which gave out up-to-date scores, took 1.6 million calls during the match, and in the closing minutes BBC Television took the unprecedented decision to break away from its early evening news broadcast.

'I have never seen a more exciting culmination to a Test,' Jim Swanton wrote. 'What palpitations! What a pulling at the heart strings!' Then there was the actor Leslie Howard who had watched every ball for five days. When the day died down he was still sitting in the Tavern Bar wearing his tattered MCC tie: "I'm working with some Americans tomorrow. My God, where do I start to tell the story? They'll never understand."

Micky took a less romantic view. "It was hugely disappointing that we didn't win. It would have brought us level in the series. It was a difficult pitch, with a ridge on it, the light was never good, and we batted so well. Closey was outstanding, so brave, and Kenny too. He never gets the credit he deserves for his part in that match. He got 80 and 60, and he played magnificently. He really got stuck in."

Walter Robins, chairman of selectors, was glowing with pride: "It was the greatest match I've seen or ever hope to see. I'm very proud of Brian Close. One has only to see his battered body, with ten bruises on it, to know what guts he's got."

Micky was never one to get carried away by the emotion of it all and, in the dressing room, he ribbed the Yorkshireman: "There was no short leg. Instead of taking all those balls on the body, you could have got a run round there every time. We'd have won the match but for your bloody bruises."

*

Despite Walter Robins' promise Edrich was dropped from the team for the third Test at Edgbaston which, thanks to some superb bowling by Trueman, was won decisively by England. It was not an easy pitch on which to bat. "They tried to take the pace out of the wicket," Micky says. "It moved off the seam all match."

Micky made scores of 39 and 27, batting when conditions were at their most difficult. They were important contributions in a low-scoring match, but he does not look back on them with pride: "I batted a long time in both innings, but I got out when I'd barely done half the job. That's no good." Nevertheless, the runs took his tally in five Tests to 368 at an average of 46. He was fast becoming an established member of the side. In fact, he was starting to pick up murmurs that he might be in line for more than that. One evening at the hotel the assistant manager of the West Indies, HL Burnett, told him what he had been hearing. "You'll be the next England captain," he said. "Take it from me. They're talking about you. They consider that you're the best one tactically."

The previous winter EM Wellings in the *Evening News* had floated the idea, writing of Micky's infectious keenness and his eagerness to listen to advice. 'Together with personal charm he has tact and determination.'

Now Godfrey Evans was adding his support in *The People*:

> *I reckon you can safely say Stewart is captain-elect ... He is popular and shrewd and gets 100 per cent effort from his Surrey men ... Micky Stewart would make a grand skipper for England, and I hope the selectors go on with their plans for him.*

The previous winter MCC had abolished the distinction between amateurs and professionals so there was no longer a Gentlemen-Players fixture at Lord's. In its place, falling between the third and fourth Tests, was a match between the MCC team that toured Australia the previous winter and the Rest. Ted Dexter captained the MCC touring team, and the selectors turned to Micky to lead the Rest.

It was a grim game, played on a grassy pitch that was wholly unsuitable for the occasion. Fielding first, Micky asked Derek Shackleton to take one end, and such was the medium-pacer's metronomic control on the awkward pitch that at one stage he bowled 13 consecutive maidens, mostly at Ken Barrington who was, in the words of *The Times*, 'at his most obdurate and unbecoming, repeating time and again his forward defensive prod to Shackleton.' Within an hour of the start, parts of the crowd had taken to barracking.

Immediately after lunch Barrington started swishing wildly at Shackleton. *The Times* suggested that he 'had grown tired of his imprisonment'; in fact, he had received a hand-written message, something to the effect of 'Hit out or get out', from Lord Nugent, that year's MCC President. Inevitably Barrington got out, bowled by Shackleton, and no sooner had he taken off his pads than the next three batsmen were back beside him, leaving the innings to be patiently rebuilt. In what was supposed to be an exhibition of cricket by the best 22 players in the country, MCC's total after 65 overs was 105 for five.

It was no more entertaining on the second day when 20 wickets fell for 226 runs. Jim Parks, with 25, made the day's highest score while Dexter, the great entertainer, was beaten five times in an over by the 38-year-old Shackleton.

You might think that the selectors would take little heed of performances in such a game. Yet, for the next Test, they called up the Somerset seamer Ken Palmer, who had successfully exploited the green wicket, and the Notts opener Brian Bolus who had hit a gritty 69. So it is fair to assume that, with the Rest beating the England touring side by two wickets, they had also noted Micky's tactical success as captain. 'In two and three winters' time,' Denys Rowbotham wrote in the *Guardian*, 'MCC must select teams to South Africa and Australia. A new captain may well be needed. Already Stewart has shown a lot of the required attributes.'

It was not to be. At Headingley, where England lost badly, he made 2 and 0, caught in the gully off Griffith and bowled by an in-swinger from Sobers. As he returned the second time to the pavilion, a Yorkshire voice greeted him: "That's your f---ing lot, Stewart. You'll never play for England again." They were harsh words, but they were so nearly proved right.

Micky was picked for the fifth Test, but he went down with a virus during the previous match and did not play cricket again that summer. Then he found himself omitted from the party to tour India after Christmas. "I was livid, especially as India was one of the easiest places to bat. Kenny Barrington had been out there two winters earlier, and he was always on about it. 'You can really fill your boots out there,' he said."

During that autumn of 1963 Micky went on an MCC tour of East Africa under the management of the England selector Willie Watson. On the plane going out Watson told Peter Parfitt, the Middlesex batsman, that he was the first reserve for the Indian tour. Yet a week later, when Cowdrey withdrew from the party, saying that his fractured arm had not sufficiently recovered, his replacement was not Parfitt but Micky.

Dexter was taking the winter off, familiarising himself with the Cardiff South-East constituency that he would be fighting for the Conservatives in the following year's General Election, so Cowdrey had been appointed tour captain, with Warwickshire's Mike Smith his deputy. With Smith's promotion to captain, a fresh vice-captain was required, and that tipped the scales in favour of Micky. A good tour of India, and who knows what might lie in store for him?

India were not considered strong opponents at that time. The previous winter England had undertaken a six-month tour of Australia and New Zealand, and the schedule for the next two winters sent them to South Africa and back to Australia. So the party for India was well below full strength. The selectors asked Trueman to take a rest and, as well as Dexter, at least five players declined the invitation, including Statham, Graveney and Close.

In an attempt to keep the tour as short as possible, MCC agreed to play five five-day Tests and five three-day matches in the space of seven and a half weeks, the schedule not always allowing a day off between fixtures. All ten games were in different cities, involving journeys that ranged between 250 and 1,000 miles, mostly by plane but sometimes by rail. With a party that contained only 15 players, there was little provision for the emergencies of injury and illness.

Their first game was in Bangalore against the President's XI. "When we arrived there, practice was optional," Micky recalls. "It was my only major tour, and that's how it was organised. There was no net at the ground so Kenny, I and a couple of others went to a school ground nearby."

Despite Barrington's enthusiasm for India and the runs he scored on his previous visit, he was not the most cheerful of tourists. "Bangalore was lovely, but Kenny never stopped moaning about the conditions on his previous tour. 'Come on,' I said to him. 'What's wrong with this? Look, there's a snooker table there.'"

With no sign of any equipment other than the table itself, Barrington reluctantly summoned an elderly bearer, only to find that he did not speak English. "Kenny started making all these gestures, indicating that he wanted balls and cues. The bearer seemed to get the idea, and off he went. We sat there for about half an hour waiting for him. Then finally he reappeared with a basket full of oranges and a flit gun."

Micky made the best of starts to the tour, scoring 119 and 82. From there without a day's break they flew 300 miles north to Hyderabad where in his only innings he was bowled off his pads for a duck. Then it was down to Madras, where after a one-day break they began the first Test, losing the toss and fielding under a hot sun while India made 277 for two on the first day.

That evening David Clark, the England manager, remarked cheerfully to reporters how well his team had adapted to the change of climate and diet. The next morning, as India piled on the runs, they started to go down with a flu virus. India declared on 457 for seven, and by the following morning, when England lost their third wicket at 116, five of the six men still to bat were in bed in the hotel. For much of the day only the number eleven, David Larter, a man with a batting average of 6, was ready to come in.

To much surprise the first to rise was Jim Parks, a man you never asked "How are you?" when you were in a hurry. Then Barry Knight and Fred Titmus. Micky, however, had a temperature of 102 and was in no fit state to get up – though, according to the *Guardian* correspondent Henry Blofeld, 'a car was on standby to rush him to the ground if the worst came to the worst.'

For most of the day Ken Barrington and Brian Bolus were at the wicket, with no alternative on a slow pitch but to stay in at all costs, in the hope that the others would appear. At one stage the slow left-armer Bapu Nadkarni bowled 131 balls, almost 22 overs, without conceding a run. At the end of the day he came off with figures of 29 overs, 26 maidens, no wickets for 3 runs.

A rest day saved England from humiliation. They all recovered sufficiently to bat, even Micky, who came in at number ten with 21 runs still needed to avoid the follow-on.

Titmus greeted him. "None of your bloody nipping between the wickets," he said. "Use your crust. You're nothing like a hundred per cent."

"Inside three balls," Micky recalls, "I'd had to dive into the crease because he'd called for a stupid run. I was covered in dirt."

A runner for Micky was agreed, and he lasted for 85 minutes, providing little entertainment for the large crowd but at least saving the follow-on. "Then I had a swing at Chandra Borde, got stumped and went back to bed. It was a circus."

JON'S SPORTING TYPES

" I'm his runner "

Michael Melford summed up his innings in the *Daily Telegraph*:

> *The under-nourished Stewart, though playing quite well, lacked the strength to penetrate the field.*

The next match was 800 miles away in Ahmedabad. The plan had been for Micky to captain the side, giving Mike Smith a short rest ahead of the second Test in Bombay, but now it looked as if Micky was the one who needed a rest – except that Micky, being Micky, was keen to get back into action. "I was livid with what had happened in the first Test. I was in very good nick, I was feeling better by the end of the game, and I wanted to play again. So I said to Mike, 'You have a rest, go straight to Bombay. I can take the team to Ahmedabad.' Looking back, it was a stupid decision. The air was all smoggy there, and I didn't score any runs. Then on the last day, when the game was dead, Kenny broke a finger, dropping a catch at slip off John Price."

Worse was to follow. On the plane down to Bombay four of them – John Edrich, Phil Sharpe, John Mortimore and Micky – started to complain of feeling ill, with upset stomachs and with flu. Then Ken Barrington's finger was examined closely in Bombay and declared to be worse than originally thought. So, when it came to a count-up, there were only ten men fit to take the field for the Test the following day, and they included the slow left-armer Don Wilson who was complaining of a bad back.

At the end-of-the-afternoon press conference the manager David Clark took Henry Blofeld aside. The 54-year-old Clark, a batsman with a modest record, had captained Kent as an amateur, last playing in 1951, while Blofeld had got no further than Cambridge University and Norfolk.

"You and I are the only two to have played first-class cricket," Clark explained, "and you're a great many years younger than me. So, if it comes to it, you'll be the man." He then added a little advice: "Try to get to bed before midnight."

Cowdrey and Parfitt had been sent for and would arrive in time for the following Test. But Blofeld, milking the moment, wanted to make one thing clear. "If I make a fifty," he said, "I'm damned if I'll stand down for Cowdrey."

Micky was sharing a room with Ken Barrington. "I got given some pills and a glass of orange juice. I remember waking in the night, feeling rough. I thought I wouldn't disturb Kenny by putting the light on. So in the dark I put the tablet in my mouth and, when I went to take a sip of orange juice, I felt this cockroach crawling across my lips."

The next morning Micky was a little better, making his feelings plain when he heard the news of Blofeld's selection. "You're kidding, aren't you? Even if I'm only a quarter fit, I've got to be better than him." They were fighting words but, as things worked out, they did not prove to be true.

On another hot day England fielded first. Shortly before tea, with Titmus bowling, the batsman nicked the ball onto his pad and it went straight up the wicket. Micky was at forward short leg. "It bounced well in front of me so there was no chance of catching it, but I dived forward, landed on my chest and with the impact I threw up all over the wicket. I had to be escorted off."

Deprived of Edrich, Sharpe, Barrington and now Micky, England found themselves playing the rest of a five-day Test match on a slow Indian pitch with a ten-man side that included four quick bowlers, two wicket-keepers, two spinners (one of whom had a bad back) and only two specialist batsmen. Somehow they managed to escape with a draw.

"I should never have gone to Ahmedabad. I copped it twice in ten days, and I was very weak. I lost pounds and pounds, and I wasn't carrying any weight in the first place. I had to stay for a few days with a nice couple in Bombay before I was fit to fly home. And it took me a while to recover when I did get home."

When Micky was escorted off the field, he was taken to the local hospital where he was put on the same ward as Mortimore, Edrich and Sharpe. Shortly afterwards they were joined by Ken Barrington who, with his broken finger, was passing the time, waiting to go home. "He'd heard the food in the hospital was pretty good, better than in the hotel, so he turned up, saying he'd got a sore throat, and they kept him in. They put him in the bed opposite me."

Barrington was in good spirits, thinking he had wangled himself a good deal. Then suddenly a group of nurses arrived and pulled the curtains around his bed. "We could all hear him. 'No, no, no,' he was saying. 'It's just my throat. My throat.' It turned out they were administering an enema. And he'd only come in for the food."

*

Micky had, alas, not 'filled his boots' in India, and the selectors' thoughts turned elsewhere. The following summer the Australians were over, and for the first Test England opted to open the innings with John Edrich and the young Yorkshireman Geoffrey Boycott. Then when Edrich dropped out with a twisted ankle, they did not call up Micky, though he was only twenty miles away, preferring instead to ask Fred Titmus to fill in at the top of the order. It was much the same story for the second Test, when Boycott was injured and Dexter himself opted to go in first. Later in the summer they called up Bob Barber, and for the winter tour of South Africa they took Boycott, Barber and the young Mike Brearley. In twelve months Micky had gone from being 'the next England captain' to just another opener on the discard heap.

It was a Test career of eight matches, four against the might of Hall and Griffith. It had begun at Lord's, when for the only time he had let his nerves get the better of him, and it had ended at Bombay when he had vomited on the pitch: "my last contribution as an England cricketer."

Was he unlucky not to play more? Unlucky that David Sheppard came back when he did? Unlucky that he played so many of his Tests against a great West Indies side? Unlucky that the tour of India, where his technique against spin should have brought him runs aplenty, ended as it did? Unlucky that Geoffrey Boycott then emerged?

"I don't see it like that," he says, repeating what he says about his time as a footballer at Charlton. "It was down to me as a batsman to score the runs, to put in the performances so that they couldn't leave me out. And I didn't do that. I've got no excuses at all. That was entirely down to me."

9

A PROFESSIONAL CAPTAIN

'Brighter Cricket' was the order from Lord's for the summer of 1961. Away with negative play! Bring back the crowds with a greater spirit of adventure!

One contest that certainly lived up to all that was the Whit Bank Holiday match at Trent Bridge between Nottinghamshire and Surrey. In three pleasantly warm days the two teams bowled 362 overs, scored 1,114 runs, including a sparkling century by the now semi-retired Reg Simpson, and took the match all the way to a last-over finish.

John Clay, the Notts captain, looked back on it forty years later as the best game of cricket he ever played, while Simpson himself glowed with enthusiasm in his column in the *Nottingham Evening Post*:

> *If all games were played in that spirit and with the same disdain displayed by both sides for the possibility of defeat, there would be no need to worry about the game of first class cricket as a spectacle.*
>
> *I have never seen any other side continue to attack right down their batting order to the extent that Surrey did on the last afternoon, especially when the odds were heavily stacked against them. Many lesser cricketers would have thrown in the sponge – but not this new look Surrey captained for the first time by Michael Stewart.*

In the previous match Peter May had pulled a groin muscle, while David Fletcher, a possible stand-in captain, had fractured a finger. With Alec Bedser having retired, the obvious solution for May and the county coach, Arthur McIntyre, was to turn to the experience of Eric Bedser or Bernie Constable but, instead, they opted, to general surprise, to send for Micky. "It came right out of the blue," he says. "I hadn't expected it at all."

Among the senior players there were some rumblings. "They've only asked you because you went to public school," one of them said. But moaning was a built-in part of life at Surrey, it did not signify serious discontent, and at Trent Bridge they fell in line behind their new leader – at least, up to a point.

Nottinghamshire were a poor team in those years. They were bumping along in the foothills of the championship, without a victory at Trent Bridge for almost two years. Micky had played against them eleven times and never been on the losing side. So it would not be the most challenging introduction to captaining Surrey.

Yet Surrey themselves were not the force they had been. Jim Laker and Alec Bedser had gone, Tony Lock with his remodelled action was not as penetrative, and Peter Loader was starting to lose pace. On the final morning the Notts batsmen, especially Simpson, cut loose, allowing Clay to declare. For Surrey to win, they would have to score 291 in 190 minutes.

They were up with the pace during a second-wicket partnership of 99 between John Edrich and Ken Barrington. Then wickets fell, a lull followed, and once more the chase was taken up. The crowd of five thousand was enthralled as they watched runs, wickets and spilled catches, and all the while the hands of the pavilion clock moved steadily towards the five o'clock close.

No one can quite remember the order of events in the closing minutes, but we do know that, when Tony Lock was caught, the seventh man out, there were still 57 runs to be scored and only 25 minutes remaining. We also know that Roy Swetman was at the wicket and that at some point, before or after the fall of Lock's wicket, Micky went onto the balcony, caught Swetman's eye and signalled that the chase was over. It was time to play for the draw. Brighter Cricket or no Brighter Cricket, it was what any county captain of that time would have done.

Micky might have been to public school, but he was a professional in everything he did, unlike Swetman whose schooling had not been as grand but who, in Micky's view, "approached the game in a more irresponsibly happy-go-lucky way."

Swetman had joined the Oval staff in 1949, at the age of 15, a promising young wicket-keeper, but his progress into the first team had been blocked by Arthur McIntyre. Indeed he was still McIntyre's understudy in the summer of 1958 when the England selectors chose him for that winter's tour of Australia. Mac, now 40 years old, was persuaded, a little unwillingly, to retire, and soon enough Swetman succeeded Godfrey Evans as England's keeper.

It did not work out as planned, for England or for Surrey. On the 1959/60 trip to the West Indies Swetman fell out with the tour manager Walter Robins and was told he would never play for England again, while at Surrey he played just three summers, then at the end of 1961, disillusioned by the loss of his England place, he announced his retirement. Micky recalls the conversation they had.

"I'm going to be working for a company that publishes children's books," Swetman explained.

"Oh? What are you going to do?"

"I'm taking people out to lunch, old boy." He then gave details of his salary, a considerable jump up from that of a county cricketer.

"What? For taking people out to lunch?"

"Yes, old boy."

"Well, good luck."

Some while later, however, he returned to the game, keeping wicket for Notts, then after another break for Gloucestershire. McIntyre lived to be 90, right to the end complaining that he should not have retired when he did. He could have played for at least two more seasons.

"Roy was an outstanding keeper," Micky says. "He had good, quick hands. He looked the part, little and dapper, and he could bat. But he enjoyed his time off the field too much. He'd start off the season in good nick, but after a few weeks back he wouldn't be so sharp. He didn't have the strength and stamina to maintain that lifestyle. It was sad, really."

When the sign came from the Trent Bridge balcony, Swetman ignored it. Perhaps it was the cavalier in him: "I'd rather lose going for a win than play for a draw," he says. "What's the point of cricket if not to try to win?" Perhaps it was the rebel: "If you said 'Block it out' to Swetty," according to team-mate Michael Willett, "he'd go and slog. He'd be thinking, 'Sod them up there, I'll show them what I can do.'" Or perhaps it was because Micky was captain: "Micky's a great friend of mine," Swetman says, "but he couldn't captain a rowing boat."

Bomber Wells was bowling, hurrying through his overs off a one-pace run-up. Reg Simpson in his column called him 'the most complete off-spinner in the country. If we wanted a genuine England side with character, Wells would be in my side every time.' Swetman hit him for a six and a four, and suddenly it was only 35 to win. Then he played a shot too many and dragged the ball onto his stumps. Soon enough a ninth wicket fell. Then off the first ball of the very last over, the tenth.

Nottinghamshire had beaten the mighty Surrey, and the crowd stood and clapped them into the pavilion. 'My heartiest congratulations to Surrey,' wrote Reg Simpson. 'May you continue to play in this spirit and prosper as a result.'

John Thicknesse in the *Daily Telegraph* was rather less impressed. 'Surrey donate 12 points for Brighter Cricket' was the headline on his report:

> *The Christmas spirit was abroad today, with Surrey cast as Santa Claus, going bald-headed for their target long after it had become a practical impossibility. ... Whether one approves of this sort of result depends on*

how one thinks cricket should be played. Personally I subscribe to the view
that a match should be saved if it cannot be won.

Micky, in the Surrey dressing room, was very much of the same view, and the sparks flew. "I had quite a bit to say to Swetty," he recalls. "I pointed out to him that it was a team game."

Micky captained 16 championship matches that summer, only one of which was won. Surrey were in free fall, finishing 15th in the table, the lowest position in their history. No one blamed his captaincy, but with the bat Micky had a poor season, averaging just 26 in a dry summer that for others was full of runs. The previous year he had finished in the top ten in the national batting averages; now he was down in 100th place.

Off the field it was a hard summer, too. In June Sheila's father died. Then in August Micky's father, only 61 years old, underwent surgery for cancer. Micky was captaining Surrey against the Australians – "Your dad would want you to play," his mother told him – and after the operation the surgeon Frank Henley came to the Oval to report that things were looking good. Then in the next session of play Micky, fielding at short leg to the bowling of David Sydenham, dropped a little dolly of a bat-pad catch from Richie Benaud – "the easiest catch I've ever dropped in any cricket in my life" – and came off to learn that his father had taken a sudden turn for the worse and died.

It was not a good year: for Micky or for Surrey.

*

The summer of 1962 was quite different. Micky returned to the top ten of the national batting averages, scoring more than 2,000 runs and making his Test debut, while Surrey regained their spirit, remaining in contention for the championship till the closing days of the season. In fact, as it worked out, they would have been champions if they had won their final two matches. In the first, at home to Yorkshire, the eventual champions, they lost a crucial toss and found themselves in the field till well into the second day. Then at Southampton, still with an outside chance of the title, they paid dearly for a single dropped catch. The culprit was David Sydenham, a left-arm swing bowler whose rise that summer had been a vital element of the county's regeneration.

Micky was in charge at Southampton. He remembers the conversation as Danny Livingstone, Hampshire's left-handed batsman from Antigua, made his way to the middle. "Locky was on a hat-trick, and he called out, 'Come on, everybody in.' I said, 'Hold on. Danny Livingstone's a big lapper of the ball. Let's leave Syd on the square leg boundary, in case he goes for an escape route down there.' And sure enough, first ball, he swept at it and it flew up in the air, down to just where Syd was standing. I can see Locky now. He spun round with his hands in the air. And Syd dropped it."

It is a story that David Sydenham also enjoys telling. "I got him myself in the end," is his punch-line. "Caught by Micky at long off. For 200."

Hampshire, at one stage 128 for eight, finished on 358, and Surrey had to settle for fifth place in the final table.

*

The 1960s were years of great change in English cricket. Hardly a season seemed to pass when there was not some new initiative, designed to bring back the lost spectators. The most significant of these came in 1963 with the introduction of a one-day knockout competition, featuring games in which each innings was limited to 65 overs, of which an individual bowler could contribute no more than 15. It started out as just a bit of fun, to attract back the crowds, but its effect on the game in the years that followed was immense: not just in its impact on the skills of batting and bowling but in the way it shifted the whole emphasis of cricket from the display of those individual skills to the over-riding importance of the result.

"As each year passed," Micky says, "cricket became more and more of a result-centred game."

Surrey's first experience of the new game was not a happy one. Chasing 230 for victory at Worcester, they slumped from 82 for no wicket to 115 all out. It was a game in its infancy, and Micky had much to learn. "In the field," he remembers, "I ran the game as if it were a championship match, looking to take wickets at every opportunity."

The summer of 1963 saw a second momentous change in the world of cricket: the abolition of the distinction between amateurs and professionals. Once, the ideal of amateurism had been about men of independent means, free spirits who played their sport without the influence of financial reward. But war and social change had put an end to much of that. Now the system had become riddled with hypocrisy, often sustained by counties arranging non-existent jobs for their amateurs – or, in the case of overseas tours, by MCC paying the amateurs 'broken-time earnings', compensation for lost income. In many cases the payments were considerably greater than the touring professionals received. In addition to all this, most of the more prominent amateurs were also paid for advertising products. As Jim Laker, never one to let such matters lie, would say: "I think I'll become an amateur. I can't afford to play as a professional any more."

The last team to represent the Players, Lord's, 1962
Standing (left to right): John Edrich, Phil Sharpe, Norman Gifford,
Peter Walker, Micky Stewart, Peter Parfitt
Seated: Fred Titmus, Derek Shackleton, Fred Trueman, Tom Graveney, Keith Andrew

The change coincided appropriately with Surrey's announcement that their new captain, taking over from Peter May, would be Micky, the first professional cricketer in the county's history to hold the office. The social order was shifting, though at the Oval there was some reluctance to embrace that shift. "They wanted me to change upstairs in what had been the Amateurs' Room. I said no, but the dressing-room attendant only had one year left before retirement and I would be putting him out of a job. So for that first year at the start of a match I'd change up there, then take everything downstairs. If we were batting, I'd watch from the downstairs dressing room."

Promotion to the captaincy was not that great a step up for Micky. He had had plenty of experience of it over the previous two summers and, before that, he had led sides at school and during National Service. "I don't know why, but they even picked me to captain that London Under-14s side at Lord's."

As a youngster coming into the Surrey side Micky had never been one to concentrate only on his own performance. "As the game was going on, the strategy of how to win was always in the front of my mind. Even back when I was playing weekend cricket at West Surrey, I would sit in the bar in the evening, perched on a chair, listening to them all talking about the game. It would be an all-day match, and I'd be there till 9.30 or 10, just sipping an orange juice and listening. County cricket was the same. It totally absorbed me. There was so much discussion at the end of the day – with the other team, too. The money you earned was very little so it was all about your ambition and your love of the game."

Before the start of the 1963 season he was invited to lunch by Maurice Allom, the former England bowler who was chairman of the cricket committee. "I'd prepared some thoughts," Micky recalls. "Some headings on a piece of paper. How I saw the way forward. He was most impressed. 'You've got it all there,' he said."

It was not an easy summer. Micky was away with England for the first four Tests; then he was taken ill in August. The side was in transition, and the Oval pitch was growing increasingly unhelpful to the bowlers. In that summer, as in the previous two when he stood in for Peter May, he was having to adjust the ideas he had developed in Surrey's golden championship-winning years. "It took a while for me to realise that we didn't have the ammunition we'd once had. The attack was different; the surface was different. So we had to go about winning games in a different way. I had been brought up always to attack, always to have people round the bat. Now I had to learn to be more patient, to build up pressure, restrict the other team's scoring."

For all that, he was determined to be a winner. "At Surrey we always set out each summer to win the championship, just as Yorkshire did. Maybe Glamorgan did when Wilf Wooller was captain, though for most of the time they didn't have the resources. But very few of the other counties did. I talked to John Murray about it. I said to him, 'When you were playing for Middlesex, at the start of the summer, did you talk about winning the championship?' He said, 'No, never.' Most counties, they just had this lovely existence where they went round the country, playing the games. In many ways it was an extension of club cricket."

Some of that was starting to creep into the Surrey side, particularly with those players who, during the championship-winning years, had spent too long grazing in the easier pastures of the second eleven. In the words of one player of that time, "It had all got a bit too light-hearted, too pallsy-wallsy, with some of them. In the second team they'd been allowed to get into a bit of a lackadaisical attitude. And Micky had to change their mentality, to say 'This is the championship side now.'"

One who had spent too long in the seconds was Michael Willett, who had joined the staff in 1949 but who did not establish himself in the first team till 1961. He was a gifted all-round cricketer and a great competitor for whom Micky had much admiration. "But his lack of first-team opportunities in those years," Micky says, "was detrimental to his natural approach and attitude. It slowed his progress." He was also, like Roy Swetman, one who, as Micky puts it, "enjoyed the peripherals too much. You need relaxation but only up to a degree."

Willett's father Aubrey, a haulage contractor who played his cricket for teams such as Herne Hill Wanderers and the Croydon Pawnbrokers, was as frustrated as Micky: "I keep saying to Michael, he should have the same approach and attitude as you."

On one occasion, playing for the Club and Ground side, Willett bowled his off-breaks indifferently and ran into Andrew Sandham at his most severe.

"The ball was wet," he pleaded in self-defence.

"Never mind that," came the unforgiving reply. "You should practise more."

"Next time there were nets," Micky remembers, "he walked out with his kit and with a bucket of water."

In one of his rare first-team appearances, Willett was out for a duck at Leicester. "While he was waiting to bat in the second innings he wrote a poem about getting a pair." It lightened the mood in the dressing room, though not everybody thought it reflected well on him when in due course the poem proved prophetic.

By 1964 Micky had finally got through to the 31-year-old Willett. "He was always a huge competitor, but he could have been single-minded much earlier in his career." That summer Willett hit four centuries, including the season's fastest, and finished in the top ten of the national batting averages: "the best number five in the country". At the end of it all he gave an interview to *Playfair Cricket Monthly*: 'Willett, fine team man that he is, has nothing but the highest praise for his skipper – Michael Stewart.'

By this time Roy Swetman had gone. So had Laurie Johnson, whom some at Surrey thought a better keeper than Swetman. He had moved to Northampton, in the mistaken belief that Keith Andrew was soon to retire, and was stuck in their second team. So at the Oval there was an early opening for the young keeper Arnold Long, a key member of the Surrey side throughout Micky's years as captain.

"He was a bit like Arthur McIntyre," Micky says. "A no-fuss keeper. Reliable. Good hands, good footwork and a good team player. He wasn't a big appealer but, like Mac, if people didn't walk, he'd get very uptight. He was a big help to me as captain, and he was no mug with the bat."

'Ob' Long had come through Wallington Grammar School and the Beddington Club, one of a string of promising youngsters whom Arthur McIntyre as coach had identified in his work around the county. Another was the 17-year-old fast bowler Geoff Arnold from Malden Wanderers, a raw and aggressive swing bowler who provided excellent back-up that summer to David Gibson and David Sydenham, who each missed almost half the matches. "Syd and David Gibson were outstanding bowlers," Micky says, "but they were injury prone. With different bodies they could both have played for England."

There were even more exciting developments on the spin bowling front. The retirement of Eric Bedser had left the off-breaks in the hands of Ron Tindall, a front-line batsman, but at the start of August 1964 a tall and talkative 17-year-old from Merton, Pat Pocock, was introduced, and he was taking wickets straightaway. He was a big spinner of the ball, and it was not long before the members were talking of him as the new Jim Laker. It was also not long before the Pat became 'Percy', a creation of the ever-mischievous Sandy Tait.

At the other end in 1964, in place of Tony Lock, was the slow left-armer Roger Harman, a bespectacled 22-year-old from Hersham whom they called 'Airy'. He had none of Lock's fiery temperament or histrionic appealing, but his tally of wickets for Surrey that summer was greater than anything Lock had achieved in his final years. In the second championship match, at Trent Bridge, he destroyed the Notts second innings with figures of 17.1 overs, eight wickets for 12 runs, and three weeks later, against Kent at the Oval, he took eight wickets again, this time for 32 runs.

"He did everything right," Micky says. "In the first innings, if the pitch was good, he would bowl economically, with good control. Then when the pitch started to wear, he'd take wickets. He wasn't that experienced. Yet it went on like that all summer."

At one point he looked like being the first bowler in England to reach 100 wickets, Stuart Surridge turning up in the dressing room with two crates of champagne in readiness for the celebration. In the event he was pipped by the veteran Hampshire seamer Derek Shackleton, who was the only bowler to end that summer with more than Harman's 138 wickets.

The previous summer, at a second eleven game, Michael Barton, the former Surrey captain, had watched Harman and Pocock in tandem. "I've just seen England's next spin combination," he declared, and now the members at the Oval were starting to say the same. Harman and Pocock were going to be the new Lock and Laker.

It was all starting to come together for Micky. Barrington, Edrich, Willett and Micky were all having good summers with the bat. They had a capable all-rounder in Stewart Storey, a lively young keeper and bowling options aplenty. In early August they stood in third place in the table, behind Worcestershire and Warwickshire, and Micky started to calculate. If they could win five or six of their last eight matches, starting at Lord's, maybe they could bring that championship pennant back to the Oval.

Lord's, alas, did not bring joy for Micky. It brought a broken nose and a fractured cheek bone – courtesy of a John Price bouncer that Micky, ever ready to hook, top-edged into his face. For nearly three weeks he walked round in dark glasses, watching as his Surrey side lost their way: one win in five games while Worcestershire were victorious five times in a row.

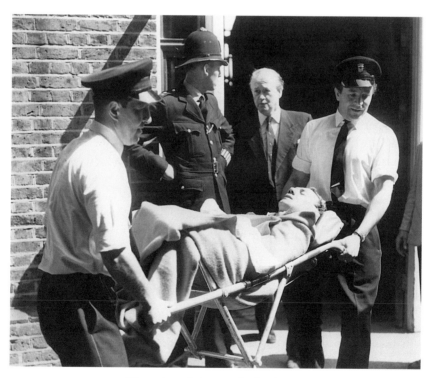

The price of playing the hook shot
Off to hospital with a broken nose

Surrey might not have won even that one game if Micky had not controversially intervened. It was Ken Barrington's benefit match, against Yorkshire at the Oval. Yorkshire/Surrey games renewed plenty of England friendships, with Trueman, Illingworth and Close on one side, Barrington, Edrich and Micky on the other, but somehow the fixture was starting to acquire some ill-feeling, much of it stemming from the game in June in Bradford when Brian Close had not accepted Roger Harman's word that he had caught him in the leg trap.

"He's caught you, Closey."

"Ah, I'm not so sure, Micky."

Yorkshire were on the verge of defeat. The umpire, unsighted, said 'Not out', and Close went on to save the day with a century. "The catch was almost knee high," Micky says, still irritated by the episode nearly fifty years on.

At the Oval it all flared up again. Barrington, captaining the side in Micky's absence and keen to make a score in front of the Saturday crowd at his benefit match, edged a ball from Illingworth onto his pad, only to watch as Trueman in the leg trap dived, rolled over and came up, claiming the catch. Off walked Barrington, for just eight runs, and thought no more of it. Then a photographer arrived in the dressing room, brandishing a picture that made it quite clear that the ball could not possibly have been caught.

"Well, look, Ken," Close said when Barrington, parading the photograph, let off a tirade of swear-words in the Yorkshire dressing room. "If Fred said he caught it, then he did catch it." The incident upset Barrington so much that four years later he devoted six pages of an autobiography to it.

As at Bradford Yorkshire got the worst of the contest and were reduced to holding on for a draw. Their ninth wicket fell with more than half an hour remaining, but Richard Hutton and Mel Ryan were solid in defence against the Surrey spinners and the minutes ticked away. Suddenly Micky appeared on the field, carrying a tray of drinks. "Get Richard Jefferson on," he suggested. "Get him to bowl his off-cutters." Moments later Hutton was lbw to Jefferson. "Yorkshire were not at all happy."

Surrey and Yorkshire. They had some wonderful fun in those years. On one occasion Syd Buller, the umpire, summoned Close and Micky. "If it had been a football match," he wrote in his report on the game, "I'd have sent the pair of them off."

Jim Parks and Alan Oakman watch as Micky hits a six,
one of 27 which he scored in the summer of 1964.

"At Surrey I had always used Stuart Surridge bats, but the previous winter, before going to India, Reg Simpson had given me a Gunn and Moore. It felt really good so I started the summer with it. I hit a big hundred at the Oval and, while I was taking my pads off, somebody told me Stuey had been telling people proudly what a good bat it was, thinking it was one of his. Then I heard he was coming down to the dressing room. I had to hide it quickly in a locker."

Micky returned for the last two matches of 1964, both of which were won. The first was at Bournemouth where he was keen to find out how he would react after his injury. "I'd played for Malden Wanderers in a midweek club game to see if I was OK, but there was nobody of real pace playing. Down at Bournemouth 'Butch' White opened the bowling. I remember standing there as he ran in, saying to myself, 'Bowl me a bouncer, bowl me a bouncer', just to see what I would do. And he bowled this big bouncer that sailed miles over my head."

Micky scored 34 and 89, then 47 back at the Oval where Warwickshire were beaten by an innings. Their captain Mike Smith had just been appointed England captain, and his dismissal on the last day, the vital breakthrough, still remains in Micky's memory.

"Roger Harman was a very quiet chap, quite different from Locky. He only appealed when it was absolutely plumb. He bowled his arm ball, and it hit Mike on the pad. Nobody said anything, and Longy threw the ball back to Roger. The umpire was Lofty Herman. I was at short extra cover, and I saw the look on his face. I said, 'How's that, Lofty?' Roger was ready to bowl the next ball, and Lofty put his finger up. 'That was out,' he said. Mike Smith looked absolutely astonished. He wasn't very happy when he went off."

'Airy' Harman took ten wickets in the match, a triumphant ending to his glorious summer. It was clear that in his first two years as captain Micky had forged a new spirit at the Oval. 'Surrey now have a fine young team,' their annual handbook said, 'and must stand a very great chance of topping the table in 1965.'

*

Organised fitness training had never been a part of life for the professional cricketer. In the 1950s, when Surrey were winning championship after championship, the team, when they arrived in the morning, would warm up with a cup of tea and, in some cases, a cigarette.

At the start of one summer, when Micky had not been playing football, he decided to get in early each day and to build up his fitness with fifty minutes of interval running across the ground. Arthur McIntyre was the senior professional, responsible for upholding team discipline. "What's all that about?" he interrogated Micky. "You can do that at home. If you start doing it here, we'll all be asked to do it."

Times had moved on by 1964. Arthur Mac was coach, and during pre-season practice he introduced a little football on the outfield grass: the Capped Players versus the Non-Caps, with Ron Tindall the Chelsea centre-forward the man to have on your team. "He was brilliant in the air and quick.

Jimmy Greaves thought a lot of him." Then before matches Mac had them doing a few stretching exercises in the Long Room. Micky, though, with his background in football, wanted to take it all to the next level.

"I knew from my own experience that being fitter and stronger was a great benefit to me – in my reactions, my sharpness, my agility and mobility. It helped me to maintain the right standard when I spent six hours in the field. And, if I played a long innings, I didn't tire so quickly. I also used to wish I had more upper body strength. So I had a chat with Mac. I said to him, 'We're not going to be a worse side if we're fitter and stronger.' I suggested that we got people together in the winter for training sessions. 'It will be good for morale,' I said."

Micky found an ally in a new committee member, Brigadier Geoffrey Rimbault. "He was very much of the same thinking as me, from a military view. 'I'll see if I can get somebody for you,' he said."

Major Alec Greaves of the Army Physical Training Board was recruited, a man who had become a hero in Malaya where his fitness work with the national badminton team had led to their beating for the first time the world champions Thailand. Two school gymnasia, at Wallington and Carshalton, were booked, and a 12-week programme was devised, with two nights a week of circuit training from February 1965.

As far as Micky is aware, it was not something that any other county had ever done. 'I know this is something entirely new in pre-season training,' he wrote to the players, 'and in some cases might not be too popular, but I am certain that every individual will benefit as well as the team as a whole.'

The younger players were keen – Pat Pocock, Geoff Arnold, Stewart Storey, Arnold Long – but it was not so well received by some of the older ones, people such as Ken Barrington who reckoned he had managed fine so far without it. "What's all this bloody circuit training lark? Why have we suddenly got to do this?"

It was Micky's benefit year, a chance for him to gain some financial reward after ten years in the first team. Barrington, together with Sandy Tait, tried to persuade Micky to drop the circuit-training idea on the grounds that it would distract him from organising his benefit.

"I used to say to people," Micky says, "'I don't know why cricket is called a professional game. A, There's no money in it, and B, The general approach isn't professional at all.'"

He cites the standard of running between the wickets and the fielding.

"The running between the wickets in the English game was generally some way behind what it was in Australia and South Africa.

Pre-season training in the Long Room, supervised by Arthur McIntyre

Standing (left to right): Bill Smith, Mike Edwards, Roger Harman, Geoff Arnold, Richard Jefferson, Pat Pocock, Stewart Storey, Arnold Long   Seated: Ron Tindall, Ken Barrington, Micky Stewart, John Edrich, Michael Willett

People used to say, 'I can't keep running these singles if I'm looking to bat all day.' Running between the wickets was bracketed with dashing around in the field. It wasn't part of the English game."

He remembers Ken Barrington in India. On one occasion the sprightly Fred Titmus joined Barrington at the wicket towards the end of a long day, calling him several times for sharp runs.

"What are you doing?" Barrington admonished him. "It's a hot day. We'll have no energy left if we don't cut out some of these quick singles."

"All right then," Titmus replied. "We'll only run mine."

"Fielding was the same. I remember when I was at school, reading that Clive van Ryneveld's Oxford University side were diving in the field. 'Diving?' I thought. 'What are they doing?' Then he came over with the 1951 South Africans, and they were all diving around. But there was considerable resistance to it in England. 'Oh well,' people used to say. 'They're from the southern hemisphere. They've got the sun on their backs.'"

Micky was a natural athlete and he loved fielding. He had been inspired by watching Learie Constantine at Lord's during the war. So as captain he had no compunction in trying to change the attitude to fielding.

"It doesn't matter how good a bat or bowler you are," he would tell the Surrey team, "the thing you're going to do most in the game is field. So why not enjoy it? Regardless of your build, every one of you can be an average to good fielder."

Fielding was team work, and that was another vital aspect of the game for Micky. "If you're in the field all day and it's hot, you haven't had the greatest day and the bowler is in his 20th over, and if he pulls one down short and the batsman smacks it away, if somebody dives and gets a chest on it and, instead of it going for four, it goes for one, that's a tremendous fillip for the bowler. That's where the team work comes into good sides."

Micky set up organised fielding practice in the mornings before play. "The only county I was aware of who did anything regularly like that was Essex when Doug Insole was captain. They used to go out and practise close catching and skiers."

"I started it when I was captain at Cambridge," Doug says. "Blokes were turning up straight from lectures, and we got moving with a bit of fielding practice."

The rise of one-day cricket, with its emphasis on team work and result, would soon see all the counties adopt this new approach to fielding, and in 1965 Surrey showed its relevance by reaching the final of the knockout competition, the Gillette Cup. In three home games at the Oval they beat Glamorgan, Northamptonshire and Middlesex, relying each time on a seam attack, with no Pocock or Harman.

The final at Lord's pitted them against Yorkshire. Overnight rain led to a delay of an hour and a half at the start, and the long wait did not do the Surrey side any favours. "It was a big occasion, a full house at Lord's. We had a young side, and some of them didn't have the greatest self-confidence. It was the most nervous I've ever known a dressing room."

Micky asked Yorkshire to bat first. "I didn't think it was going to be easy to score runs early."

His reading of the game looked astute for twelve overs, during which the Yorkshire openers Ken Taylor and Geoff Boycott managed only 22 runs. Then came Brian Close, promoting himself to number three and bristling with purpose. He had strong words with Geoff Boycott, and in the eleven further overs before lunch the total leapt from 22 to 87.

Micky had talked with the team about Boycott. "He was very strong off the back foot so I said to the bowlers, 'Whatever happens, don't bowl short. If you're going to stray at all, bowl a fraction too full.' Whether it was nerves I don't know, but we kept bowling half-volleys, and Boycs timed them beautifully."

Close made a belligerent 79, Boycott a thrilling 146, and Micky, with his predominantly seam attack, was powerless to halt the cascade of runs. He tried Ron Tindall's off-breaks, but they yielded 36 runs in just three overs. Then in desperation he turned to Ken Barrington's occasional leg-breaks. His five overs, with several long-hops and full-tosses, went for 54, and Barrington threw in the towel: "I don't think it's my sort of wicket, skip," he said.

At the end of their 60 overs Yorkshire had reached 317 for four, the highest total in three years of the competition. In fact, it would be another ten years before a first-class county would concede more runs than Surrey did that day at Lord's.

In reply Surrey were 27 without loss when Trueman struck three times in an over. They recovered to 76 for four, then Illingworth repeated Trueman's feat. With almost 20 overs remaining, Surrey were all out for a meagre 144.

"It was a poor decision to put them in," Micky says now, in as matter-of-fact a voice as he can muster. Or, as Jim Laker put it, 'Instead of going down in history as an utterly unselfish batsman and a brilliant close catcher, Micky will be remembered as the skipper who put Yorkshire in to bat in the 1965 Gillette Final.'

*

It was Micky's benefit year in 1965, county cricket's way of rewarding their underpaid professionals after long years of service. The previous year it had been Ken Barrington's turn, and his had been a great success, passing £10,000 at a time when a Surrey cricketer, even with plenty of win bonuses, would not earn £1,000 in a summer. A great lover of cars, he arrived at the start of 1965 in a brand new Rover.

"For the first away game he gave Roger Harman a lift," Micky says. "It belted down with rain, and there was a leak on the passenger side that dripped onto Roger. He arrived with his trousers soaking. During the match somebody went off to the shops and, when it came to the return journey, there were half a dozen of them standing there, all wearing these pac-a-macs. 'We're all ready to go with you, Kenny,' they said."

The beneficiary could organise eight Sunday matches around the county which, even in those days of six-day-a-week cricket, the players found time to support. In May at Beddington, with BBC2 showing the whole match, a Surrey eleven played the International Cavaliers, who were captained by Trevor Bailey and included three overseas cricketers yet to be seen in the county game: Mushtaq Mohammad, Keith Boyce and Intikhab Alam.

Then there was a fixture against Sterling Cables at Aldermaston, where the day was renowned for the superb spread of food the hosts laid on. The ground was pleasantly situated, with terraced cottages alongside it, though the facilities in the small pavilion were rather basic. "There was only a little wash basin," Micky says. "We played there on a baking hot day one year. Percy Pocock hadn't been in the side long, and he batted up the order. He hit a few runs, and he came off dripping with sweat."

"Where are the showers?" he asked.

"There aren't any," Ron Tindall replied. "But don't worry. They've made arrangements for us to wash in the cottage over there. Don't bother to knock; just walk in that side door."

The gullible young Pocock did as instructed. There was no shower but he found the bathroom, ran the hot water and lay there, singing away cheerfully. After a while a man's head appeared around the door, and the naked Pocock thanked him for his kindness.

Relaxed and well scrubbed, he returned to the pavilion where the astonished Tindall almost dropped his drink in disbelief. "You did what? Surely you realised I was pulling your leg."

Geoffrey Howard was now Secretary at the Oval so at least Micky did not suffer the fate that befell Alec Bedser in his benefit year in 1953. The hero of that summer's Ashes series, Bedser pinned up a notice at the Oval inviting Surrey supporters to attend his next Sunday match, only for the Secretary, the autocratic Brian Castor, to tear it down.

"One of the last times I saw Alec," Micky says, "the week before he died, he brought that up. He was still complaining about it."

Micky's benefit raised £7,000. He was not as big a name as Ken Barrington, it was a much wetter summer and, in truth, he found much of the fund-raising rather embarrassing: "It was like saying to your best friend, 'Will you give me twenty quid?' I wasn't at all comfortable with it."

The day following the Lord's final against Yorkshire Micky was at Merstham, where rain fell for much of the day. As a consequence he had to speak to their annual dinner later in the year, where they asked him to give a full account of the Gillette final, his worst day in twenty years as a Surrey cricketer.

"I think Yorkshire were going to give me the freedom of Bradford and Leeds for putting them in to bat."

*

Surrey's success in reaching the Gillette Cup Final in 1965 was the highlight of what was in many respects a disappointing summer, one in which the county failed to live up to the pre-season predictions of championship success. Ken Barrington had a lean year, Michael Willett – just as he had broken through to the front rank of batsmen – missed most of the season with a knee problem and, worst of all, Roger Harman's slow left-arm bowling went backwards, bringing him fewer than half the wickets of the previous summer.

The enigma of Harman's decline still troubles Micky. "Every year up till then he'd progressed but, once he was capped and became the number one left-arm spinner, he never really performed. You'd get on a turning pitch, and you'd go out for the last innings, saying 'Airy will knock them over', and he didn't produce the results."

For Micky it did not help that the members were forever harping back to the days of Laker and Lock. "It raised the expectations too high. An 18-year-old Pocock would be compared with a 36-year-old Laker, a 22-year-old Harman with a 34-year-old Lock. Then when things didn't go well, they'd say, 'He's not as good as Tony Lock was … not as good as Jim Laker.' I'd say to them, 'Did you see Jim Laker at 18?'"

For Pat Pocock, a bubbly, self-confident character it was not a great problem, but for the quieter Roger Harman the pressure grew too great.

"Whenever the pitch started to take turn," he says, "they'd lob the ball to me. 'Come on, Airy.' And they'd expect me to bowl the other side out.

When you're bowling well, you never think about what your body's doing; you think about what you're going to do with the ball. 'I'll toss one wide of off stump' or 'I'll bowl one quicker on leg'. But I got to the point where I couldn't do it, and I was thinking about what I was doing wrong. And of course I became tight, and that made things worse. The previous year, when I was taking wickets, the members would all acknowledge me. Now, when I walked through them to the dressing room, they looked the other way. Progressively I lost confidence in my own ability."

"I used to field bat-pad to him," Micky says, "and towards the end it wasn't too enjoyable."

Harman's last summer on the staff was 1968 when, recalled to the first team, he gave one final reminder of what might have been. Already told that he was not being retained, he travelled to Ilkeston where he bowled tidily on a slow-paced pitch to take six wickets in the Derbyshire first innings. Then second time round, when the top of the pitch became broken, he took eight wickets, including a hat-trick, for just 16 runs.

His next appearance was at Nottingham where before play on the Sunday he went for a stroll along the River Trent with Ken Barrington and Micky. "It was a lovely morning," Micky recalls, "and we sat down. There was a couple with a picnic basket, and Roger said, 'Look at them. How lucky can they be, and we've got to play cricket.' I lost my rag, I'm afraid. 'People would pay anything to be in your position,' I said, 'and you're saying you'd rather be over there.' You rely on somebody to win you matches, and he's thinking that way. That's no good."

Micky is not one who will readily admit fault. It is part of his belief that leaders should not do so. "As a captain or a manager you're bound to cock things up sometimes but, if you're responsible for a group of players and you keep telling them you've made a mistake, they'll soon lose confidence in you. But then I don't find that too difficult because I'm not often wrong!"

"When I married Mister Right," Sheila chips in cheerfully, "I didn't realise his first name was Always."

Yet, reflecting on the career of Roger Harman, Micky is uncharacteristically self-doubting. "What could I have done better?" he asks. "Perhaps I didn't handle him right. Maybe I was too hard on him. On reflection I think I could have done more to boost his confidence. He was a highly talented bowler, and he's a much stronger person than you might think. He did well in business, and he's done some great work off the field for Surrey cricket. In recent years I've become very friendly with him. He jokes to me, 'You gave me the sack.' And I do feel a bit guilty about it."

10

IN SEARCH OF A CROWD

The success of the Gillette Cup led cricket's administrators to further change. An advisory committee recommended that the championship include a number of one-day matches, but this proved a bridge too far. Instead, for the summer of 1966, they tried to speed up the three-day format by limiting the first innings to 65 overs in about half the fixtures.

It was not a universally popular move. It marginalised the spin bowlers, and it did nothing for the equanimity of Ken Barrington in a summer when Charlie Griffith was already haunting him. At Trent Bridge, in the 61st over of their 65-over allocation, he played out a maiden, finding himself sent to Coventry when he returned to the dressing room.

Two weeks later Barrington found himself at the centre of another brouhaha. Surrey, moving forward under their Secretary Geoffrey Howard, had finally overcome the opposition of the Lord's Day Observance Society and arranged to play the second day of their championship match against Kent on a Sunday. The hours of play were two to seven, with spectators – necessarily admitted free – encouraged to buy a scorecard for two shillings and sixpence.

They piled in, eight thousand of them, and they were treated to a display of unadventurous batting by Barrington who took three hours to score 42. Colin Cowdrey set a defensive field and, according to *The Times*, 'play seemed to lose momentum altogether.' At one stage Barrington, enduring slow handclapping and barracking, offered his bat to the crowd.

"The pitch was doing a bit," Micky says by way of defence. "I know Kenny drove them all out the Hobbs Gates, but technically it was an outstanding innings."

"It was a disaster," Geoffrey Howard said. "It was the best Sunday gate in all my time at the Oval, better than we ever got for the Sunday League, and by the end they were going out faster than they'd come in."

Surrey were in deep water financially, and Geoffrey Howard was not one to hold back if he felt the players themselves were contributing to the decline in spectators. Two years later, at the end of another grim day's cricket, this one not involving Barrington, he sent Micky two typed pages listing some 33 points, among them:

Surrey v Middlesex, Saturday 13 July 1968. An awful day's cricket.
Weather Cloudy. Atmosphere – climatically dull and oppressive.

Cricket equally dull.

Crowd small and apathetic. Very few handclaps all day.

Catering unimaginative at best – at worst unbelievably inefficient.

Wicket good and true: little deviation seen yet Parfitt bowled 8 overs for 10 runs.

The president of Danish Cricket Association left thoroughly disappointed with English batsmanship.

The Taverners Bar was about 75% flop.

The "frustration of the opposition" skills have become very competent. As they advance in competency and ingenuity the spectators steadily go out the door.

The game is said to lack characters. But three-day cricket is only a game of character and charm if played with enterprise. Otherwise it is too long drawn out to compel interest.

Micky's hand-written reply pointed out that Surrey had lost early wickets and needed to consolidate, also that the main culprits were inexperienced batsmen who 'couldn't break out from the pressure of accuracy that Titmus and co put on them ... I don't accept that there is a <u>general</u> lack of first day urgency but I do accept that at times there is a lack of <u>positive</u> approach whatever the day, unless of course there is a run chase on.'

"Geoffrey was aware that the crowds were dwindling and that the game was in a parlous state," Micky says now. "He wanted it to be entertaining, and that's understandable. But we were approaching the game from the point of view of its being a competitive match, trying to retrieve the situation after losing early wickets. Whenever as captain I went out to toss, my only thought was to win the match and, once that became impossible, to make sure we didn't lose it. If you don't go out with that attitude, you're doing the game a disservice."

On another occasion, Micky remembers, a breathtaking victory in a third-day run chase was followed next morning by some cautious Surrey batting on a greenish pitch. Suddenly, after five successive maidens, there was a crackle on the tannoy, and Micky heard the Secretary's voice: "Ladies and gentlemen, after yesterday's thrilling victory, I have to inform you that the surface and the playing conditions for today's match are totally different."

Undoubtedly the pitch had become a problem. "You'll never win a championship here at the Oval," Brian Close regularly told Micky. Yorkshire, by contrast, played at Bradford, Hull, Harrogate and Sheffield, grounds where the wickets had life. "The square had got more and more tired," Micky says. "It was always hard work at the Oval."

*

Another development followed in the spring of 1966, with the death of Sandy Tait, the veteran masseur. He had been at the Oval since the days of Jack Hobbs, and little had changed in his work during that time. He had a massage table, a heat lamp and a strong pair of hands to rub out the aches and pains, but that was all. If somebody reported a niggle in the thigh or hamstring, his response was simple: "Take short steps, son. Don't stretch out."

Micky knew how much the world of football had moved on from this, and he was instrumental in the appointment of David Montague, a properly qualified physiotherapist. Now the club, despite its parlous finances, was setting aside a special room with various new pieces of equipment including two kinds of heat lamp and a Faradism machine for electrotherapy.

"With Taity, if you came in with a bruise, he'd get you on the table. 'I'll rub it out, son,' he'd say. Sometimes he'd be rubbing it too early, increasing the bleeding."

The team was moving forward, too. A talented teenaged Pakistani, Younis Ahmed, arrived in 1965. He had to serve a two-year residential qualification before he could play in the championship, but he had an outing in the first team when Surrey played the South Africans that July, showing the promise of his left-handed batting with scores of 21 and 66. "I was at the wicket when he came in," Micky recalls. "Even at that age he played in a very aggressive, confident way, looking to establish his ascendancy over the bowlers. He became a real match-winner. He could always score runs, all round the wicket, even when it was difficult."

Unfortunately, much to Micky's frustration, Younis never became a good fielder. "He was hopeless. When we played at Lord's, the Middlesex side used to pile onto the balcony, waiting to see how long it would be before I gave him some stick."

"Micky could be a bit in the football mould at times," Pat Pocock says, "running it like a football squad, giving out bollockings. Forty years later, I'm still trying to work out whether that was a good approach or not."

"That's rubbish," Micky says. "It was nothing to do with football. At Surrey, when I started under Stuart Surridge, we had a team strategy where every individual went onto the field knowing what they had to do, what their responsibility was. As captain I carried that on. If people didn't live up to their responsibility, or ventured outside it, as Percy was inclined to do, I was quick to point that out. Maybe I did sometimes explode, but the occasions were few and far between."

Nevertheless, for all this, Pat Pocock's assessment of Micky's captaincy is unambiguous. "Mike Brearley was the best captain I played under. I went on an Under-25 tour to Pakistan when he was captain, and he was brilliant. And he got better and better after that till he became a genius. Micky wasn't a genius, but as a captain he was right up with the best."

Pocock's cricket advanced at a rapid rate, taking 112 wickets as a 20-year-old in 1967 and being selected for England's winter tour of the Caribbean. He was an outstanding prospect, even if he did drive Micky to distraction with his endless experimentation. "He was absolutely dedicated to off-spin bowling, still is. But if, for example, you had Fred Titmus bowling at one end, everything would be simple, common sense. Percy at the other end, he'd be making it all complicated, trying out variations, bowling four different deliveries every over. There were crucial times when all you had to do was spin it and put it in the same place. He'd do that four times, build up the pressure, then he'd try something else and give the batsman a way out."

Micky was forever trying to drill a more conventional approach into his young protégé, but Pocock, with all the joy of youth, could not resist experimenting with the unknown. "He always looked to learn," Micky says, "but he wasn't the greatest listener."

"I was a slow learner," Pocock admits now. "I did experiment too much. I realise now that I must have been wrong and he must have been right, because everyone was saying it. They wouldn't all be wrong. For a non-bowler, Micky was extremely knowledgeable about bowling."

Micky was not so knowledgeable about Pocock the batsman. His error of judgement stemmed from a match early in Pocock's career, a match that found Micky caught up in a newspaper furore. "We were playing at Bath. The games there were the big money-spinner for Somerset in those days, but the pitch could be terrible. Before the match I went out to look at it, and I couldn't believe what I saw. 'This isn't conducive to first-class cricket,' I said, and somebody from Somerset told the *Daily Express*. They made it sound as if I'd said it later and I was moaning because we'd been bowled out cheaply. I found out later that the pitch had been prepared by an AA motorbike rider – for a first-class match."

In a low-scoring game that was over by tea on the second day Micky was dismissed for a pair, the first of his career, and he watched in despair as the Surrey second innings disintegrated to 39 for nine, only to have his spirits revived by the young Pocock who hit 45 out of a last wicket partnership of 68 with Roger Harman. "I'll tell you this, Stew," Micky said to Stewart Storey, sitting beside him. "This lad will do the double before his career is over. You can have what you like on that."

"You're on," Storey replied without hesitation.

Micky's prediction was not to be. Pocock rarely rose higher than number ten in the order, only once passing 400 runs in a season. "I soon realised my folly," Micky says, "but I refused to pay up till he retired."

In the summer of 1969 Pocock, now 22, suffered two setbacks. First, Ray Illingworth was brought into the England side as captain, blocking the young Surrey bowler's path into further Test cricket. Secondly, the 40-over Sunday League was introduced, with its emphasis on negative, run-saving bowling.

Micky's instinct was not to play Pocock but to nurture his progress in the longer game. But the crowds were turning up on Sundays, it was becoming a major part of the summer, and the young off-spinner wanted to be part of it.

"At first I hardly played so I had a meeting with Micky. I said, 'Sunday cricket is here to stay. It's becoming very important. And I want to play. So I'm going to work on a different technique.' I deliberately made my action different so that I could divorce one from the other. Six years earlier I wouldn't have had the experience to do that, but I developed a different run-up, delivery stride and arm action. I used to hit the wicket much harder. I was lucky. If I hadn't been a big spinner of the ball, I couldn't have done that."

Micky disagrees adamantly. "The John Player League didn't do him any favours at all. I'm absolutely convinced that, if it had never come along, he'd have played a lot more Test cricket, and his Test record would have been top drawer. He was a very fine bowler, but his one-day style did disturb the simple rhythm of his bowling in championship cricket."

One for whom the Sunday League was definitely not designed was Ken Barrington, but sadly he had been forced to retire the previous winter. In October he had flown to Australia to represent England in a series of double-wicket contests, and in the Melbourne pavilion after one such game, against a West Indian pair that included his old adversary Charlie Griffith, he suffered a mild heart attack.

It was perhaps inevitable that when Surrey embarked on their first summer of the Sunday League somebody in the dressing room, with a typical cricketer's humour, would speculate about how Barrington would have coped with the new format. "It's a good job he's finished now. I reckon this would have given him another heart attack."

In their first Sunday match, at the Oval, Surrey made only 147 in their 40 overs, yet they still managed to beat Worcestershire who were all out for 142 with one ball remaining. It was a new cricket, bringing in the crowds, and in his end-of-season report Micky recalled how in the first weeks, before he acclimatised to the pace of it all, he would go home after the game and 'slump in the armchair, unable to unwind till about eleven o'clock – with the last two days of the championship match still to think about. I soon discovered many players were experiencing a similar thing.'

In that first match Tom Graveney stroked an elegant 45, but he was a fish out of water, as was Micky whose 22 that day was his highest Sunday score of the summer. "I was hopeless. Instead of playing my natural game I was trying to whack it. I even cocked up the bowling in that first game. Younis Ahmed had to bowl an over."

Tom Graveney was filled with foreboding, predicting to Micky that in two years the technique of batsmen would be showing signs of deterioration. Micky agrees: "In Test cricket it's always been about the batsman going out there and accepting their responsibility, looking to get big runs. You don't give it away. You play yourself in, then you try to take control and dominate the bowling. But in 40-over cricket you're giving the batsman an excuse for getting out."

He recalls John Edrich returning to the Oval after a glorious winter in Australia in 1970/71. "He was a big run-getter from when he first started, but like all left-handers, because of the angle, he would miss or nick balls outside the off stump. He had a great temperament; he never let it worry him. But that year, when he came back from Australia, it was the best I ever saw him bat. He was middling everything. Then he got back into playing one-day cricket, having to run the ball down to third man, and soon enough, when he was playing in the first-class game, he was back to missing and nicking it again."

As the years passed, Micky became more and more aware that there was a marked change in approach to batting. "I remember going to watch Neil Fairbrother in a county game when he was under consideration for the Test team, and he got off the mark by hitting the ball over cover. I thought, 'Blimey! Would he do that in a Test match?'"

It was the dilemma that English cricket faced – still faces. On the one hand the crowds were deserting the three-day county game, yearning for more of the excitement of the limited-over format. On the other hand county cricket was supposed to produce Test cricketers, with appropriate skills for the five-day game.

"I would never want to bowl a young bowler in a 20-over or 40-over game," Micky says. "You work with them to build up their control, to create sideways movement, to exert pressure. They get to the point where they can land six balls in the same place, and in a championship match that's a maiden. In a Twenty20 game the same over might go for 18. That isn't the best environment when you're learning how to bowl."

Surrey won nine of their first thirteen 40-over games, challenging to be the first champions of the league, but, as Micky's end-of-season report made clear, there was much about these Sunday games that could be improved, not least the hastily prepared pitches, often on the edge of the squares. At Hove in May the groundsman gave them a pitch with a boundary of 38 yards on one side, and there was a lengthy delay as Micky insisted on a fresh strip being cut. Then at Leyton in August, playing fellow title contenders Essex in front of a full house of several thousand spectators, the surface of the pitch broke up so quickly that no batsman on either side reached 30. The crowds were back, but in Micky's view they were not being treated to the entertainment, the display of batting skills, that they deserved.

In Micky's report he also questioned the wisdom of the regulation limiting bowlers' run-ups to fifteen yards:

> The only sight I don't like in the Player's League is a young bowler of genuine pace having to bowl off a restricted run with consequent loss of speed and rhythm, just trying to contain batsmen. This, I think, is a great shame.

Surrey lost their last three matches, finishing fifth, a position which remarkably they did not better till 1992. In Micky's years as Surrey captain they contested 15 one-day tournaments, and they never came closer to a trophy than the disastrous Gillette Cup Final of 1965 – though they were only one ball away from returning to Lord's for the 1970 Final.

The semi-final that year at the Oval lasted till almost eight o'clock at night, the long day ending with the sun dropping low across the River Thames. A tight contest between Surrey and Sussex went down to the very last ball, with Sussex – in the person of John Snow, on strike for his first and only ball – needing two runs to bring the scores level and to win the match on fewer wickets lost. Geoff Arnold was the bowler, while the non-striker was the Sussex captain Mike Griffith, a quick runner between the wickets.

"Whatever you do, if they run, throw it to the end Snow's running to," Micky instructed, and he took himself off to the mid-wicket boundary. "I thought to myself, if anybody's going to drop it, it had best be the captain."

The ball was a good one, just the right length, and Snow drove it hard into the off side, straight to the fielder Intikhab Alam. "I remember jumping up in the air," Micky says. "We'd won it." Then a sorrow creeps into his voice. "Everything was in slow motion after that. My arms came down. Oh dear."

Younis Ahmed distracted Intikhab by running towards the ball. Intikhab momentarily looked up at the batsmen, allowing the ball to go through him. Then finally, as Snow struggled to complete the vital second run, the throw came in to the wrong end.

With another opportunity gone, time was running out for Micky. It seemed that Surrey would never win a trophy under his captaincy.

*

From early 1966 Micky was spending his winters working for Slazenger in their Allied Products section, reviewing and developing the range of their equipment. "For my first task I was asked to reduce the number of different cricket pads they offered. I looked at it from a cricket point of view, and I eliminated the one I thought was superfluous, which turned out to be their best seller. The sales manager wasn't best pleased. He immediately put it back. I also designed a range of football boots."

It was a job in which, apart from the kudos to Slazenger of being the Surrey captain and an England cricketer, he showed both organisational ability and flair. Yet the cricket still came first for him, and twice his winter's work was interrupted by overseas tours, both of which he was asked to captain.

The first of these, from 15 January to 10 April 1968, was an extraordinary enterprise, sponsored by the British-American Tobacco Company and organised by Joe Lister, the Worcestershire Secretary. They spent a fortnight in Sierra Leone in West Africa, playing four matches, then flew across for a fortnight in East Africa, where they played in both Uganda and Kenya. From there they went on to four-day games in Karachi, Bombay, Madras and Colombo, followed by a final three weeks in Singapore, Malaysia, Thailand and Hong Kong. In all they travelled 32,000 miles, played 46 days of cricket in ten different countries and staged numerous coaching clinics, all with a squad of only 14 players, one of whom, Gamini Goonesena, missed the first month in Africa while another, Tony Greig, was out injured for the second half of the trip.

Most of the party would in time become Test cricketers, three of them – Keith Fletcher, Mike Denness and Tony Greig – future England captains. So it was a tour that provided great learning experiences for the party, even if many of the games were one-sided. In all, they played 21 matches, winning 15 and getting the better of the draw in the other six.

Derek Underwood took wickets galore: nine for 53 off 40 overs in the two innings of the match against a strong Chief Minister's XI at Madras, then fifteen for 43 in 37.4 overs against the Ceylon President's XI in Colombo. "I gave him some stick at Colombo for bowling a flighty delivery," Micky remembers. "I said, 'On a pitch like this, Locky would never have bowled that ball.' And Jack Birkenshaw said to me, 'He's just taken eight for 12, and you're giving him a bollocking.'"

It was the happiest of tours, though Micky was not one to let the fun get in the way of maintaining standards. "He was a tremendous leader, a great enthusiast," the wicket-keeper Roger Tolchard recalls, "but it wasn't an off-season jolly. It got bloody hot in places, and we weren't allowed to sit down on the field. 'We are professional cricketers,' he'd say."

In the game at Colombo he did relax, however. "We batted first on a beautiful pitch," Micky says, "and at lunch we were 90-odd for no wicket. Several of them came to me; they said they'd been invited to go and look at some cheap jewellery. It was only ten minutes away. Was it all right to go? Just five of them. I said, 'Hold on a minute. Numbers nine, ten and eleven can go. That's all. And come straight back.'"

Inevitably, no sooner had they gone, than wickets started to fall. 99 for none became 135 for six, and Tolchard joined Micky in the middle with no sign of the rest of the batting order. "I said to Roger, 'You get out now, and you'll be on the first plane home.' The first ball missed his outside edge by a whisker. If he'd have touched it, I'd have had to declare."

A few minutes later there was a sudden rush of activity as the remaining batsmen reappeared. Tolchard was bowled and, after a long delay, Harry Latchman, Middlesex's Jamaican leg-spinner, made his way to the middle, wearing one pad and carrying the other. "We should have scored a million on that pitch, and we were all out for 179." Then it poured with rain during the night, and under a burning hot sun next day Underwood was unplayable. Their total of 179 turned out to be more than enough.

They had Dennis Amiss: "He was always going to be a big accumulator of runs." A young Tony Greig: "Technically you could fault him here and there, but he had everything." Harold Rhodes: "A really top bowler, with that bit of extra pace. I was on the committee that had to decide whether he threw, and I voted that he didn't. In my view it was hyper-extension of the elbow."

And Micky's Surrey team-mate GG 'Horse' Arnold, with his fast bowler's aggressive energy: "At Kowloon he stayed with the boss of the

Post Office. A smashing fellow, he was willing to take us all shopping, and he took us out to lunch. Then in the game he comes in to bat against us, takes guard with a cap on, and first ball Horse bowls him a bouncer and hits him straight on the head."

Often on the tour they stayed not in hotels but with families, and by the end of the three months they were almost dizzy with the places they had been and the people they had met. The last game was in Hong Kong, where the sun beat down from a cloudless sky. Micky scored 40, then had a shower, emerging into a darkish dressing room where he was greeted by a man who seemed familiar but whom he could not place

"You haven't got a bloody clue who I am, have you?" the man said.

"I know I've seen you before."

"Seen me before?" he laughed. "That's nice. I gave you nine days of hospitality in Sierra Leone."

The only difficult moment of the tour came in the one game in Pakistan, at Karachi against a Board of Control XI captained by the great Hanif Mohammad. With the pitch breaking up, the tourists were well placed on the third evening, 255 ahead with five wickets in hand. Then the next morning they arrived to find that all the cracks in the pitch had been filled in.

"I got Hanif out there. I said, 'This is a first-class match. This is going to Lord's.' I got the groundsman, and we removed all the stuff they'd added overnight. 'We'll chase the total right down to eleven,' Hanif said. 'I'll do that if you don't report to Lord's.' I said, 'You're too late, Hanif.'"

They did chase to eleven, losing by 43 runs, and the row blew over.

Three years later Micky returned to Pakistan, on a three-match Commonwealth tour, again organised by Joe Lister, but this was a far tougher assignment. In the first match, at Karachi, where Micky scored a confident 93, they collapsed against the leg spin of Intikhab Alam, losing by eight wickets. Then, in the second at Dacca in East Pakistan, they had Pakistan in trouble, eight wickets down in their second innings and only 128 runs ahead, and they looked set to square the series.

Three months earlier, in parliamentary elections, East Pakistan had voted overwhelmingly for Sheikh Mujibur Rahman, a nationalist fiercely opposed to the domination of West Pakistan and its leader Zulfikar Ali Bhutto. So the tensions in the country were high.

"The ground had concrete terracing all around it," Micky recalls, "and there wasn't much of a crowd. We went out after lunch with a substitute fielder, a West Pakistani lad, and I put him down on the boundary at deep

The Commonwealth tour of Pakistan, February/March 1971
Standing (left to right): Harry Pilling, Doug Slade, Younis Ahmed, Roy Virgin,
Bob Cottam, Robin Hobbs, Don Shepherd, Neil Hawke
Seated: M.U. Haq, Norman Gifford, Micky Stewart, John Murray, Joe Lister

"I've never met a more English-type gentleman than M.U.
It wouldn't have surprised me if he'd met us at the airport
in 100 degrees heat in a three-piece Harris tweed suit and brogues."

square leg. Don Shepherd was bowling and, when I looked round from my position at short leg, I saw the lad was only ten yards from me."

"What are you doing?" Micky called across. "I want you right back."

"I can't," he said. "They're throwing stones at me."

Micky turned to Norman Gifford. "You swap with him, Giff."

"Swap with him? You're joking. I'm not going down there."

Within minutes fires were burning on the terraces. Micky turned to his old friend, wicket-keeper John Murray.

"What's going on there, JT?"

"Hmmm," he said, laughing. "I think there's something up."

"Next thing I know," Micky recalls, "a large group of them were running towards me from the pavilion. So I walked across to them. They were all students."

"Captain Stewart," their leader said. "There's no danger to you or your players. But we wish the game to be abandoned. We're protesting because Bhutto has called off a meeting with our leader."

Micky was as single-minded as ever. "Can't you just wait till we get these two wickets and knock off the runs?"

No, they could not, and off the teams trooped.

"We spent two hours in the dressing room. We could hear shots firing and all sorts. Then a high-ranking army guy came in, and he led us out into a military vehicle that took us to an army camp. As we drove away, we could see several bodies lying on the ground."

From the army camp they were escorted to the hotel, where they had the good fortune to run into an airline pilot: "An impressive-looking chap, he'd just flown the last flight into Dacca."

"You are guests in my country," the pilot said, "and I must treat you as guests. I shall fly you out at midnight."

So at midnight they were driven through curfew-quiet streets to the airport where hundreds of West Pakistanis were waiting for flights to safety. "When we eventually got onto the plane, there were umpteen people sitting in the aisles."

The Pakistani cricketers did not escape that night, and for the final match at Lahore, due to start two days later, the Pakistan Board selected two elevens: one if the players got back from Dacca, the other if they did not.

"I talked to Inti afterwards. He honestly thought it was even money whether they would get out alive or not."

It was all a terrifying ordeal, and Micky's preparation for the final game was not helped when, as a boisterous prank, some of his team-mates spiked his drink. As a consequence he was in no great shape when he reached the wicket to face a young Imran Khan.

"It was the first time we'd set eyes on him, and he was quite wayward. His first four balls to me were all long hops outside the off stump, ideal to square cut, and all I could do was hit them straight down into the ground."

He was caught behind for 12, returning to the pavilion to be greeted by Robin Hobbs: "I have to say, captain, that's the worst first-class innings I've ever seen."

The match was drawn, and Micky stayed on in Lahore to do some business on behalf of Slazenger. Days after he left for home, the country was plunged into a civil war between East and West.

*

In 1968 English cricket, still looking for ways to bring back the spectators, made another major change, allowing each county to employ one overseas player who had not qualified by residence. Nottinghamshire recruited Gary Sobers, who led them to fourth in the championship, their highest position since 1932. Glamorgan prospered with Majid Khan, Kent with Asif Iqbal and Hampshire with Barry Richards. Surrey, meanwhile, still struggling financially, opted not to join the rush and fell from fourth place the previous year to 15th.

The following year, 1969, Surrey recruited Intikhab Alam, captain of Pakistan, and they were once more among the championship leaders. In truth, Intikhab was only one element of the revival. Geoff Arnold was back after missing almost a whole year with a knee injury, Younis was fast becoming a top quality batsman, John Edrich had an outstanding summer, Micky himself had his best season for several years, and the younger players – Graham Roope, Robin Jackman and Mike Edwards – were all developing.

They played good cricket through July and August and, after three weeks on the road, they returned to the Oval on the morning of Saturday 30 August. They were 13 points behind the championship leaders Glamorgan, with three games left to play, all at the Oval, the last of them against Glamorgan.

"One of the things that attracted me to first-class cricket," Micky says, "was the crowd at the Oval when I went there as a boy. Playing there was like going on stage in front of thousands of people. If you hit a ball and it ran away for four, there would be a great cheer. But that had gone by the end of the '60s. The old dilapidated Vauxhall stand was still there, but there would be hardly anybody sitting in it.

"That Saturday, when we turned up, we really believed we had a chance of winning the championship, and there was no one there. A Saturday at the end of August, and the ground was almost empty. You could feel the disappointment in the dressing room. It really did affect us when we took the field."

By close of play Hampshire had made 401 for four, and Surrey could do no more than hang on for a draw. Meanwhile in their West Wales heartland at Swansea, Glamorgan were being cheered to the echo as they beat Essex by one run in front of a jubilant crowd who ended the match full of hwyl, singing *Cwm Rhondda* and *Calon Lan*. The contrast with the Oval could not have been starker, and Glamorgan duly sealed the championship in their next match at Cardiff.

It led Micky to say in an interview that he thought Surrey should play more matches away from the Oval, in the heart of the county where there was more support. His comments provoked several letters of protest to the club from members who had paid to see their cricket at the Oval, and nothing came of the proposal.

"When we played at Guildford, there was always a good crowd. It wasn't a big ground, but there was so much more atmosphere, compared with playing in front of empty terraces at the Oval. It wasn't as intense as Yorkshire playing at Bradford, but you could definitely feel the support around you. And people in the field responded to it."

As if to bear this out, Surrey's best victory of that summer came at Guildford, their only home game away from the Oval, when Leicestershire, set 137 to win, were all out for 134 off the penultimate ball of the match, the third run-out of a brilliant fielding display. Micky had led the way with scores of 97 and 64, but his main memory of the match was of a less inspired fielding performance the previous day.

"Between lunch and tea we dropped about five catches, and I wasn't happy. The last ball before tea we dropped another one. I think it was Mike Edwards, who was usually superb in the bat-pad position. I marched off and started going up this narrow staircase in the pavilion. All the members were around and, as I went up the stairs, a voice called out. 'You want to try some high full tosses, Stewart.' And not being happy, I responded with a one-word answer. Not a very polite one, either. I didn't look at him or anything.

"Three years later I went to a wine festival in the Long Room at the Oval, and I was introduced to Percy Fender, who was in the wine business."

The 80-year-old Fender was one of the great names of Micky's childhood: scorer of the fastest century in cricket history, an inspirational and unorthodox captain of Surrey through the 1920s and author of some of the books Micky had devoured in the Carnegie Library in Herne Hill Road.

"It's a pleasure to meet you, Mister Fender," Micky said. "I don't think we've ever met before."

"We haven't actually been introduced," Fender replied, "but you have addressed me."

"Addressed you? When?"

"At Guildford. Do you remember a suggestion about bowling full tosses?"

11

CHAMPAGNE STOPS PLAY

Part way through the summer of 1971 Micky decided that he would call it a day at the end of the season. He was coming up to 39 years old, he was in his ninth year as Surrey captain, and Slazenger were keen for him to work for them all the year round. In addition, he was upset by a dispute between the club and the young fast bowler Bob Willis.

Willis had been flown out to Australia during the winter as a late replacement for the injured Alan Ward. It had been a shock selection – he was not playing regularly in the Surrey side and was still uncapped – and it shocked Willis himself. "He came round my house after he'd been selected," Micky says. "I said to him, 'They're not mugs, the selectors. You've been picked on your ability.'"

The Ashes were regained in Australia, under Ray Illingworth's captaincy, and Willis played in the last four Tests, taking twelve wickets, most of them key Australian batsmen. He had broken through to the next level and, when he returned to the Oval, he asked for a pay rise, amounting to about five pounds a week. Surrey operated a rigid system of remuneration, based on whether you were capped, and Stuart Surridge, the chairman of cricket, said a firm no, at one stage banging the table and saying that Surrey expected Willis to earn his wages, not demand them. "I had a heated chat with Stuey," Micky says. "I said to him, 'It's ridiculous. He's playing for England, and he's still on second-eleven wages.'"

It was a clash of generations and, though Willis did eventually receive a small increase, the dispute contributed to a disaffection that led to his moving to Warwickshire at the end of the year.

"At that stage," Micky says, "Bob was very inconsistent as a bowler. As he wasn't a robust build, he incurred niggling injuries. But he'd got pace, and he'd got bounce. Sometimes he'd frighten the death out of batsmen. Other times, when he didn't keep his hand behind the ball, it would just float down. I remember him running up first over and Clive Lloyd whacking him over his head into the pavilion.

"He wasn't the most confident young lad. But he learned and he kept at it. He wouldn't shirk hard work. He turned into a very fine bowler. But I don't know. He finished up listening to these hypnotising tapes, didn't he? Evidently they helped him no end, but I don't know what my dad would have said if I'd had to play tapes telling myself how good I was."

There were other problems for Willis at Surrey. The Oval pitch was not responsive to fast bowling, and there were too many bowlers competing for places in the team.

Geoff Arnold was first pick, now a mature bowler who generated a lively pace, swung the ball both ways and was a keen observer of the weaknesses of batsmen. In 1971 he had the season of his life, finishing at the head of the national bowling averages, though only 24 of his 83 wickets were on the lifeless Oval track.

There was Robin Jackman: "A real hundred percenter," Micky says. "It's a little derogatory to say he was a fine county bowler, but he was. He was just what you needed in six-day-a-week cricket, accurate, shrewd, a hard worker. He wasn't so tall or quick, he was more of a skiddy bowler, but you could always rely on him. He was a really good English pro bowler."

Then there was the medium-pace of the all-rounder Stewart Storey, the last Surrey cricketer to do the double. "An entertaining batsman, a brilliant slip and a more than useful bowler. A real team player, with a quiet determination."

If Willis was to play, most times it would have to be in place of Jackman, and that was not an easy decision for Micky to make.

There were selection problems with the slow bowling, too. Pat Pocock was the off-spinner; that was simple. But the popular Intikhab Alam spent the first half of the summer captaining Pakistan on their tour of England, and in his absence the young slow left-armer Chris Waller had great success. In mid-July a choice had to be made between the two of them.

At least the wicket-keeper was straightforward: Arnold Long. Also the five batsmen: John Edrich, Mike Edwards, Graham Roope, Younis Ahmed and Micky, with Dudley Owen-Thomas and Roy Lewis in reserve. It was a team that Micky had been developing over several summers, a team that he knew had the potential to win the championship. Could they do it in his last year with them?

On 25 June the answer seemed to be yes. At Hove Stewart Storey glanced the last ball of the match to the fine leg boundary to complete a four-wicket victory that took them to the top of the table, with six victories in their first eleven games.

By 14 August they had sunk to seventh place, having won none of their next six matches. Yet again they had shown that they had the potential to win the championship, only – it seemed – to be found wanting as the long weeks of high summer separated the victors from the rest.

Yet Micky, never a man given to great mood swings, did not become downcast. He looked at the remaining fixtures, and he did some calculations. "If we can win five of the last seven games," Pat Pocock remembers him saying, "we can win the championship from here."

He had already made one crucial decision: to opt for Intikhab ahead of Chris Waller. On paper, looking at the averages at the end of that summer, it was a decision that did not look quite right. But Micky was not one to base his thinking entirely on averages. Indeed, early in his reign, when the averages had started to appear on a board in the pavilion, he had insisted on them being removed.

"It was hard leaving out Chris. I felt sad doing it. He was young, and he'd taken a lot of wickets, at a good average. But the majority of those wickets came when batsmen were attacking him. He'd bowl with a slip and a ring of fielders, and he'd get his wickets by frustrating the batsmen. That wasn't enough if we were going to have a chance of winning the championship; we had to be able to take wickets when batsmen were defending. Inti could do that; with him you could put fielders round the bat and attack."

Five wins out of seven was Micky's target for Surrey, and they met it with ease, winning five in a row. First, on a wearing track at Lord's, where Pocock and Intikhab took crucial wickets. Then on a green one at Kettering, where Micky decided to pick both Jackman and Willis and to leave out his second spinner. "Inti was very good about it. He was captain of Pakistan so he could understand my position and what I was thinking."

In a low-scoring match, won by an innings, Micky scored 81, the game's only fifty, and had a never-forgotten encounter with Sarfraz Nawaz, Northants' Pakistani bowler. "It was seaming all over the place, a pitch for getting on the front foot, and at one point he bowled three consecutive bouncers at me. I used not to say anything, but with the third one I did have a word. Sarfraz followed through, right down the pitch, till he was standing in front of me. 'I want to see your blood, Micky,' he said with a smile. 'I want to see your blood.'"

At Bristol it was Graham Roope's turn to play the match-winning innings, 105. "Roopy was a great stroke-maker, a fine driver off the front foot, a very good timer of the ball." And he followed it up with four slip catches in the Gloucestershire second innings. To many observers Roope was by this time the best pair of hands in the country, and his 59 catches in the shortened first-class programme of 27 games was, in catches-per-match, not far short of Micky's 77 in 34 games in 1957. "Mind you," Micky says, "If he dropped one, it was never his fault. I remember one that hit him smack in the middle of his chest, and he turned straight to Stewart Storey next to him. 'That was yours, wasn't it?' he said."

Back at the Oval Roope made a career-best 171, then they bowled out Yorkshire twice to win by an innings, the only time all summer when they took all twenty wickets on the unresponsive Oval pitch. Yorkshire, in their first year under the captaincy of Geoff Boycott, were – according to John Woodcock in *The Times* – 'wretched', with 'no spirit to speak of, no will to resist'. "I remember going out to toss with Boycs at the start of the match. They'd been at Bournemouth, and I asked him how they'd got on down there. I was expecting him to tell me about the game, but all he talked about was his own batting. He took me through his two innings."

At the Oval Boycott was out twice in the day: first to Pocock's arm ball, then drawn out of his crease by Intikhab's leg break. For the first time since 1866 Yorkshire would go a whole season without an away victory.

The last wicket falls
Bore caught Stewart bowled Pocock 0

Surrey, meanwhile, made it five out of five by beating Derbyshire at the Oval. This time it was Stewart Storey's turn to hit a career-best, 164, and Micky's decision to opt for Intikhab ahead of Chris Waller proved perceptive when the Derbyshire batsmen had to be winkled out on the final afternoon. That was certainly what John Woodcock thought:

> *Surrey won because they had a leg spinner to tickle out the tail. Without Intikhab, who took five for 63, they could not have done it. Without Pocock, who took three for 54, they might not have done. And without Willis, who took Derbyshire's first two wickets in his second over, things could have been different.*
>
> *They got home with ten minutes to spare and to win the championship they need 14 points from their last two matches, against Glamorgan and Hampshire.*

"If we can win five of the last seven games," Micky had said, "we can win the championship from here." And they had won five in a row. The championship was theirs for the losing.

They returned, after a four-day break, to the Oval to play Glamorgan. Twelve months earlier, almost to the day, Colin Cowdrey had scored his 94th century at the Oval and in so doing had secured the championship title for Kent, for the first time since 1913.

Around the counties the captains were coming and going, only two of them in post for more than five years: Cowdrey at Kent, in his 15th summer, and Micky in this his ninth and last. So, with its echo of Cowdrey's success a year earlier, there was something rather special when on the first day of the Glamorgan match Micky took Surrey to the verge of the title with the 49th century of his career.

In Micky's nine years at the helm so much in county cricket had changed: the abolition of the amateur, the start of one-day cricket and its expansion into the Sunday League, the strange one-year experiment with a 65-over first innings, the introduction of overseas players and now a complicated system of first-innings bonus points. Under Micky's captaincy Surrey had to a great extent ignored these points, to the criticism of many observers, and this had now created a situation in which, with 11 wins, they were still uncertain of overtaking Warwickshire, who had completed their programme with only nine.

Victory over Glamorgan would render such calculations irrelevant. At the end of the second day, Thursday, that seemed highly likely, so much so that the Glamorgan all-rounder Peter Walker, following his father's footsteps into journalism, chose to make Micky the subject of his weekly interview for the *Guardian*. The assumption behind his questions was that he was interviewing the captain of the champion county.

Friday, however, brought frustration for Surrey. With 15 overs to be bowled and three wickets to take, Arnold Long dropped the last recognised batsman, Roger Davis, off Intikhab. When the ninth wicket fell 12 overs later, Davis was still there. The number eleven, Lawrence Williams, was a true tail-ender, but he only had to face two deliveries. Micky took the new ball for the final two overs – one by Geoff Arnold, the other by Intikhab – and Davis resolutely made sure of the draw. There was no feature in the *Guardian*. Surrey, heading to Southampton, still needed six points.

"It was very disappointing," Micky says. "We wanted so much to win in front of our own crowd."

"I remember coming off the field," Pat Pocock says, "thinking, 'Have we blown it? Has that one wicket cost us the championship?'"

Yet for John Woodcock:

> *It had been a day without a dull moment. Of its kind it was every bit as exciting as the Gillette Cup final. The prize, too, was the most valuable in the game. Surrey will probably win it still. And yet six bonus points are no formality. It is an awkward number. And is the weather breaking up? And did poor Arnold Long turn restlessly last night? No, it is not quite over yet.*

There were more twists at Southampton. Morning rain, delaying the start for an hour, was not a good omen, but a century by John Edrich, supported by Micky and Graham Roope, took Surrey to 190 for one off 62 overs, leaving 23 overs to take the total towards the vital bonus points: 275 would give them five, 300 the all-important six. They reached 240 for three, yet somehow contrived to be bowled out for 269.

"That was terrible," Micky says. "It was a good pitch, too. I think I was stumped off Peter Sainsbury in both innings. I bet I'm the only person he did that to in his whole career. He only gave the ball one and a half revs."

There followed an anxious Sunday, checking weather forecasts and hearing rumours that the Hampshire captain Richard Gilliatt might declare at three wickets down, thereby depriving Surrey of the vital point and forcing them to go all out for victory.

At the start of the match Micky had made one of the hardest decisions of his time as Surrey captain, opting for the raw pace of Bob Willis rather than the wholehearted contribution of Robin Jackman. "I think Jackers' heart was the shape of the Surrey feathers. But Southampton was always a good batting pitch. We had Geoff Arnold and Stewart Storey to swing it. Bob was a 'horses for courses' bowler, and for that game we needed his extra pace and bounce. Jackers was almost in tears when I told him."

According to Jackman, "Bob Willis kept me out of several games, and every time I queried the selection Micky had an answer – and every time he was proved right, which of course didn't make it any better. At Southampton I had the sulks and he quite rightly came down on me. 'I don't want the twelfth man behaving like a child,' he said. 'I expect you to play your part for the team.'"

And part he played, a memorable part on the Monday, though it was not at all what Micky expected or, for that matter, approved.

The Hampshire opening pair, Barry Richards and Gordon Greenidge, were the first obstacles to overcome, and they both fell with the score on 30. Then the difficulties began. David Turner, a stocky left-hander with a short, punchy backlift, and Roy Marshall, the veteran West Indian stroke-maker, took root. Micky ran through his bowling options but, as lunch approached, the wicket tally on the board was still stuck on two. Crucially the over count had now risen to 44, more than halfway to the all-important 85.

A great Surrey crowd had gathered, people whom in some cases they had not seen for a long time. They packed the trains out of Waterloo, and they saw Bob Willis, summoned for a quick burst before lunch, knock back Turner's stumps. Now, barring the rumoured declaration, just one wicket stood between Surrey and the title.

Gilliatt himself appeared, and the game went on wicketless to lunchtime and through the first forty minutes of the afternoon. Then Intikhab, bowling from the city end, got a ball to take the outside edge of Gilliatt's bat and Arnold Long's glove was there to grasp it. Surrey's 13-year wait was over.

Alan Gibson in *The Times* was full of praise for the new champions:

> *I would say that Surrey are the most convincing champions for some years. We have known for a long time that they have all the talent required, but it has not knitted together, under pressure, until these last couple of months.*

"I think I jumped on Longy's back," Micky says. "Then, and I didn't know anything about it, on comes Robin Jackman with a tray of champagne. They'd arranged it all with the umpires. There was quite a stoppage in play. At one point I saw Sheila so I walked towards her and gave her a kiss. Jim Swanton was there for the *Daily Telegraph*. He didn't take too kindly to it at all."

(top) The vital wicket: Gilliatt caught Long bowled Intikhab
(below) Micky starts the celebrations by jumping on Arnold Long
(top right) The champagne celebration

'The champagne was brought out,' Swanton wrote stiffly, 'and a lady, reputedly Mrs M.J. Stewart, broke the long cricket custom of wifely anonymity and embraced the triumphant captain while the wine was being drunk.'

"Get on with it," the Hampshire members started to shout.

"I didn't agree with the lull in play. I wanted us to focus on winning the match."

They did not focus. Marshall made 142, Sainsbury 52, and Hampshire declared, 26 runs ahead, without losing another wicket. Then, when Micky went to pad up, he found himself escorted by Stuart Surridge to the far side of the ground, to give interviews for the television and radio. "I said to him, 'I want to be in the dressing room.' I should have been stronger really. We were halfway through the match, and I was supposed to be opening the batting with John Edrich. John was livid as well."

*

Next day the *Guardian* carried Peter Walker's interview, in which Micky extolled the match-winning virtues of the bowlers: Intikhab 'the world's best leg break bowler', Pocock 'potentially his equivalent as an off spinner', Arnold 'the best opening bowler in the country bar none', Willis 'still very raw but the best young fast bowling prospect in England' and Jackman 'a tremendous competitor who through sheer guts and determination has overcome the handicap of being on the short side for an opening bowler.'

He spoke of the consistency of the batting, the crucial role of the all-rounder Storey and the high quality of the close catching: 'Around the wicket I don't think there's a team in the world to compare with us.'

Most of all, however, he attributed their success to 'what is fashionably called these days professionalism. I prefer to label it efficiency. We play at maximum output as often as humanly possible.'

Then, conscious that his language could be interpreted as an attack on individual flair, as it was twenty years later when he was England manager, he went on:

> I don't believe in having eleven faceless people in the side. I have encouraged every player on our books to play in his own way.
>
> We're a youngish side, and these days young people aren't afraid to express themselves. There are certainly far fewer dull mediocre cricketers around now than there were five years ago. The overseas players have helped encourage this, too.

*

In Surrey's second innings at Southampton John Edrich made 95, completing a wonderful summer with the bat, but nobody else made runs. On the last day they lost by four wickets, leaving them level with Warwickshire in the final table and only winning by virtue of having won more matches. "We batted hopelessly in the second innings," Micky says. "I don't like losing a game of cricket at the best of times, but to lose like that when you've just been crowned champions, I'm still unhappy when I think about it."

Nevertheless he had taken Surrey back to the top of the tree, where many thought they might remain for several years, becoming in the 1970s as dominant as Yorkshire had been in the 1960s.

Yorkshire, under Boycott, were down in 13th place, their only cause for celebration a last-day century by their captain, making him the first Englishman ever to end a summer with a batting average above 100.

John Edrich was a different character. As a batsman he was single-minded but, according to Micky, in a run chase he always played for the team. "In those years he played so many match-winning innings. When we opened the batting together, we had a great understanding. When we built a partnership, we were good for each other."

In the Southampton dressing room, as they all packed up, the players presented Micky with a silver inkstand. "I was just about to have a bit of a moan at them, for the way we'd played, but I was stopped dead in my tracks. In the end it was all a bit emotional."

12

AWAY FROM CRICKET

Surrey persuaded Micky to stay for one more summer. At one stage he was going to enjoy a season without the cares of captaincy, but finally he agreed to carry on as before. There was no natural successor, and the committee felt he could build on their championship triumph.

"Arthur Mac and Stuey both put pressure on me to stay, they offered me a testimonial, and Slazenger said, 'It's up to you. It's always nice to refer to you as the Surrey captain.' So I finished up playing another season. On all counts I shouldn't have done."

It did not help that Bob Willis had gone or that Geoff Arnold, the lynchpin of the attack in 1971, took only 15 wickets in just seven games. Several others had less good summers, and Micky himself scored fewer than 500 runs. They achieved little in the one-day competitions and finished twelfth in the championship.

"Since taking over as captain, the one thing I'd wanted to do was to win the championship. But that last year my performance was hopeless. Anything you achieve is history. Now you've got to move on to the next goal – win it again. That's how I'd been brought up. And I definitely didn't have that single-mindedness in my last year."

Micky's status at the Oval, especially with those he captained, was not tarnished. "One of the most pleasing things from my time in cricket is that even now, to this day, the majority of the people who played under me still call me Captain."

"He was a great captain," Geoff Arnold says. "I played under quite a few captains with Surrey and England. As a handler of players and a tactician of the game Micky was second to none."

So does he call Micky 'Captain'? "No, I don't," he replies. "I went back to the Oval when he was the manager there. So I call him Manager – or Boss."

Micky laughs. "I say to him sometimes 'This is silly. Just call me Micky.' And he says, 'I can't, Boss.'"

*

In the summer of 1972 Micky was approaching his fortieth birthday and, with a testimonial to organise, the relentless schedule of the county game was becoming a strain. That summer a third one-day tournament, the Benson and Hedges Cup, was introduced, and the Sunday League games were no longer conveniently tucked into the middle of a three-day match at the same venue; they were often a long car drive away.

In early August Surrey played the first day, Saturday, of a county match at Lord's, then drove almost 150 miles to Weston-super-Mare. "We got to our hotel quite late, maybe even midnight. Then, when we were fast asleep, the fire alarm went off and we all had to troop out. I remember Jack Hill, our scorer, coming down in a dressing gown and cravat."

They returned to Lord's for Monday and Tuesday. Then the fixture list took them to Scarborough for three days, from where they drove down to Eastbourne to start again on Saturday. "No sooner were people off the pitch than they were getting into cars. And the last thing you want to do after a day's cricket is to spend four or five hours cramped up in a car. The quality of the cricket was playing second fiddle to the commercial considerations."

On Sunday morning Micky drove up to Surbiton for a testimonial game, then back to Eastbourne to complete a match that had a denouement as astonishing as any he ever played. Micky had set Sussex 205 to win and, with three overs remaining, they had reached 187 for one.

"Jim and Albert Plummer, my friends from West Surrey, were there. I remember chasing a ball down to the boundary where they were sitting. 'You've lost this one, Micky,' one of them said. I finished up having a bet with them that we wouldn't lose. However well you're batting, if you're near the end of a limited-over game, which in effect this one was, the last twenty runs are always the hardest to get."

Pat Pocock bowled the third last over. At this stage he had figures of 14 overs, nought for 65, but his six balls brought three wickets for two runs and suddenly there was a different kind of buzz around the ground. Normality resumed with 11 runs, off Intikhab, in the penultimate over. Now, with six balls left, Sussex were 200 for four. Just five to win.

The Surrey twelfth man took a call from Arthur McIntyre at the Oval. "How's it going down there?" The twelfth man started to explain the position, breaking off in mid-sentence. "Just a mo. Percy's taken another wicket." That was five down and it was still five to win.

"I'll hold on then," Mac said, only to be told "Percy's got another one."

Mac was starting to smell a rat. "Are you taking the micky?" he asked, only for the twelfth man to shout, "He's got the hat-trick."

"I'll get you for this. Just you wait till you get back to the Oval."

The batsmen managed a single off the fourth ball. Then Pocock struck again with the fifth, his seventh wicket in eleven balls. Sussex were 201 for eight, needing four runs, and off the last ball the new batsman was run out. During Pocock's final two overs eight wickets had fallen.

"Whenever I'm listening to a match," Micky says, "and the commentator says, 'They're coasting it now,' I always think of that day."

*

Micky's last match as a first-class cricketer was against Nottinghamshire at the Oval in late August, a three-day match that was broken by a Sunday game in Swansea. Micky scored 24 and 3, taking his final tally of first-class runs for Surrey to 25,007, one of only seven Surrey batsmen to pass the 25,000 mark: along with Jack Hobbs, Tom Hayward, Andrew Sandham, Bobby Abel, Ernie Hayes and, later, John Edrich.

His first game as captain had been against Nottinghamshire, when they set Surrey 291 to win and they went down in a blaze of Brighter Cricket. Now, older and wiser, Micky set Nottinghamshire 296 to win and, with Pocock and Intikhab in tandem, he masterminded a thrilling 21-run victory, the last batsman appropriately caught by Micky himself at backward short leg. It was his 604th catch for Surrey, a total that will almost certainly never be surpassed.

*

No sooner had Micky left cricket, settling to full-time work at Slazenger, than an attempt was made to woo him back. This time it was not Surrey but Sussex in the form of their newly appointed, forward-looking captain, Tony Greig. Five winters earlier Micky had captained him on the tour that ran from West Africa to the Far East. Now Greig saw him as someone who might help to shake things up at Hove.

Arthur Dumbrill, the Sussex Secretary, rang Micky one day, asking him to come down and meet the Chairman.

"Tell me," the Chairman asked Micky over lunch. "What do you think of Sussex County Cricket Club?"

"Well, you've always had top players," Micky replied, not certain where the conversation was heading, "but …"

"But what?"

"But it still seems as if the club is in the 1920s."

They pressed him to elaborate, and his further comments were greeted positively. "I'd like you to meet some other committeemen," the Chairman said finally. "Tony Greig has told us all about you."

On the appointed day Micky drove to the meeting at the headquarters of the Lewes Building Society. His car broke down on the way, making

201

him almost an hour late, and he arrived to find the full Sussex committee sitting around a board-room table, staring at an empty seat, in front of which sat a cup of cold coffee.

"I'd like you to repeat what you told me about Sussex cricket."

"Is this fair?" Micky replied.

"No, please carry on."

They asked him to become the county's cricket manager, a newly created post that would encompass much more than the role of the traditional county coach. But Micky turned it down. His work at Slazenger was going well, and he could not bring himself to join a county other than Surrey.

Six years later, when Surrey came to him with a similar request, his heart strings were pulled, and he returned to cricket.

*

Micky was with Slazenger part-time from 1966, at which point the managing director was 'Buzzer' Hadingham. Buzzer was the son of Tony Hadingham, the company's first MD, though he did not succeed his father directly. In fact, when he returned there in 1945 from a tough war, his father's successor gave him a hard time.

"I gather you were the boss's son," the man said to him on his first day back. "Well, you're not now, and I've got my eye on you."

Nevertheless Buzzer rose to be managing director, witnessing much change. "We put nylon into the cloth of the tennis balls," he said. "I sent large telegrams to about 250 leading tennis clubs, advertising our new ball. It proved very successful. And I held in my hand the first metal racquet. René Lacoste was promoting it. It was a marvellous thing, but I decided it was too expensive. We would have had to sell it at about twelve pounds, ten shillings." He smiled wistfully. "I think I made the wrong decision."

When Micky started full-time as Allied Products manager in the autumn of 1972, Buzzer was still the MD, the company bearing all the hallmarks of his cheerful personality. "He made a point of visiting three departments each day," Micky recalls, "talking to people about how their work was going. 'We're all in this together,' he used to say. It was like a family."

Buzzer retired in 1975, and Ian Peacock, who had worked his way through the ranks, was appointed in his place. "We were part of the Dunlop group," he says, "which was a much more corporate business, selling tyres, gum boots and the like. We were only sports, and Buzzer was a sports fanatic. He was a wonderful boss, an inspirational leader, and he left me a very happy company. Fun and laughter was very much part of the ethos, and that was an environment in which Micky readily sat, a team player who loved the camaraderie we had."

They were years of rapid expansion. Not only were there developments in the sporting equipment but they extended their clothing range and took over Puma, the potential of whose sporting footwear had to that point not been realised. Micky had expanded Slazenger's share of the cricket market, and his venture into the design of football boots had also been a success.

Alan Mullery of Tottenham and England inspects the flexible, lightweight boot designed by Micky for Slazenger

In October 1975, when the new MD had to replace the UK sales manager, there was nobody in the sales team who fitted the bill. So he turned to his Allied Products manager, much to Micky's surprise.

"I've always wondered why he appointed me," Micky says. "At that point I had no experience in sales."

"Micky's a very personable guy," Ian Peacock explains. "Everybody liked him. He knew sport from A to Z, and he was a great enthusiast about all the things we were doing. He was well known, too, so he could walk into anywhere in the world of sport: 'Micky Stewart's coming in today,' they'd say. And we knew he was a leader of men from his days as Surrey captain. If you can lead men on the cricket field, there's no reason why you can't translate that to leading a team of 20 or 30 salesmen. To me he had the perfect cv. I was delighted to appoint him."

Micky supervised a much enlarged sales team, breaking it down into regions and matching people's strengths to the jobs to be undertaken. In his own thorough way he identified the products and the geographical areas where there was room for improvement, he set targets for sales, and the result was that in three and a half years the company's UK turnover increased more than threefold.

"It's something I'm very proud of," he says now.

In the 1980s, some years after Micky had left, Dunlop, the parent company, made a flawed takeover of Pirelli, and they tried to mend the damage by using the profits that Slazenger were making. In the end they merged Slazenger with the main company, resisting an attempt by Ian Peacock and Buzzer Hadingham to buy back Slazenger. "I left and set up my own business," Ian Peacock says. "We loved Slazengers. It was a happy family business, and it was very, very successful. We had some golden years there, and Micky was very much a part of that."

When Micky was lured back to the Oval in the spring of 1979, he had made such an impression at Slazenger that he was about to join the board.

"It was a shock when he went," Ian Peacock says, "but I guess it was a natural progression for him. He'd spent a few years learning business, and that must have helped him when he went back into the world of cricket. Sport isn't a business, but you can introduce good business practice into it. If you try to run it like a business, it doesn't really work. As we've seen with the Premiership in football, the Corinthian element is lost. The people with the most money come out on top. But having said that, if you work in sport, business experience is very valuable. I would like to think that what Micky learned at Slazengers, he was able to convert that into dealing with issues at Surrey, then with England. I'm certain his time at Slazengers enriched his management ability."

*

If Slazenger provided Micky with the experience of great success, his other main challenge in his years away from cricket most certainly did not.

In the winter of 1970/71, when he was still playing cricket, he was approached by the Corinthian-Casuals and asked if he would take over as their manager. They were deep in the doldrums, financially in a bad way and clinging to their amateur idealism at a time when almost all the other

Isthmian League clubs had gone down the 'shamateur' road, many of them with chairmen on big ego trips paying out large sums of money to their supposedly amateur players. "One day we might be a Football League club," they would say.

Micky was an occasional spectator at Casuals games and, after accepting the offer, he watched them play Sutton United. Bob Willis was in goal, but he was leaving his full backs to take the goal kicks. "Just before half time," Micky remembers, "Bob placed the ball and stood beside it. The full back ran up, and unfortunately he kicked more earth than ball. The ball dribbled out a few yards to the feet of the Sutton centre forward, who promptly struck it into an empty net. I had to leave at half-time for a sports fair in Munich, and I went off thinking, 'What on earth have I taken on?'"

They lost 4-0, Willis departed for Australia, and in mid-January Micky took over as manager. At this stage of the winter, in all competitions, they had played 26 games of which they had won one and drawn three, with a goal tally of 16 for and 88 against. There was a mountain to climb and after two games, one of which was drawn, Micky departed for a cricket tour of Pakistan.

What was it that made him accept such a formidable challenge? "I suppose I was attracted by the emotion of it, the sense of what the club had been."

His contribution to that winter's campaign, when they finished in last place, was limited, but he stayed with them for a further four years till his promotion to UK sales director at Slazenger. Each year they finished at the foot of the table, even in his last season when they were relegated to a newly formed Division Two – though in the latter part of that season they did finally enjoy a little success, with a ten-match sequence in all competitions in which they recorded nine wins and a draw.

When Micky took over at the Casuals, there were very few clubs in the league not paying their players, and one of those soon joined the majority. "Their chairman told me he'd got fed up with going in his newsagents every Sunday morning and the chap saying to him, 'I see you lost again.'"

On one occasion they were playing away to a club who were on a good Cup run, which necessitated them playing twice a week. Buoyed by the success, a good crowd had arrived, and the start was delayed as the home team players refused to leave their dressing room till the club agreed to pay them their 'expenses' – i.e. wages – per match rather than per week.

There was no way that the Casuals, with their tradition, would go down such a road. Even when the amateur/professional distinction was officially abolished in 1972, they still did not pay their players. "I enjoyed it," Micky says, "when I was with the other team's committeemen and for a change we'd just won the game. I'd call out to one of our people: 'Who's collecting the match fees?'"

Micky set out with ambition. He wrote a three-year plan for the club, moved the training from the astroturf pitch beside Wormwood Scrubs prison to the Guardian Royal Exchange ground in East Molesey, and he negotiated with Walter Winterbottom of the FA to set up home at the National Sports Centre at Crystal Palace, even attempting to buy and bring down a stand from Coventry City. The idea fell through, but he did organise a return to the Oval, hoping that this would bring back some of the atmosphere of his own season with them in the 1950s. They played their first match there in October 1972, shortly after the ground had staged an open-air pop concert. "I looked in during the week, and everything seemed fine. But on the morning of the match the sun was out, and I could see all these little things glistening on the pitch. Crushed plastic glasses. I was scratching my hand to see if I could cut myself on them. Fortunately I couldn't and, before everybody arrived, the sun went in. So nobody saw them."

The crowd at the Oval pop festival

It was not a success. Surrey County Cricket Club, a more commercial operation now, were charging considerably more than the income generated by the small crowds, and the Casuals moved on after just eight games.

It was hard work. For the return to the Oval Sheila sewed new corner flags, and each week she took the kit for the three teams to their local launderette. Meanwhile Micky, as well as taking two evenings of training, spent hours on the telephone, especially on Friday nights when regularly players in the reserve and 'A' teams dropped out.

There was no money for a team coach so the players travelled in cars, even to fixtures as far afield as Wycombe and Bishop's Stortford. Once at Wycombe they received a call that two of the team had broken down en route and were not going to make it. The substitute Martin Tyler, now of Sky Sports, was struggling with a twisted ankle, and the search to complete an eleven only ended when an occasional player, there as a spectator, was persuaded out of the bar where he had already downed two or three whiskies. Wycombe were one of the wealthiest clubs, and amazingly they were held to a 1-1 draw.

Micky worked hard to recruit new players, but many of the most promising ones were soon on their way to more powerful clubs. The ambitions of Micky's three-year plan were not realised, the club finances deteriorated further, and there was serious talk of either dropping to a much lower level of football or disbanding altogether. After a poll of all members, they resolved to battle on.

"I used to set targets," Micky says. "Just small ones. The first was that the players enjoyed their football. Then, that they all stayed positive, that they thought they had a chance of success. Another one for me was to improve the individual players to the extent that other clubs came in for them – which was, I suppose, a peculiar sort of target. We never got any transfer payments or anything.

"They were all good people; they had their hearts in the right place. But week in, week out, we had next to no chance. Football is about retention of the ball and, if your players can't do that, you're not going to win many matches."

So what did Micky take from the experience? In all his life up to this point he had enjoyed much more success than failure. He had never previously known what it was like, as his father would put it, to be an also-ran.

"You learn how to cope with adverse circumstances," he says, "how to deal with repeated loss and failure. No matter how bad a result may seem, you always have to see the things that are positive. And you have to control your reactions when you look at individual failures and mistakes."

Micky, in everything he has done, has always been the ultimate competitor – but somewhere in the mix there is also a true Corinthian, determined even against great odds to maintain the purer values of sport, not to submit to hypocrisy and cheating.

The season after Micky left, the Corinthian-Casuals had three managers. The first, a member of the side, felt the extra responsibility was affecting his performances on the field and stood down in October. The second also played, but he allowed the frustrations of his impossible task to come out on the field and, according to one team-mate, "seemed by the end to be on a mission to get sent off." This he duly achieved, for violent conduct, in the first half of a home game against Hampton. The committeemen, horrified to see their high ideals so besmirched, expelled him from the club at half-time.

His replacement, helping out for the last two matches, was … yes, you've guessed it, Micky. To this day he remains a club member, paying his annual subscription, admiring still their attempts to retain the Corinthian spirit. From time to time his son Alec plays in the side that plays against schools, along with fellow cricketers Alex Tudor and Mark Ramprakash.

For some in the world of cricket Micky brought with him to the role of England manager too strong a whiff of football, but it was football with none of the excesses and the cynicism of the big-money clubs. Corinthian football.

*

Alec was nine years old when Micky played his last innings for Surrey. It was a Sunday League match at the Oval in September 1972, and the crowd all stood as Micky went out to bat. They stood when he came in, too, bowled by Richard Hutton of Yorkshire for seven, and Alec was among them, with his twelve-year-old brother Neil and his six-year-old sister Judy.

"Dad must have been pretty good," Alec remembers thinking as the applause continued, even as Micky for the last time made his way up the pavilion steps.

Alec was already 'pretty good', too. The previous summer, at the age of only eight, he had gone with the family to watch Neil play for Surbiton in the final of the Surrey Cubs Cup. As always he put his kit in the car just in case they were one short, and to his great joy he found himself drafted in. He scored 41 of his side's 52 runs, was named man of the match by Surrey's Graham Roope and became the subject of an article in the local paper: 'Alec follows his dad's footsteps'.

"We stayed to watch," Micky remembers. "He batted very well. Always from an early age he could time the ball."

(right) Two-year-old Alec hits down the wicket at Eastwick Park

(below) Micky and Graham Roope with the winners of the Surrey Cubs Cup

Alec follows his dad's footsteps

An early age was early, too. According to Sheila, Neil had Alec playing proper double-ended cricket when he was only twenty months old. The two of them spent hours on end playing football and cricket: in the garden, in the hall, even in the sitting room. Sheila kept wicket sometimes, and Micky joined in whenever he was home. Nothing seemed to stop them, not even a pair of wasps' nests that Alec plunged into one day when fetching the ball.

"He came back covered in wasps," Sheila says. "I literally had to pick all the stings off him. For about a year afterwards he had lumps on his skin. He didn't cry, though."

They played in the local park, then Micky took them to the Pearl Assurance sports ground where he showed them different ways to kick a football and in the nets demonstrated some of the finer points of batting and bowling – though never with too much intensity.

"I was frightened to death," he says, "of shoving it down their throats, for fear of putting them off. I just wanted them to enjoy themselves."

He need not have had any fears on that score. They were both besotted with the two games, though quickly their differing personalities emerged: Neil the more easy-going, Alec fiercely determined.

"Neil needed encouragement," Sheila says, "whereas Alec needed to be told he was an idiot."

At the Pearl Assurance ground Micky would show them how to keep their hands in line with the bat when hitting through the off side, putting down cones or sweaters to set them challenges. Then he would finish with a little game in the nets, giving them thirty balls each and judging the runs they scored off each shot.

"Neil would be the first to say, 'Let's play the game, Dad.' But Alec wouldn't want to start till he'd mastered the off-side shot."

Alec's single-mindedness came through in everything he did. "When Alec was older," Micky says, "he would come home from school, go into the dining room, slap his books down and get stuck straight into his three subjects of prep. He'd beaver away until he'd finished them. Neil was quite different. He'd come in, turn on the television and sit watching the racing. At dinner we'd have to say to him, 'What subjects have you got for prep?' And he passed all his exams with flying colours."

Both passed the entrance exam for Alleyn's, but Micky and Sheila decided it was too far for them to travel and sent them instead to Tiffin, a well-regarded grammar school in Kingston upon Thames. In Neil's case the decision was accepted without fuss but, when it came to Alec three years later, he was not at all happy. Tiffin played rugby and, like his father when faced with the prospect of going to Dulwich, he wanted above all to attend a football-playing school. "He wouldn't talk to me for about a fortnight," Micky says.

In those years Alec was keener to become a footballer than a cricketer. "When he was about eight years old, I took him to Loftus Road to see Queens Park Rangers play Chelsea. There must have been 15,000 people there. He said to me, 'I'm going to be a footballer.'"

"You look around at all the people here," Micky said. "Out of all of them there's probably only one who will be really good enough to get to the top."

Quick as a flash Alec replied: "Well, that's all right. That will be me."

For a while he looked as if he might be right, scoring more than a hundred goals one winter for his side Clarion. "He used to strike the ball very powerfully," Micky says, "and with timing. He could score from outside the box, even at eleven. Also he was probably the tallest in the team. Then he stopped growing till he was about sixteen."

Alec joined the youth section of Mitcham Royals, where he played alongside the future Welsh international Glyn Hodges who, according to Alec, "didn't seem to be all that much better than me." There they were coached by the brilliant Dario Gradi, who later had great success developing young players at Crewe Alexandra. Dario Gradi had an Italian father, though Sheila for a long time thought he was an Irishman – Derry O'Grady.

Eventually Gradi told Alec to forget the football and focus on his cricket where he was already making great progress. He had made his debut in senior cricket at the age of 11, playing for Malden Wanderers 3rd XI against Old Emmanuel 3rd XI and scoring 44. "We went up to watch," Micky recalls, "and he batted really well. It wasn't just the runs he scored; it was the way he got them. He struck the ball; he didn't just run it down to third man."

Neil, an all-rounder, was doing well, too, earning selection for the Surrey Under-15s and the Surrey Young Cricketers. So at this stage, while Micky was working at Slazenger, did he start to dream that either of his sons might follow him into cricket?

"Never. I just wanted them to enjoy playing, to experience the pleasure of a team sport. I knew how much enjoyment I'd got from playing, and I hoped they'd get the same. It's a lovely game. You meet so many people, and it teaches you to be honest – and honest when you lose, too." Micky pauses. "I was pleased, though, to see how much drive they had to be successful in their own right."

211

"He didn't have to live his sporting career through Neil or me," Alec says. "So many parents are desperate for their child to be successful, and they destroy the enjoyment. Once you lose your enjoyment, you may as well give it up."

Micky was determined not to push his children counter-productively, but the voice of his own father still echoed down the generations: "Whatever you do, Mick, concentrate on being number one – or near the top. It's a waste of time being an also-ran."

In 1979, the summer when Micky returned to cricket, Neil was captain of the Tiffin 1st XI which included the future Surrey all-rounder Mark Feltham and the 16-year-old Alec. In July Neil was selected to play for Surrey 2nd XI, then to captain the South of England in an Under-19 tournament in Toronto. His team included the future England bowler Neil Foster as well as several who would play county cricket, among them Raj Maru, Alan Wells and Ian Pont. The next year, still only 19, Neil was appointed first team captain at Malden Wanderers. Unfortunately, however, he was bedevilled by the repeated recurrence of a dislocated shoulder that he had sustained on a school skiing trip.

Micky remembers popping into the Malden Wanderers ground one evening towards close of play. He walked round the side of the pavilion, and the first ball he saw was bowled by Neil. The batsman edged it, Alec behind the stumps caught it, and Neil threw his arm up in appeal. "And that put his shoulder out again. I had to drive him to casualty."

After a spell at Slazenger Neil threw himself wholeheartedly into cricket coaching: first at the East Molesey Cricket School, then from a base at Ewell Castle School and with the City of London Freemen's School in Ashtead. He runs the Surrey Under-15s and Under-17s, is active in the county's Academy and remains a regular point of help for the professionals who have progressed from his tutelage. "He's passionate about it all," Micky says proudly.

*

Back at the Oval, in the autumn of 1978, things needed sorting out. In the six years since Micky's departure the dressing room had become unhappy in a way that it had never been when Micky was there.

Micky had recommended that the captaincy pass to Arnold Long, with Stewart Storey as his senior professional. In terms of seniority John Edrich was the obvious successor, but he was still in the England side and he had made it clear to Micky that he did not want to be captain. The committee, however, did not follow Micky's advice, persuading Edrich to take it on. It was a decision which did not work out well. Edrich, though a great batsman and a hard competitor, did not find man-management easy.

"I'd be in my office at Slazengers," Micky remembers, "and the phone would go. Three o'clock in the afternoon, during a match. People in the team complaining about things. Some of the calls would go on for half an hour and more. I said, 'It's nothing to do with me now.'"

Surrey finished as runners-up in the championship in Edrich's first year in charge. Then in the second they won the Benson and Hedges Cup, with Edrich himself winning the Man of the Match award. But gradually the results declined and the side, for all its talent, fell into a habit of mediocrity. It did not help that key experienced players – Storey, Long and Arnold – left, all three of them ending up at Sussex.

"Looking back now with an older, wiser head," Pat Pocock says, "we let the thing gnaw away at us. Micky left a hole; there's no doubt about that. But, to be fair, there's far too much importance put on the captaincy. We could have won the championship whoever had been captain, if everybody had just got on and done their job."

"That's rubbish," Micky says. "The history of the game, both domestically and internationally, shows that every successful cricket side has had a strong leader. There were plenty of talented individuals in that Surrey dressing room. What they needed was somebody to get them competing as a team."

When Peter May became chairman of the full committee at Surrey, he co-opted Micky onto the cricket sub-committee. Micky's first meeting took place in the winter of 1977/78, just after John Edrich had stepped down as captain, and the agenda included the appointment of a replacement.

Roger Knight was the man lined up for the job. He had played some games for Surrey in the late 1960s while studying at Cambridge. Now he was playing for Sussex, which he combined with winter-time work as a teacher of modern languages at Eastbourne College. In the eyes of the committee he had much to commend him. He was an accomplished all-rounder and an upstanding character, he had a Surrey background and, as captain, he would be a fresh broom, one not infected by the recent travails.

"I was in the office of the headmaster's secretary," Roger remembers, "when this call came through out of the blue. It was Alf Gover, asking me if I'd be interested in coming back as captain."

Should he give up cricket, as the headmaster was urging, and become a housemaster? Should he, as Sussex wanted, take over from Tony Greig as their captain? Or should he return to the county of his birth? "Hove suited my cricket," he says, "but my heart was always with Surrey."

Around the table of the Surrey cricket committee went the question: "Roger Knight, do you agree?" And back came the answers: yes, yes, yes. Then it was Micky's turn.

"I can only speak as I know," he said. "If we had a young side, Roger would be the ideal person. He'd set the right example. But it's not like that in the dressing room. We've got a number of talented, experienced people in there who haven't got the right approach nor are they consistent in their personality and character. Roger hasn't got the experience to handle it." Pressed for an alternative, he suggested Robin Jackman.

"We'd like to make a unanimous decision," the chairman Raman Subba Row said.

"No, I'm sorry, I can't go along with it."

The minutes duly recorded that there had been one vote against, MJ Stewart, and were distributed, with a copy to the new captain – so twelve months later, when Micky was back as cricket manager, he was working alongside the man he had voted against. "It could have been very embarrassing," he says, "but we met up, talked it through and it was fine."

Roger Knight's first summer in charge, before Micky's return, largely proved Micky right. The dressing room remained an unhappy place, not helped by John Edrich having told Robin Jackman that he was to be the captain. Not all the professionals appreciated their new leader's style: "You're too much of a schoolmaster," Roger Knight remembers Jackman telling him. "You've got to eff and blind more."

The results reflected the malaise: a worst ever championship position (16th) and poor performances in all three one-day competitions. To add to the sense of crisis, Fred Titmus, in the second year of a three-year contract as coach, resigned at the end of the summer. Seven years earlier, when Surrey had won the championship under Micky, there had been talk of a new golden age at the Oval. How long ago that now seemed!

*

Off the field Surrey had undergone a great change of attitude since the mid-1960s. Throughout the 1950s, when Surrey had won championship after championship, no effort had been made to address the increasingly parlous state of the finances. Other counties, such as Warwickshire and Northamptonshire, had introduced money-spinning football pool schemes, but Surrey had turned up their noses at such 'vulgar' fund-raising. Then came Geoffrey Howard as Secretary, and soon there was fresh blood on the committee, notably Raman Subba Row, who ran a public relations business; Derek Newton, from the world of insurance; and Bernie

Coleman, a South Londoner who in 1947 had taken on his father's pub, The Castle in Tooting Broadway, and with hard work and imagination had built up a chain of pubs and hotels. Together they recognised the scale of Surrey's problems, and they started to think the unthinkable.

At the Oval Test in 1968 the first advertising board appeared, an XS Insurance sign at the Vauxhall end.

"What's that?" asked MCC's Gubby Allen, appalled by the intrusion of such commercialism into one of the great cathedrals of English cricket.

"That, Mister Allen," replied Bernie Coleman cheerfully, "is five hundred pounds, and we're broke."

The key to Bernie's early success at The Castle, at a time when money was short, lay in staging night after night of talent shows and entertainments, all with the aid of an upright, iron-framed piano that he had bought for twenty pounds and a pianist whose nightly wage was ten shillings, a cheap bottle of British wine and a packet of cigarettes which he smoked non-stop as he played. The pub advertised Old Time Musical Hall evenings, Jazz Nights, all sorts to attract the punters, and Bernie quickly became a favourite of the Surrey cricketers when he brought his money-raising acumen to their benefit committees. In 1953, for Alec Bedser, he staged a dinner-dance at the Wimbledon Palais and sold every ticket.

Bernie Coleman (left) entertains Sheila, Micky
and among others (second right) the actor John Stride

Surrey, infused with this new entrepreneurial spirit, shook off its stuffiness, and by the early 1970s the Oval found itself staging pop concerts, Sunday markets, Christmas funfairs, donkey derbies, anything that might once more bring in people and money. "There was one occasion," Micky recalls, "when I turned up in winter to have my photograph taken between two camels. Oh, the smell of them! I'd just bought a beautiful new overcoat, and they spat all over it."

By 1978 the triumvirate of Raman Subba Row, Bernie Coleman and Derek Newton were at the heart of the club's decision-making, and their response to the problems of the first eleven and the resignation of Fred Titmus was once more to break with tradition.

Derek Newton recalls the thinking: "We realised that we had to have someone who was not only in charge of the first-class cricket but also the game throughout the county. We wanted to win competitions, that was important, but in our minds it was also important to produce cricketers from Surrey who would go on to play for England."

Titmus had limited himself to working with the Surrey playing staff and, according to Derek Newton, never did shake off his lifelong loyalty to 'the opposition', Middlesex. So they decided that they must replace him with a Surrey man. But who?

Pat Pocock told Derek Newton who: "There's only one move for you to make. You've got to get Micky Stewart back." But Derek did not think that would be possible. Micky was doing well at Slazenger, earning good money which Surrey could not match.

"How much does it cost to run the second team?" Pocock remembers arguing. "Cut that in half and spend it on Micky. That would be much better value for money."

No other suitable candidates emerged from the county's discussions, and finally Micky agreed to attend a Boxing Day meeting at Raman Subba Row's house, with snow lying on the ground. The plan was for Derek and Raman to present to Micky their idea of what the job of manager should involve, but Micky got in first. "He came in and told us what needed to be done, and it was more or less exactly what we were thinking. He said he didn't want just to be a coach and selector for the first eleven. In addition he wanted to develop cricket in the county."

Money was not discussed. Micky went away to think about it, and before making his decision he spent a weekend in Ipswich with his old friend Bobby Robson, talking through the pros and cons. It was March when he finally accepted the job.

Micky knew that, for all the talk about developing cricket in the county, the first crucial task was to sort out the playing staff. Could he do anything about that? "I knew there was the right amount of talent in the dressing room," Micky says. "If there hadn't been, I'd never have gone back."

He was to be Surrey's first cricket manager, a club appointment answerable to the full committee, not just the cricket committee, and he was to be given considerable autonomy in the way he interpreted the role. He was not going to leave Slazenger, passing up the opportunity to join its board, to return to the Oval simply as the successor to Fred Titmus.

"Traditionally the standing and profile of the county coach was very low," Micky says. "Andrew Sandham was a highly respected character, but in many cases it wasn't a question of appointing the best possible coach or man-manager. It was more to do with finding a job for a popular, long-serving player."

Micky was much more than a coach. "He was an organiser, a manager, a motivator," Derek Newton says. And Micky's essential qualities? "Integrity and professionalism. Integrity always. No one would ever willingly let him down."

Derek Newton was chairman of Surrey for fifteen years, leading the county into the 1990s by which time they were once more a power in the land. "I've not met many people in any walk of life with Micky's integrity," he says. "Mind you," he adds by way of qualification, "I did work in insurance."

Sheila and Micky
with (left to right) Neil, Judy and Alec

Micky at Buckingham Palace with Judy, Sheila and his OBE, 1993

*Judy has held managerial positions in the world of fashion
and is now responsible for the design of children's facilities at fitness centres.
At school she was in the county under-18 squad for netball.
"There's nobody in the family more competitive than Judy," Micky says.
"Playing ball or board games, even Trivial Pursuits."*

13

THE NOBO MAN

The years of the 1970s were ones of great change in English cricket, as they were in English society, and Micky was concerned by much of what he saw when he returned to the Oval after six summers away.

"More pitches seemed to favour the batsmen so there didn't seem to be the same awareness among batsmen of how to play when the ball spun or swung sideways, the areas where you were going to score your runs. Some of it had come from playing more one-day cricket. For example, quite a few batsmen seemed not to regard the dangers of hitting against the spin. Someone would be facing a left-arm spinner pitching middle-and-leg or middle stump, and he would try to hit it over mid-wicket. The ball would go straight up in the air, and he'd come in, saying 'What happened there then?'

"The ball didn't turn so consistently on the pitches so there were fewer spin bowlers about and that meant that there was less awareness of how to play the spinning ball. Also many captains didn't seem to have the same understanding of spin bowling, the situations and conditions in which you would use it. The change was so marked, just in those six or seven years, and every year since it seems to have got worse.

"The whole approach to bowling seemed to be different. Many bowlers would run in with a new ball and bowl three or four consecutive balls outside the off stump that the batsman would leave. The cry from the fielders would be 'Well bowled.' A few years earlier the same bowler would have got some stick for not making the batsman play.

"There was far more short-pitched bowling. My first year back at Surrey I saw more batsmen hit on the head than in my whole career of playing."

Micky was also surprised how much the accepted customs of the game had changed. In his later playing days there had been an increasing number of batsmen who did not walk when they knew they were out, but now that was almost the norm. Similarly fielders at short leg would appeal for bat-pad catches which they knew not to be out.

"You had your moments of disagreement," Micky says of his own time as a cricketer, "but there was always a huge respect for the game and all the important things that made it a special game. When I started, cricket was played with so much integrity. And that seemed to be changing. A lot more self-interest was evident, as it was in society."

Micky, in his time as captain, had researched the rates of pay around the counties, securing some improvements for his team, but largely, at a time when money was short, he followed his father's advice: 'Work at what you enjoy, and the money will come. Don't just do it for the money.' By the 1970s, however, attitudes were changing. The Professional Cricketers' Association was becoming a powerful force, negotiating on behalf of county cricketers, and in 1977 the Australian media tycoon Kerry Packer raised dramatically the rewards for those who reached the top.

As manager Micky recognised that attitudes had changed and took it upon himself to work out a pay structure that fitted this new age, one that sought to shake the players out of their complacency by introducing more incentives. Never again would a young Bob Willis, back from Ashes glory, be forced to accept the wages of an uncapped player.

*

As Surrey manager Micky appointed a county coach: first David Gibson, then Geoff Arnold. The initial plan was that Micky would spend 60 per cent of his time with the professional staff, mainly the first team, and 40 per cent creating an infrastructure that would bring through future players.

"At the time," he says, "there were only 27 people with a coaching qualification in the whole of Surrey."

Micky, who had never done the national coaching qualifications himself, went to Lilleshall in the autumn of his first year back, gaining a Distinction in the Advanced Course – "I wish I'd known all this when I was playing," he said, a sentiment that Clive Lloyd also expressed a few years later – and he soon had in place a scheme, sponsored by Nescafé, that grew rapidly till there were over a thousand children each winter attending centres around the county.

The problems in the first team were not so straightforward. "It wasn't the happiest of dressing rooms," Micky says. "It revolved too much around selfishness and envy. That's OK to an extent when you're winning. But they weren't, and that's when it gets testing. In those situations the majority of the problem is with the people who, if something goes wrong, will always claim that it's somebody else's fault."

His first task was to form a strong working relationship with Roger Knight. Traditionally the captain had been the focus of all cricketing decisions; now there was a manager as well, and Micky needed to play his part in such a way that he neither undermined his captain nor confused the players.

"When the team crosses the white line onto the field of play, there are so many decisions that have to be taken there and then. You have to work it so that it's the captain that the players look to, not the manager on the balcony, and that isn't always the easiest thing to do.

"The relationship between the manager and the captain has to be very good, with the right amount of mutual respect. You've got to be very honest with each other. And the team has to be aware that the relationship between the two of you is one hundred per cent. I'm sure I slipped up now and again, but I never did anything significant at Surrey without going through things with Knighty."

Together they devised a programme of pre-season training and they selected the teams, on the understanding that, in the event of a disagreement, the captain would have the final say. "And if it doesn't work out," Micky told him, "I'll never say to you, 'I told you so.'"

Micky can only remember one occasion when they had a significant difference. In their second summer together they went up to Worcester, and Roger Knight wanted to rest Pat Pocock in favour of the slow left-armer Giles Cheatle, whom Micky had signed from Sussex with the intention of teaching him to spin the ball more, a task in which, alas, he failed.

Pocock was not in good form, and as always he was experimenting too much for the liking of captain and manager. "I think Knighty was getting a bit exasperated with him. He wasn't the easiest person to captain. He just wouldn't keep things simple."

Captain said Cheatle, manager said Pocock, and for once Micky put his foot down firmly. "Whatever happens, Roger, Percy is playing."

The game was a great success. Knight scored a century, and on a responsive pitch Pocock took nine wickets. In the aftermath of victory, all that remained was for captain and manager to laugh about their disagreement.

"You're an autocrat," Roger chided.

"Yes," Micky replied, "but a nice one."

There were, however, players with personalities which required more of Micky's man-management skills than the ever-enthusiastic Pocock. Foremost among these was David Smith from Balham, whose prodigious talent was accompanied by a character which had some very rough edges. He had already been sacked at the end of one season, then reinstated, and it was not unknown for him to throw a punch at a team-mate in the dressing room.

"He was a very likeable lad," Micky says in his fatherly way. "He'd say, 'Hallo, manager.' He's never called me anything else, doesn't to this day. But there was another side to him."

On one occasion, in a Sunday League run-chase at Edgbaston when Surrey's top order had fallen cheaply, Smith looked well set and in control when he suddenly took to whacking every ball without discrimination. He was dropped one ball, then caught the next, coming into the dressing room with a tirade which began with some such words as "Do I have to do it all myself?"

Micky, not giving any ground, took him on. "Never mind about that. You just listen here. You were the person to win this game. You're in magnificent nick. And you've thrown it away. Because you couldn't stand the pressure." He did not hold back. "So, in other words, you … are … a coward."

The dressing room was utterly silent. Out of the corner of his eye Micky could see Alan Butcher and Robin Jackman reaching for their cricket bats, in case 'Smithy' blew his top. But he didn't. Without another word he gathered up his belongings, thumped the wall with great force and drove off in high dudgeon.

"I think you went a bit too far there, manager," somebody suggested. Then Micky realised that Smith was one of the not-out batsmen in the championship match which was due to resume next morning at the Oval. It seemed unlikely that he would turn up in the right frame of mind.

At the end of their day in Birmingham Micky headed off to Balham in search of Smith, arriving at the front door of his terraced house at half past eleven.

"Hallo, manager. Would you like a cup of tea?"

Smith, with his bruised hand, resumed his innings next morning – but, Micky reflects, "I probably did go a bit overboard there."

It was all part of life as a cricket manager.

*

"Micky's arrival as manager did help a lot," Roger Knight says. "People always respected him so it did settle down quite a few players. There was a lot less moaning and negativity."

In three respects Micky's return to the Oval was fortuitously timed.

First, Surrey had just recruited the Barbadian fast bowler Sylvester Clarke, who was as quick and menacing as anybody on the county circuit and who, to the amazement of many, was not a part of the West Indies Test set-up so was available every summer.

He had come for trial the previous autumn. He was suffering from a streaming head cold and turned up at the Oval after getting lost on the Underground. "We were out in the middle," Roger remembers. "Hugh Wilson was bowling, and Jack Richards was standing back, taking the ball just above knee high. Sylvester was wearing three sweaters, he came in off about six paces, and Jack was stretching to take the ball above his head. Straightaway I said, 'We'll have him.' He had this great ability to get the ball to bounce from close to the batsman."

Not only did Clarke put the fear of God into batsmen, taking wickets aplenty at a low cost, but he put so much pressure on them that at the other end the hard-working medium-pacer Robin Jackman became all the more effective. In 1980, at the age of 35, Jackman took 121 first-class wickets, still the highest total in a season by an English bowler since 1968.

"The whole side was energised by Sylvester's arrival," Roger Knight says. "Captaining a losing team is always difficult. And suddenly we were a cricket side. We started to smile."

The second bonus for Micky and for his captain was that the team was starting to change. Geoff Arnold had moved to Sussex, Younis had been released, and John Edrich had retired. Edrich was replaced by Grahame Clinton from Kent, a no-fuss cricketer, and younger players such as Hugh Wilson, Monte Lynch and Andrew Needham brought a freshness to the dressing room. The ever-popular Intikhab was still present, always offering his experience in a helpful way, and they also benefited from the New Zealand batsman Geoff Howarth.

Thirdly, to Micky's relief, the new groundsman Harry Brind had started work on relaying the square. "If you drop a ball from a 16-foot pole," Brind says, "it should bounce two or three feet. But when I arrived at the Oval, it was bouncing three inches."

The Oval was becoming a good cricket wicket again, though Micky's relationship with the independent-minded groundsman had its awkward moments, notably a game in 1981 against Middlesex. Most of Surrey's pace bowlers were out of action so Micky spoke to Brind. "Whatever happens, the pitch has got to turn," he said. "Don't worry. I'll take responsibility if anything goes wrong."

So faithfully was the instruction followed that the first ball of the match, from Robin Jackman, brought up a puff of dust. Intikhab and Pocock immediately set to work and, with David Smith batting outstandingly well against the Middlesex spinners, Surrey won in two days, the first victory over their London rivals for eight years.

One morning some weeks later the Surrey Secretary Ian Scott-Browne approached Micky. "Don't forget you've got to go to Lord's today."

"Lord's? What are you talking about?"

"You know, the pitch report."

"Pitch report? What pitch report?"

"Against Middlesex."

Micky arrived at Lord's to a meeting chaired by Freddie Brown. Ken Taylor, the former Warwickshire batsman who was now cricket manager at Trent Bridge, was also there. That year Nottinghamshire were winning the championship with pitches prepared especially for their bowlers Hadlee and Rice, so Micky greeted him by asking, "Are you on a charge as well?"

"No," he replied. "I'm on the committee."

"On the committee? But you're the worst in the country."

Freddie Brown read through the papers, stopping with astonishment at the section reserved for the groundsman's comment.

"What's this? 'I was asked by Micky Stewart to prepare a pitch …' Is this true? … I've never seen anything written down like this in my life."

"It finished in a laugh," Micky says. "I got off with a warning."

*

Micky's impact as manager was helped greatly by the immediate improvement in the team's results. From 16th in the championship in 1978 they rose to third place in 1979, second to Mike Brearley's outstanding Middlesex side in 1980. They also each reached a Lord's final in both 1979 and 1980.

The first of these finals, in the Benson and Hedges Cup, came at a bad moment for them. Sylvester Clarke was injured and out of action, Robin Jackman was struggling, and there was also a fitness doubt about their third front-line opening bowler, the exciting young prospect Hugh Wilson.

The final was on the Saturday, and Micky's only opportunity to test Wilson's fitness in match conditions was to pick him in the MCC side he was taking to Tiffin School on the Tuesday. This was the year that Neil was captain, Alec was in the team as well, and they were nearing the end of a summer in which they had not lost a game.

Micky also took the Surrey batsman Monte Lynch, who scored a century when MCC batted first. Then Micky gave the new ball to Wilson who ran in and bowled gently at the schoolboy openers.

"What are you doing?" Micky asked.

"I can't let it go against these lads," replied the six-foot-four-inch Old Wellingtonian.

"But this is no good. We've got to find out if you're fit or not."

So Wilson ran in hard and took a hat-trick, with the young AJ Stewart the second of his victims. "Sheila was so angry she wouldn't talk to me." And Tiffin lost their unbeaten record.

Surrey did not win the final, losing to Essex on a fast pitch, nor did they win the following year when Middlesex beat them in the final of the Gillette Cup. The summer of 1981, Micky's third in charge, brought a third appearance in a Lord's final, and this time, with Clarke once more not fully fit, they could not contain Somerset's Viv Richards who hit a powerful and imperious century. They had lost three finals, but they were not downhearted. Rather, Micky thinks, morale was improved by their reaching Lord's so frequently. At least they were now in contention.

"It helped a great deal that we got into those finals and that we did well each year in the championship. It's always easy to get people believing in what you're doing if you're getting positive results, but of course you can only do that if you've got the right number of quality players. After that, as long as the players are good enough, it comes down to man-management and to being honest. You can't kid people in the dressing room. If you're not straight, you soon get found out." He pauses for a moment, thinking about the implications of what he has said. "Mind you, there are ways of being straight that don't help."

Micky liked to analyse each session of play. Sometimes he would gather them together as a group, giving them feedback and focusing them on the challenges of the session ahead. More often he would offer quiet and encouraging advice to individuals.

At the start of each summer he would bring out his Nobo flipchart and paper, challenging each of the team to say how many runs and wickets they thought they could get that year. Just as in his early days under Stuart Surridge, the ambition was always to be the champion county.

"If you want to win the championship, you need to win at least ten matches, maybe twelve. And to do that, over the summer, you need to score 8,000 runs and take 300 wickets. So let's see how we're going to get those. I want each of you to write down your figures, what you feel is a reasonable target for you for the summer."

He had seen the same approach applied in football – "Who's going to score those goals then?" – and, of course, he had done all this with spectacular success with his sales team at Slazenger: "So, if we're going to increase our sales by 20 per cent, where are those extra sales going to come from?"

The whole Surrey staff took part in the exercise, and Micky pressed them. "We're still the best part of a thousand runs short. Can anybody think that they might get a few more?"

"It helped me no end, and it made them more individually responsible for their contribution to the whole team performance."

The flipchart was such a crucial part of Micky's approach to the job that the young Grahame Clinton invented for him the nickname of 'Nobo'.

Micky thought that funny, though he did not see the funny side of it when at Chelmsford in 1983 they were bowled out for 14 by Essex. Two ties were produced – a 'Fabulous Four' for those who got off the mark and a 'Magnificent Seven' for the ones who didn't – but Micky banned the players from wearing them. Such abject failure was no laughing matter.

"I must admit," Micky says, "I lost my sense of humour over that. At one point I thought we weren't going to get ten."

On a happier note Surrey returned to Lord's in September 1982, their fourth final in four years. In the early morning conditions of a ten o'clock start their bowlers were much too strong for the Warwickshire batsmen, and they won the NatWest Trophy by nine wickets with more than 26 overs to spare.

Roger Knight
with the NatWest Trophy,
Lord's, 1982

Surrey failed to push on to greater triumphs in the years that followed, though they were one of the stronger sides on the circuit. The frictions within the dressing room never quite went away, and there were several changes of captaincy after Roger Knight stood down at the end of 1983. The New Zealander Geoff Howarth led them in 1984. In Micky's view, he was "an attractive stroke player all round the wicket, an excellent all-round fielder and as a captain very tactically aware". Unfortunately, at the start of 1985, Sylvester Clarke was ruled out for the summer, and Howarth, fresh from a tour of the West Indies, recommended as his replacement the Trinidadian Tony Gray – "in full knowledge," Micky says, "that under the new regulations for overseas players he himself couldn't appear in the same side. He was a most unselfish cricketer."

Micky was still a powerful figure at the Oval, too powerful perhaps for some, and by the summer of 1986 there were murmurs that one or two committeemen would like to start afresh with someone more malleable.

Nevertheless, Micky's work out and about in the county was bearing rich fruit: not only in a much more extensive programme of coaching activities but in the creation of a flow of promising youngsters, notably Martin and Darren Bicknell, David Ward and Keith Medlycott – and, soon to follow, Alistair Brown, Graham Thorpe, Mark Butcher and the Hollioake brothers. Within the county the seeds of future greatness had been sown.

One of the most promising of the Surrey youngsters in these years was Micky's own son, Alec. In 1980, aged 17, his run-scoring in school and club cricket started to attract attention, and he was invited for a week at Sussex where he turned out for their second team. Stewart Storey was the coach there, and Micky wanted his independent opinion on Alec's potential.

In late June Alec was picked to play for Surrey seconds, being driven to the game at Horsham by Sheila as soon as he had completed his History 'O' level paper. He batted once, coming to the wicket with seven to win and making nought not out during which he had to survive several balls of unfamiliar pace from Garth le Roux.

At the end of the summer several counties, including Sussex, Nottinghamshire and Hampshire, were interested in signing him, and Micky talked it through with Roger Knight.

"I was very keen to have Alec," Roger remembers. "He was talented, and he had a bit of chirp about him. Not unlike Micky, though not quite the same personality."

Roger related to Micky how his father had been a master at Dulwich College while he was a pupil there. It caused no problems, though another boy in the same situation had a terrible time. "But that was because his father wasn't respected." It hardly needed adding that, on that score, Alec would be fine at the Oval.

"I don't know that my saying that to Micky made any difference. He probably wanted that as my answer."

"This is the form," Micky explained to Alec. "I want you to play for Surrey. But, because of me, that gives you another problem. Some people will say that you're only there because of who your father is."

Alec was clear: "You know I've always wanted to play for Surrey, and that's what I'm going to do." So they fell into a way of life in which at home he called Micky 'Dad', at work 'Manager'.

"I remember him coming home one evening," Sheila says, "and he was talking about something that had happened that day. 'Don't tell the manager,' he said. Then straightaway he asked, 'Is Dad going to be in for dinner?'"

"In team meetings," Micky says, "I always referred to him as Alec Stewart or 'Stewie'. And he called me 'manager', even in the car when we were talking cricket. 'What do you think, manager?' he would say. When I was coaching, I deliberately didn't do the regular one-to-ones with him. I'd make suggestions sometimes, but I always got David Gibson and Geoff Arnold to work with him."

Alec made his first-team debut in 1981, played once in 1982, then had a run in the team in the latter half of 1983, averaging over 40. Yet to his disappointment he did not start in the side in 1984. "Go and score some runs in the second team," the manager told him – and, when he did regain his place in June, he was surprised to be left out of the side for an important NatWest quarter-final match. He recalls questioning the decision, only to be given a brisk reply: "This is the team we're going with. You haven't been selected."

His great leap forward came in 1986, Micky's last year at the Oval, when, still only 23, he topped the county's batting averages. Such was his progress that he came under consideration for the last batting place for that winter's tour of Australia, a place that went to the 24-year-old James Whitaker of Leicestershire.

The Stewarts are the closest of families, yet somehow the two of them handled the situation so well that there was no resentment. "I always asked myself, 'Am I being too hard on him?'" Micky says. "I didn't want to push him forward too fast, but also I didn't want to hold him back."

"If he had to go one way or the other," Alec says, "he'd have gone the tougher route with me."

"As it worked out," Micky says, "whenever there was any doubt about his selection, he came up with the result so it was never a problem."

"Alec made it easy for Micky," Pat Pocock says. "He was the archetypal perfect pro so Micky never had to speak to him. I'm not saying Micky didn't sometimes say 'You played the wrong shot', but Alec's approach to everything was right: his relationship with practice, his attitude in the side, his presentation of himself on and off the field. Never, ever would Alec have given Micky one moment of difficulty.

"Micky handled it so well, too. A stranger could have come into that dressing room and spent a week with us. If he hadn't heard the names, you could have asked him at the end of the week, 'Which one is the son of the manager?' And he wouldn't have known."

The only exception to this, Pocock reckons, was a game at the Oval at the end of 1983 when Michael Holding, playing for Derbyshire, bowled a short ball that bounced less than expected and broke Alec's jaw. "Micky came running out, and he looked much more concerned than if it had been Clint or Butch or one of the others. That's the only time I've known him give any inkling of the blood relationship."

Some years later, though, Micky was making a joke of it. "Michael Holding's a lovely fellow. I introduced him to Sheila in Antigua. 'You haven't met Sheila, have you, Michael?' I said. 'This is Michael Holding, Sheila. He's the fellow who broke your little boy's jaw.'"

"That's hardly fair," Holding protested.

"All through playing and working," Micky says, "I was always able to detach the emotional ties and concentrate on what I was trying to do – to make the right decisions and win the game."

14

TRIUMPH IN AUSTRALIA

Followers of English cricket in the 1980s endured a roller-coaster ride of extraordinary highs and lows. Ian Botham, with his inspirational feats against Australia in 1981, caught the imagination of the general public as no other cricketer had done for many years, while David Gower, a graceful throwback to another age, delighted the traditional supporters, leading England to further triumph over Australia in the summer of 1985.

Yet among those uplifting victories there were humiliating failures, none greater than the 5-0 defeats inflicted by the powerful West Indies side in both 1984 and 1985/86. The latter of these defeats occurred on a tour of the Caribbean that was not only a cricketing disaster but a public relations one as well. Once the defeats started to accumulate, questions were asked about the approach of the tour party under the captaincy of Gower and the management of Tony Brown, the former Gloucestershire captain, and his assistant Bob Willis.

To a large extent England were simply up against a much better team, to whom it was no disgrace to lose, but they did not help their image by spending days off relaxing in sailing boats and by organising optional net sessions which senior players, including the captain, did not attend.

The British press was changing fast, with a bitter circulation war developing between the red-top tabloids. No longer were England's tourists travelling cheerfully with writers concerned to uphold the image of the game; now there were reporters in their midst with a radically different agenda. Their prime target was the hard-living Ian Botham, and a story duly appeared linking him with a local beauty queen. It was all ghastly for the English cricket authorities, who were unprepared for such publicity. They concluded, in the words of *Wisden*, that 'much went wrong that with firmer captaincy and management might not have.'

Things did not improve greatly the following summer. Botham was banned for admitting to the *Mail on Sunday* that he had smoked cannabis, Gower was stripped of the captaincy after losing the first Test to India, and by the end of August England had lost not only to India but also, for the first time in a home series, to New Zealand. With a tour to Australia next on the schedule, something needed to be done.

On 1 August, at its summer meeting, the Test and County Cricket Board decided to appoint an assistant manager for Australia, somebody whose responsibilities would include players' fitness, practice facilities and day-to-day discipline. Then, after the tour, the Board would decide whether to extend the role into the English summer and to make it permanent. Australia had just appointed their former captain Bobby Simpson to a similar position.

Many assumed that the front-runner was Raymond Illingworth. He had captained England to victory in Australia and had had some experience in a managerial role at Yorkshire. Furthermore, though born in 1932, three months before Micky, he had been playing for Yorkshire as recently as 1983 and knew most of the England cricketers. But, without being offered the position, he ruled himself out, saying that the job lacked real power. He thought he would be little more than a glorified bag carrier.

Micky took a different view and attended two interviews with Doug Insole, chairman of the TCCB's Cricket Committee, and Donald Carr, its chief executive. The job was only initially for the winter, but Micky knew that, if he made it work, it would develop into something more long-term. "I remember saying to somebody at the time, 'If I hold the job for three years, the guy who takes over from me will be in a better position – and the guy after him should be running it totally.'"

For English cricket it was a significant development, one that Micky had long thought necessary. "During my early years as manager at Surrey, seeing how the game was changing, I felt that every county required a cricket manager. And even earlier, before my playing days were over, I thought that England required one."

His only battle at that stage was about his title. The Board wanted Assistant Manager; Micky wanted Team Manager. "They thought Team Manager was too close to football. The decision had to go to a full Board meeting. At lunchtime they said 'Assistant Manager', and I said, 'Forget it.' Later in the day they came back: 'Team Manager.'"

There was no desire at Lord's to bring anything of football into the game of cricket, and undoubtedly Micky's tracksuit regime raised hackles in some quarters. Nevertheless the interviewing panel made clear where his priorities were to lie: "There was some talk of working with the players technically, but the first priority was organisation, preparation and discipline."

Micky, freshly appointed but not yet in post, attended the final Test at the Oval and, as was his wont, he began his day by training on the ground for fifty minutes. "You don't expect me to do that, do you?" Phil Edmonds had said. "Because I couldn't."

"Everybody's different," Micky replied, though it was clear that this did not entirely allay Edmonds' anxieties about the regime the new team manager was planning for the winter ahead.

The party for Australia had largely been chosen already, but Micky sat in when the selectors finalised their decisions. His only significant contribution came when they discussed Surrey's Jack Richards as the second keeper. They were uneasy about his temperament, and Micky reassured them: "Don't worry. I'll look after that part of it."

Micky had been 'looking after' Richards for eight years at the Oval. Richards had come up from Cornwall, a young lad with emotional insecurities, and he was not always the easiest person when things were not going well. "He didn't have the level of confidence he should have had," Micky says, recalling an occasion in his first year as Surrey manager when the team reached the semi-final of the Benson and Hedges Cup, a Wednesday match at Derby. "On the Sunday beforehand, we were playing a benefit game at Aldermaston. We had a good day, and at the end of it I went into the dressing room to pick up my gear. And there was Jack, sitting by himself, in quite a state. 'I keep thinking of Wednesday,' he said. 'If we don't win, I don't know how I'll be able to stand it.' He was living on his own in digs, and Sheila said, 'We can't leave him like that.' So we took him home for the night."

The full party for Australia consisted of sixteen players and a scorer, plus Lawrie Brown as physio, Micky as team manager and Peter Lush, the TCCB's Head of Public Relations and Marketing, as tour manager. It was another world from the party that toured Australia twenty years later when there were, among others, an operations manager, a media relations officer, a physiologist as well as a physiotherapist, two team doctors, a massage therapist, a team analyst and several coaches.

"I was very fortunate," Micky says, "to be working to a manager Peter Lush and with a physio Lawrie Brown who were both absolutely first-rate. We blended very well as a team. The players had great respect for both Peter and Lawrie."

Wisden acknowledged this, referring to 'the efficient, friendly partnership of Peter Lush and Micky Stewart' and 'the good team spirit that resulted'.

The two players most unlucky to miss out on selection were Richard Ellison, the Kent bowler who had played with such success in the last Tests against Australia the previous summer, and Greg Thomas of Glamorgan, who could bowl at great speed. Both were considered to have technical problems so Micky, anxious that they did not feel wholly discarded, offered to work with them at the Oval at the end of the summer.

Unfortunately Micky's assistance did not yield rewards for England. Ellison missed the whole of the following summer with a pelvic injury while Thomas, a softly spoken schoolteacher, seemed to lack the inner fire to go with his exceptional pace. His attitude was nothing like Peter Loader's, that was for sure.

"I bet you frightened them to death when you played cricket at school," Micky said to him. "You must have taken hundreds of wickets."

"Not really."

"What about club cricket? Some of the pitches there, they wouldn't have fancied facing you."

"I wouldn't say so."

"Well, how many wickets did you get for Glamorgan this season?"

"Thirty-nine."

Micky shook his head. "So what you're telling me is, you hardly take any bloody wickets."

Micky's next task was to sit down with the captain, Mike Gatting. How were they going to avoid the problems of the previous winter? How would they manage the big egos in the team? There were plenty of them.

Neither had been on an England tour of Australia, nor had their paths crossed much, but they were determined to start out with purpose. There was no question of a 'Let's see how things pan out' approach.

"I'd heard quite a lot about Micky," Mike Gatting says, "and I understood him to be a pretty straight, honest bloke who was passionate about the game, and all of that was to be very true. I didn't know how the established players would take to somebody like Micky coming in, but he was brilliant. He'd worked in teams all his life, and he'd come from the Oval where he'd had a lot of difficult characters. We both knew that it was going to be a long, long trip and that we'd have to stick together."

"When I came in," Micky says, "I could see that the confidence in the side was very low. They'd just lost three series on the trot, and they'd put up with so much media criticism. I've never known a group of such talented people, in sport or in business, where the level of confidence was so low."

There was tension in the team, too, with Gatting struggling at times to command the respect of all the players. "Phillipe Edmonds was a bright chap," Micky says, "and he would refer to Gatt as 'The Plumber'. I think

Frances his wife had come up with the nickname. Now 'The Plumber' doesn't matter if you're successful. But it matters a lot if you're on the wrong end of things, and the next session you need the captain to be the number one. Mike hadn't had the education that Edmonds had had, but he was strong on the pride of playing for your country and we had that in common. So I always talked everything through with him and, whenever I addressed the team, I always referred to Gatt and me as 'we' – 'We have come up with this programme.' I had to make sure that he was respected."

Gladstone Small was a young fast bowler on his first England tour, and he thinks Micky made a great difference. "He bridged the gap between Mike Gatting, who was an experienced player but a newish captain, and the strong players in the team: the two ex-captains Gower and Botham and Phil Edmonds the intellectual. Micky was a mediator and a very good one, too. If there was any confusion about selection, for example, he would calm the waters."

"Micky's role was a new one," Chris Broad, another newcomer, says. "At first, for want of a better phrase, it was all about massaging some egos, to make sure the team worked."

The night before departure the tour party stayed at the hotel at Heathrow airport, where Micky summoned the senior players to a meeting: Gatting, Botham, Gower, Lamb, Edmonds, Emburey, possibly Dilley.

"Man for man, on paper," Micky told them, "we're a better side than any the Australians can put out. The success or otherwise of this trip is down to you. If you all produce par-for-the-course performances, we'll be successful. Any contributions from the others will be a bonus. It's going to revolve around you."

The greatest challenge for Micky and Mike Gatting was to get the best out of Ian Botham. So much was happening in the big man's life: charity walks, a brief foray into Hollywood, the lurid headlines during the Caribbean trip, his column in the *Sun*, the drugs ban, now a great schism at Taunton that would lead to his leaving Somerset. He was overweight, not as fit as he needed to be, and he had the potential to undermine the best efforts of captain and team manager. So it was decided that Mike Gatting would sit down with him.

This is how Mike remembers the conversation: "I asked him if in the early weeks he'd work with the young bowlers, Small and DeFreitas, and he thought that was a nice idea. Then I said to him, 'How do you want to play the trip? If I tell you what I want, you tell me if that's OK.'" He outlined

Captain and manager

a programme in which Botham worked hard till the first Test, then they judged what he needed to remain fit for the rest of the series. "'How does that sound?' He said, 'That's brilliant, Gatt, thanks very much.' And off we went. To me that was a huge hurdle out of the way."

Then there was David Gower, the team's most talented batsman. A year earlier he had celebrated Ashes victory on the balcony at the Oval, but since then he had had a terrible time: his mother had died, he had endured intense criticism in the Caribbean and had lost the captaincy. Now he had been passed over as vice-captain for John Emburey and was not even on the tour selection committee.

At the start of the trip Gower was out of sorts, and it came to a head during their first match, a three-day up-country affair at Bundaberg in Queensland. One evening they were invited to a social club where the entertainment on offer was the local rum and a series of lengthy monologues, one of which after a while Gower uncharacteristically took to heckling. It shocked Micky, who was all set to be stern till Allan Lamb and John Emburey came to see him next morning, explaining how low in spirits their team-mate was.

Lamb himself was another who could occasionally be hard work for a team manager responsible for discipline. At the end of the evening in the Bundaberg social club, he was late back to the coach, then made them stop at a petrol station so he could have a pee. "He'd been messing about at the back," Micky says, "so I said to the driver, 'Drive on fifty yards.' He came out, and there was no coach there. Then he started trotting. He got to within five yards of the coach, and I said, 'Drive on another fifty yards.'"

All the time there was a tightrope to be walked: harnessing the positive energy of the senior players, who believed that they played better when they were enjoying themselves, and nurturing the younger men who needed to feel they were not second-class members of the team. "The gap between the senior and the junior players was huge," Bill Athey, on his first England tour for six years, says. "Micky didn't want an 'us and them' situation, but mostly what he did was to let things flow. The tour was that bit more organised, things were planned in more detail than they had been on previous tours, and that took huge pressure off the captain."

An early letter home to Sheila was upbeat about the spirit in the party, with just one aspect of his job causing Micky anxiety, an aspect which in the following years would become something of an Achilles heel for him:

> *The biggest concern to me so far is the press. They are never away from the lads, neither in practice nor in the hotel, and they are searching for a story*

the whole time. Some of their angles are so childlike it is untrue. I feel that none of them can be really trusted, due to the pressures from their editors.

Inevitably his principal concern in this respect was Ian Botham.

"Both" has been nothing other than good although I know he has to work all the time to conform which is even more creditable. ... You can't possibly imagine his popularity out here. He is a real "megastar" which makes things very difficult for him – but then he really loves it and who wouldn't??

In practice sessions Micky's attempts to get Ian Botham fit included a fair amount of football, which Botham enjoyed greatly. "We played five-a-sides, and he'd never stop till his team had won. Quite often he was one of the last to finish training."

Micky tried to make their fielding practice fun, injecting little competitions into the routines. "I think some of them were a bit apprehensive that I was going to take them for ten-mile runs. And I played up to that a bit. They didn't know me socially at that stage, whether I had a sense of humour. So I kidded them I'd done my National Service in Korea. 'You think this is hard,' I'd say. 'You should have been in a trench out there. That's real team work, knowing your life is in your mate's hands.'"

"Micky had this sergeant-major way about him," Neil Foster, the Essex fast bowler, says, "but he's not a sergeant-major at all, far from it. It's just how he sounds. If you didn't know him and you heard him announce that fielding practice was starting, you'd think he was a right bully, but that's not how it was at all."

"He's an orderly, disciplined fellow," Gladstone Small says. "Everything had to be in place. He was always fiddling to make sure his shirt was straight. He was well organised, and that was the way he did things. He always had the right word at the right time for the right situation. But you could share a laugh with him, and he could take a joke. He was a lovely man."

There was not the level of individual coaching which the England cricketers today enjoy. Micky did what he could, but mostly he was organising the team, making sure that each and every one of them felt part of the trip, not just the established players.

"Micky took me under his wing," says Phil DeFreitas, one who was enjoying his first contact with the England set-up. "He often said, 'Don't look at this tour as just a bit of fun. Don't just carry the drinks. Make a name for yourself.' I remember he encouraged me to eat whatever I wanted. As much as I could. That was quite unusual, but I was only ten and a half stone."

Wherever they went, it was Micky's job to make sure that the practice facilities were in place, even for wet days. This had been a problem the previous winter in the Caribbean, though – to be fair – there were never going to be the same difficulties in Australia. "There was one ground in the West Indies," Mike Gatting recalls, "when the groundsman came up to us when we arrived. 'I'm sorry, guys,' he said, 'the cows have got on the wicket.' Well, how do you deal with that?"

During the warm-up matches Micky watched intently, making notes in blue hardback books. There were no computers then but, Mike Gatting says, "Micky was almost like a computer himself, with all his copious notes about our opponents and their weaknesses. He'd talk to the bowlers, get them to think more about where they should be bowling at different batsmen, but he didn't make it too complicated. Mostly we tried to play to our strengths. Keep things simple wherever possible."

So far, so good. Unfortunately, for all the newly forged team spirit, the greater organisation of practice and Micky's debriefing sessions, the cricket they played in the warm-up matches was poor, culminating in a dismal performance against Western Australia in the last match before the first Test. Micky was back in the hotel, in bed with flu, so he could not offer feedback during the game. But he received full reports. On a fast bouncy pitch they bowled too short, they dropped several catches and they batted badly, with Gower, yet to find any form, dismissed for a pair. As they flew the width of Australia to the tropical climate of Brisbane, Martin Johnson of the *Independent* wrote his famous report saying that England had only three problems to overcome: 'they can't bat, they can't bowl, and they can't field.'

Such humour was not to Micky's liking. "After the debacle in the West Indies, whenever you went to a dinner in England, the speaker or comedian always used to take the mickey out of the England cricket side. You can say I'm a bit miserable if you like, but I couldn't stand that." Nor could he stand it when, at a lunch for the two teams in Brisbane, the host congratulated the Australian side for their recent performance in India. "Now we welcome the Poms," he went on. "The form our lads are in, I feel sorry for them."

Back at the hotel that evening Micky spoke to the team. "Well, after that welcome, I don't have to say too much, do I? I don't know about any of you, but I'm not here to have Australians feeling sorry for us – or to be a laughing stock for our own countrymen."

Micky had suggested to Ian Botham that he spoke to the team at the eve-of-match meeting, and his contribution caused some surprise among the more experienced members of the side. "I'd sat in a few of Beefy's pre-match talks," Mike Gatting says. "He'd say things like 'I'll bounce him out … I'll smash him around … Yashpal Sharma, he can't play. I'll sort him out.' Then next day Yashpal gets 140. But at Brisbane it was different. It's the first time I'd heard him get up and say something sensible."

This is the gist of Botham's speech, as Mike remembers it: "The practice games have gone. We can't do anything about them now. Tomorrow's the Test match, and that's when it's all going to start. Eleven of us against eleven of them. If we play to our potential, we can beat them. So let's forget what's happened and think about that. Let's turn up tomorrow and be ready to beat them – because we can."

They were not strikingly original thoughts but from Botham they carried an elemental force. "His words were heartfelt," Mike says. "You could see they meant something to him, and it got through to the lads. At that point we all needed something like that."

*

On the morning of the Brisbane Test Micky was hard at work.

First, he led some fielding practice out in the middle, as close to the square itself as they were allowed to go – so that the slip fielders would grow accustomed to the background and the light. Already the plans were in place, with each team member allocated specific roles in the field, roles that made the best of their particular strengths. It would not be like Micky's first Test back in 1962 when, as the best close catcher in the country, he found himself in the outfield.

Secondly, he had to deal with the team's lack of confidence and, in several cases, their nerves as the big moment approached. "In the dressing room I sat down for a few seconds with each and every member of the team, not just to talk to them generally but to remind them what their job in the team was. John Emburey told me afterwards that that had gone down very well."

Thirdly, there were the final tactical discussions, the decision to put the Australians in if the toss was won and also the last-minute switching of the batting order. "David Gower was going to be number three, Allan Lamb four and Gatt at five. But, with the form David was in, I felt Gatt should be three. So he and David switched. If Gatt had been there by himself, I don't know whether or not that would have happened."

Finally, there were the players not in the eleven to be looked after. Gone were the days when Peter Loader could come back from a six-month tour of Australia complaining that the captain Len Hutton had barely spoken to him. "Micky and I talked about that," Mike Gatting says. "We'd got to make everybody, all sixteen, feel part of it – and not just 'make them feel'. They *were* part of it."

"It's always important," Micky says, "to spend time with the players who are disappointed at not getting picked, to emphasise to them that they're still important, so that they're ready if they do get the call."

Then, his main tasks performed, Micky sat and watched the England batsmen, put in by Allan Border, reach 198 for two before a storm ended play shortly after tea. Bill Athey batted with great patience to reach 78 not out, and he received good support from Mike Gatting and Allan Lamb. It was a day to settle English nerves.

"Bill Athey was passionate about England," Micky says. "He had a little union flag tattooed at the top of his arm. On that tour I tried to build up his confidence. The game of cricket never saw the best of him. He was such a good all-round player."

The following morning brought an immediate crisis. Lamb was lbw to the first ball of the day and, with the total still stuck on 198, Athey edged a swinging delivery to the keeper. "I was in the nets, working with James Whitaker," Micky recalls, "and I heard the roars." The two of them hurried to see what was happening and were in time to watch David Gower slash hard at an off-side delivery and send the ball into the hands of Chris Matthews at slip. 198 for five – or it would have been, if the ball had not fallen to the ground. Perhaps it was the crucial moment of the whole series.

"What Matthews was doing fielding in the slips, I don't know," Micky says. "If David hadn't been dropped on nought, it would all have been much, much harder. At that point he wasn't in good nick, and he needed to be in nick the way he played."

Gower, with hardly a run all tour, slowly found his touch as he struggled his way to 51, while Botham at the other end seized the day with a magnificent 138, at one stage setting a new Ashes record with 22 runs off an over from Merv Hughes. "Ian played really well," Micky says. "He was canny early on, then he slaughtered them. And they wilted. That was the good part. I saw them wilt. That confirmed what we were saying beforehand, that we were a better side than them.

"When you're in the field and the pitch is flat and someone starts taking you on, all you can do is to bowl meagrely, bowl maidens – get back to sanity, as they used to say. If you can't bowl the ball where it's supposed to go, you can't stop it."

Jack Richards, picked to strengthen the batting, was bowled first ball by a full toss, but Phil DeFreitas rose to the occasion of his debut with a confident 40 that took England's final total to 456 – well past what Micky calls 'the magic figure' of 400. Then DeFreitas took the first over with the new ball and before close of play he had removed David Boon to a mistimed pull to mid-wicket.

"For me," DeFreitas says, "Micky was a superb man-manager. Everything he did before Brisbane, his thoughtfulness, forced me to get into the Test team, and I opened the bowling. I was so naïve, I could easily have exploded and gone the other way, but Micky made me feel very comfortable. I have so much respect for him."

Micky had seen the way England had been bowling the previous summer, and he was determined that it would not be like that. "Against India and New Zealand you'd get overs where there would be two length balls that moved away and beat the bat. Then the bowler would get frustrated and bowl a bouncer that didn't get up much and went for four. Then another one that beat the bat. Then a yorker that wasn't quite full enough and went for another four. Then another one beating the bat. The bowler had beaten the bat four times, and his over had gone for eight." Perhaps there is a touch of exasperated exaggeration in the description, but the conclusion was clear: "In Australia we set out to bowl the ball down the channel, ball after ball, and set the field accordingly."

"Micky and I saw eye to eye on that," Mike Gatting says. "He'd seen Alec Bedser bowling over after over; he knew the importance of consistency. And it helped the younger bowlers greatly. Someone like 'Daffy' DeFreitas. 'Just run up and try to swing it,' we'd say to him. 'Off stump and just outside. Don't do anything else.' And that's what he did. Daffy was a huge bonus for us in that series."

On the third day Graham Dilley took five wickets, another success for the new regime. "He was well built, but he wasn't strong," Micky says. "At the start of the tour he'd bowl for 20 or 25 minutes in the net, then he'd think, 'That's it; that's what I'm used to.' I had to say to him, 'You can have a break, but you've got to bowl another 20 or 25 minutes.' Initially he didn't take too kindly to it. But all credit to him, he worked at it, and the results showed in that first Test at Brisbane. We went on to Perth, and straightaway he said, 'When are we going in the nets?' I didn't have to say a thing. His bowling was crucial in the whole series."

By close of play on that third day Australia were following on. In the second innings John Emburey took five wickets, DeFreitas three, and

England left Brisbane victorious. It was only the third time that England had won at the Woolloongabba ground – and, as John Woodcock pointed out in *The Times*, Gatting was following in the footsteps of two other men of Middlesex, Gubby Allen and Mike Brearley. In six tours since, there has still not been a fourth victory there.

More significantly it was England's twelfth Test match of 1986 – and the first which they had won. Micky's first hurdle had been cleared, with the confidence of the players flowing back. They were one up in the series, confounding all pre-match expectations.

One up in the Test series
Now Ian Botham's 33rd birthday to celebrate

The second Test at Perth was drawn, with England batting first and making 592 for eight declared. Chris Broad, with 162, and Bill Athey, with 96, put on 223 for the first wicket, and there were centuries on the second day for David Gower, back to his best after his morale-boosting fifty at Brisbane, and Jack Richards, justifying his selection as batsman-keeper.

"When we flew out," Micky says, "the thinking was that Jack would be a better bet in the one-day games and Bruce French would keep in the Tests. Frenchy was always the better keeper day in, day out, though Jack had the stronger hands. But we played Jack in the Tests for his batting, and he kept

243

The day before the third Test at Adelaide
Ian Botham, after failing a fitness test, with Micky

very well. He had an outstanding match at Melbourne. Then he lost his batting form, and Frenchy finished up playing in the one-dayers."

This time the Australians saved the follow on, though only when their last pair was at the crease, and the game ended in the cul-de-sac of a draw. The one setback occurred on the final day when Botham, straining to send down a fast bouncer, tore an inter-costal muscle and left the field.

The third Test, on a flat pitch at Adelaide, was another high-scoring draw, in which James Whitaker played in place of Botham. So it was still one-nil to England when they arrived at Melbourne for their Christmas Day party ahead of the Boxing Day Test.

They trained at the ground on Christmas morning, then they returned to the hotel for lunch. David Gower was the tour's social secretary, organising a draw in which each player picked out a letter and had to come in fancy dress related to that letter. Micky, with C, came as Julius Caesar: "'Both' said Laurie Brown, the physio, and I looked like a pair of char ladies." Gower himself, chairing the lunch, was an SS officer.

"I got the Z," Gladstone Small remembers. "I mean, what on earth can you do with a Z?" A trip to the fancy dress shop solved his dilemma: he would be Zorro with a mask, flat-brimmed sombrero and flowing cape, a dashing outlaw with a mysterious identity. That, it seemed to him at the Christmas lunch, was as dramatic a role as he was destined to play on the tour.

The next day Small was in the dressing room, quietly preparing the pre-match drinks, when Mike Gatting appeared at his side. Graham Dilley had hurt his knee while warming up and, with the captains about to toss, a last-minute change to the team was required. "You can leave the drinks now, 'Stony'. You're playing."

All through the tour the players outside the team had had drilled into them that moments like this might arise – "Make sure you're ready when the chance comes," Mike Gatting remembers saying repeatedly – and now was such a moment. Neil Foster was not happy, expecting to be the one chosen not Gladstone Small, and the captain, heading out to toss, left Micky to sort that out. "There are times as captain," Mike says, "when you don't say the right thing, and it's up to the coach to smooth things over. Micky was very good at that."

"I thought I was ahead of Gladstone in the pecking order," Foster says. "When I didn't play, it was a huge disappointment. So I sulked. And Micky gave me some time away from the cricket, which had never happened to me before. So again he wasn't the sergeant-major; he was more of an arm round your shoulder."

Christmas Day: Micky as Julius Caesar, Frances and Phillipe Edmonds as prisoners

Boxing Day: Gladstone Small in the wickets

Micky and Mike Gatting, looking up at the overcast sky, decided to put the Australians in. "I was in the viewing area," Micky remembers, "where there was a television on. Ian Chappell was commentating. The Australians were 40-odd for one, and he was saying, 'I can't understand why the Poms have put us in' and all the rest of it."

There followed three hours of play as good as it gets for England supporters. With more than 58,000 spectators in the ground Gladstone Small, after a nervous first over, settled to a steady line, moving the ball enough to induce edges, while at the other end Botham, though still not fully fit, also for the most part bowled a full length. Richards behind the wicket took five catches, Botham in the slips took three, and by tea the Australians were all out for 141 with five wickets each for Botham and his young stand-in partner.

After tea, when England batted, the left-handed Chris Broad looked as secure and determined as ever. "Broady made a huge contribution on that tour," Micky says. "He was a good player of pace bowling, very strong on the on-side."

Long before the close of play the Australian crowd was streaming out of the ground, a sure sign that England were on top, and many of them did not return on the following days. Instead, attention switched up the road to the Melbourne Park Tennis Stadium, where Australia were beating Sweden in the final of the Davis Cup. "Bob Hawke the Australian prime minister was at the cricket," Micky recalls, "but, as soon as we got on top, he nipped over to the tennis."

The next morning Chris Broad followed Jack Hobbs and Wally Hammond into the record books, scoring his third hundred in consecutive Tests in Australia. England took a first-innings lead of 208 and on the third day they bowled Australia out for 194, to win by an innings and ensure victory in the series. The final wicket, a catch in the deep, was held appropriately by the last-minute call-up, the mysterious Zorro himself.

"Edmonds was bowling," Small recalls, "and he liked to move his fielders around. One pace this way, three paces up. Mark your position with a cross. Most of it was just for his own humour. He moved me, Merv Hughes swept him and the ball came down right into my hands, without my having to move an inch. I threw it in the air and ran off. And the party started."

"At the end of the game," Micky says, "I had to go over to see all the top brass at the Melbourne Cricket Club, and who should be there, draped in a union flag, but Elton John. He was very close with 'Both' and David Gower. At the celebration party back in the hotel he was the disc jockey."

And I think it's gonna be a long, long time
Till touchdown brings me round again to find
I'm not the man they think I am at home
Oh no, no, no, I'm a rocket man.

"I like his music. I suppose I shall always associate it with the success of that tour. We went to a concert of his in Perth."

Micky had more than cricket in common with him, too. "He owned Watford Football Club. When I visited there, everybody was trained to be courteous and welcoming. He told me he was going to give the club to Graham Taylor, the manager. 'You *are* a Corinthian,' I said to him."

*

The schedule of the tour now became more complicated. Between the fourth and fifth Tests was a nine-day interlude in Perth where they played a one-day tournament, the Benson and Hedges Challenge, involving not only Australia but also Pakistan and the West Indies. There were four games, including the final, and England won them all.

"After that," John Emburey says, "we just thought we would win every match. We had a huge amount of self-belief. The trepidation, the doubt that had been there in the early stages had all disappeared."

"The fielding was unbelievable on that trip," Mike Gatting says. "I don't think we dropped a catch in the whole Test series, maybe one half-chance. Bill Athey was outstanding: the runs he saved when Embers and Edmonds were bowling in the one-dayers. And Daffy, too. Embers at slip, David Gower, Phillipe Edmonds, they were all superb. Micky was a stickler for fielding, and it really paid off."

Martin Johnson, author of 'can't bat, can't bowl, can't field', was forced to admit his error. "The line was right," he said. "I just got the team wrong."

After the Perth one-dayers it was off to Sydney for the fifth Test where, with the series already won, England opted on the final day not to play out the draw but to chase 320 for victory. On a turning pitch Gatting hit a fine 96, but they lost their way in the last hour and were all out for 264, losing with just one over remaining. "We should never have lost that game," Micky says with a lingering exasperation. "That was very disappointing."

There then followed a further four weeks of one-day cricket, playing for the Benson and Hedges Series Cup, a triangular tournament involving Australia and the West Indies. After eight matches, zig-zagging around the continent, they qualified for a three-match final against Australia. They won the first game at Melbourne and were on top at Sydney till Australia's

248

Simon O'Donnell launched a counter-attack late in the run chase and looked like taking the tournament to a decider back at Melbourne.

"By that stage of the tour," Micky says, "we had so many injuries we'd have been pushed to put out a team for the decider. We had two or three off the field, including 'Both', and it got to the point where the only people who could throw were Gatt and John Emburey, captain and vice-captain. So they were out on opposite boundaries, trying to run the show. At one point, when O'Donnell was hitting out, Gatt sent this message across to Embers on the other side. 'Ask Ernie, what does he reckon next?' It went through three fielders, and back came the answer through the same people: 'F--- knows.' At the end Neil Foster bowled a crucial over, and we won by eight runs."

After four months it was all over. Micky sat on his own in a hotel room for one last night when a knock came at the door and in walked Phillipe Edmonds. In the great cross-section of personalities on the trip he was one who could so easily have been awkward, but he had not been. "I'd just like to say," he told Micky, "I've really enjoyed this tour. I was a bit apprehensive at the start. I wondered what it was going to be like. But it's been great. Thank you."

What a tour! Three tournaments, three victories. No other England team, before or since, has achieved as much. No wonder they were greeted by a cheering crowd when they arrived back at Heathrow. For a while at least England's cricketers would not be the butt of every comedian in the land.

*

Micky's first assignment as England team manager had been an unqualified success. Perhaps the team would have won just as triumphantly if he had not been there. Or perhaps that myriad of little deeds and words, which he performed behind the scenes, made all the difference. There is no way of knowing.

"I know," Micky says emphatically.

The unanimous opinion of the Test and County Cricket Board, reviewing the tour and comparing it with events in the Caribbean twelve months earlier, was that Micky's contribution had been a highly positive one. At their spring meeting they offered him a three-year contract as a full-time, all-the-year-round England Team Manager with a place on the panel of selectors, which was chaired by Peter May.

Hopes were high that English cricket was once more moving forward.

15

PROBLEMS, PROBLEMS, PROBLEMS

At the start of July 1987, with Micky in place as full-time team manager, English cricket was on top of the world. Not only had they won the Ashes and both one-day trophies in Australia but in April they had sent a second-string side to the United Arab Emirates and, against the odds, won the Sharjah Cup. Then in May they beat a strong Pakistani side 2-1 in the start-of-season Texaco Trophy matches. The first two Tests were ruined by rain, but in both matches England played well. Mike Gatting was now a confident captain, commanding respect, and in the Queen's Birthday Honours he was awarded an OBE.

It did not take much to puncture the euphoria. Under a sunny sky at Headingley, in the third Test, Gatting opted to bat first, as Pakistan's Imran admitted he would have done, and in no time, with the ball swinging awkwardly, England were 31 for five. When Pakistan batted crucial catches were dropped, and England succumbed to an innings defeat early on the fourth day.

At Edgbaston, at the start of the fourth Test, Gatting won the toss again and this time asked Pakistan to bat first. By close of play the visitors had made 250 for three and Gatting, for all his successes, was slated in the press: 'GATT THE PRAT' in the *Star* the worst of the headlines.

Micky was a forward-thinking man when it came to cricket, pioneering a new professionalism in the England set-up, but he was not equipped to deal with the press when they were in this mood. "I should have played it more coolly," he says, looking back to a stormy press conference on the second evening. "I got much too emotional."

"What's all this about?" he challenged the *Star*'s cricket correspondent, Ted Corbett. "As an Englishman, are you proud of this?"

"I don't write the headlines."

"I'm not concerned about who wrote what. What about your piece? Are you proud that you wrote that?"

"We all have to pay our mortgages."

"Well, Gatt's got a mortgage, too. So what are you saying? You're happy to write him out of his job so you can pay your mortgage."

There was more to come, hostile questions about a silly misunderstanding when the England team were slow to realise that the umpires had gone back out after a rain break, and Micky maintained his belligerence. "Looking back," he says, "I should have done things differently. From that point onwards, I wasn't a favourite of the media."

As events turned out, England's decision to bowl worked out well. With a little more luck, they might have won on the last afternoon when they were left to score 124 runs in 18 overs. In a frantic run chase, littered with run outs, they ended on 109 for seven. "We should have got those runs," Micky says. "It was all the more frustrating not to win after all the flak we'd taken."

In the fifth Test at the Oval they were outplayed, drawing the match and thus losing the series. This was the first setback of Micky's time with England – but it was far from the last and far from the worst.

*

The schedule for the winter of 1987/88 was a heavy one. The fourth World Cup, in India and Pakistan, would run from early October to the second week of November. Then, in the six weeks up to Christmas, England would remain in Pakistan for three one-day matches, followed by three Tests. After a short break at home they would then fly to New Zealand for two months, playing three Tests and four one-day internationals, also taking in a Test and a one-day international in Australia to celebrate the country's bicentenary. In all, 48 days of international cricket were scheduled, more than England has ever undertaken in a winter, before or since.

Nor did it help that, following straight on from a home series against Pakistan, a series which contained its fair share of acrimonious moments, England were in the same qualifying group as them in the World Cup, then staying in the country for a Test series. Among other festering sores a dispute was rumbling over the appointment of umpires. In England the Pakistanis had requested that David Constant not stand, remembering a bad decision he had made against them at a crucial point of the deciding Test five years earlier. This request was turned down by the Test and County Cricket Board, who insisted that Constant was an experienced umpire, which he was, and that it was not for the visitors to dictate on such matters.

The Pakistanis' sense of grievance was not abated when on the final day at the Oval, in a tense contest in which they were pressing for victory, Constant gave a number of not-out decisions. Gatting hit a determined 150 and Botham, wholly out of character, resolutely kept out the deadly leg spin of Abdul Qadir, batting over four hours for 51, an innings that impressed Micky.

251

"To a degree 'Both' used to play up to his image," Micky says. "He always wanted to dominate, which is a good thing. That's the way I think you should play – in your own way, whether it's running the ball for singles or hitting it over the boundary for six. 'Be the Guv'nor,' as my dad used to say. But that innings against Pakistan showed that he could play in the other way as well. There were things that had gone on in the series, and he was absolutely determined that they weren't going to win."

There was, however, a wider context to the fraught cricketing relationship between Pakistan and England. Pakistan had been under the military dictatorship of General Zia-ul-Haq since 1977, and he was in the process of returning the country to civilian rule, with elections approaching. Before leaving England Micky and the tour manager Peter Lush were summoned to two meetings in London with the British High Commissioner in Pakistan, Nicholas Barrington. The message he delivered was straightforward: the region was a sensitive one, of vital importance to British interests, and nothing must happen on the tour to disturb good relations between the two countries.

It was the first World Cup not to be held in England. The hosts, India and Pakistan, were twin favourites, especially when they had reached the semi-finals by topping the two qualifying groups. At Lahore Pakistan would play Australia; at Bombay India would play England.

Gower and Botham had opted out of the winter's cricket, but Graham Gooch, after sitting out the Australian tour for family reasons, was back, and he scored a match-winning century in the semi-final at Bombay. "The preparation for that match was vital," Micky says. "The pitch was obviously going to turn, and up to that point it had been a problem for us scoring our runs fast enough against good spinners. So I enrolled six or eight local spinners, paid them plenty of rupees to bowl in the nets, mostly against Goochy. For hours Goochy swept and swept, finding out what he could do against the spin when there wasn't much bounce. And, when it came to the match, he played a magnificent innings."

Against all the odds the final at Calcutta was between Australia and England and, after their recent encounters, England fancied their chances. Unfortunately Australia, batting first, got away to a good start and, despite tight bowling in mid-innings, a late burst took them to a 50-over total of 253 for five. "We conceded about 25 runs more than we should have done," Micky says, "but even then we were well set up with our batting so we were confident we could win."

Graham Gooch during his innings of 115 in the World Cup semi-final

In Micky's view their problems started when the second-wicket pair of Gooch and Athey took 17 overs to score 65 runs. "Bill didn't knock the ball into gaps to run singles enough, and he's as quick as anything between the wickets, is Bill. We just didn't accelerate when we should have done."

After Gooch's dismissal Gatting got the scoreboard moving, taking the total to 135 for two off 31 overs. That left a target of 119 runs in 19 overs, with eight wickets in hand, and there were signs in the field that the Australians were losing control. Their captain Allan Border introduced his own left-arm spin, and to his very first ball Mike Gatting attempted a reverse-sweep which he top-edged onto his shoulder, from where it looped into the wicket-keeper's gloves. It was a fateful moment. Allan Lamb hit a brisk 45, there were some late heroics from Phil DeFreitas, but England lost by seven runs, and the journalists were quick to place the blame on Gatting's 'wretched shot'. It was a shot that Peter May, the chairman of selectors, disliked intensely, but not Micky.

"Peter was adamantly against the reverse sweep, but Gatt used to play it pretty well. 'If you can play it well, play it,' was what I used to say. Perhaps, if we'd had more runs on the board at that stage, Gatt wouldn't have played it. It was silly to say that it was that one stroke that cost us the match. The Aussies played well, they kept their heads, and we didn't do the job. It was very disappointing."

Worse was to follow. England beat Pakistan 3-0 in the one-day matches. The last of these was at Peshawar, near the border with Afghanistan in the North-West Frontier, and the plan was for the two teams to fly together from there to Lahore where the first Test would start three days later. Yet, long before they were due to depart, Micky found himself in the vicinity of the Pakistani dressing room where there seemed to be a great deal of hubbub and hurry.

"What's all the commotion?" he asked one of the players.

"We've been summoned to a meeting in Lahore," came the reply. "We're got to leave right away."

An explanation for this reached Micky later in Lahore. In strict confidence he was told that General Zia had ordered the whole team and its manager to appear before him. They had all been lined up in front of the president, who delivered an uncompromising message. Cricket was vital for the nation's self-esteem. They had lost the World Cup. They had lost the three one-dayers. The nation was depressed, and there were elections coming up. Under no circumstances were they also to lose the Test series. Micky's informant spelled out plainly the meaning of it all: "You must expect anything to happen from now on."

Micky shared the conversation with Peter Lush and Mike Gatting but insisted that the rest of the players not be told. In a team meeting on the eve of the Lahore Test Mike Gatting warned everybody not under any circumstances to get het up about the umpiring.

On the first day England were bowled out for 175, with Abdul Qadir taking nine wickets. In his blue notebook Micky recorded a few observations:

Slow turner. Qadir got it to bounce.
Struggle to pick Qadir.
We must look to be positive against Qadir.
Five batsmen sawn off out of ten wickets to fall.
Main culprit – Shakeel Khan !! (4 LBWs – 3 outside line).

It was little better in the England second innings. Chris Broad, given out caught at the wicket by Shakeel, stood at the crease for a seeming age after the umpire's finger had gone up. Graham Gooch had to usher him away. Then Gooch himself suffered the same fate.

As the players and umpires came off at the end of the session, Micky walked down the pavilion steps and stared intently at Shakeel Khan. "I tried to get him to look at me. Martin Johnson said that I behaved like a football manager at half-time."

After the success of the previous winter's trip to Australia the TCCB had awarded Peter Lush a four-year contract in the newly created position of England tour manager, and it fell to Micky and him to discipline Broad. Some observers thought that they should have taken firmer action than the issuing of a reprimand, but by this stage they were preoccupied by a strong suspicion that the umpires had been nobbled.

In all, Micky reckoned in a letter home to Sheila, 'NINE of the twenty wickets to fall were umpired out. FIVE out of ten in the first innings and FOUR out of ten in the second.'

More sinisterly, the letter went on:

> *I have had two phone calls from former Pakistan players saying that they have definite proof that the umpires were "fixed"!!*

The game was lost, there were public recriminations about the umpiring, and the tourists moved on for a quiet three days at Sahiwal where they played a Punjab Chief Minister's XI and stayed in dormitories in the Montgomery Biscuit Factory. For English cricketers accustomed to life in luxury hotels, this was as basic as it got, with nothing much to do after the day's play was over. "I asked Bill Athey to organise some entertainment. Over the three days we must have played about ten hours of 'Give Us A Clue'."

The match provided them with a first sighting of the leg-spinner Mushtaq Ahmed, only 17 years old but already good enough to take six wickets in England's first innings. Then word came through that Mushtaq might have to replace Abdul Qadir in the next Test and, to prevent the English batsmen having a further look at him, he hardly bowled when they batted again.

And so to Faisalabad. The Second Test. The one after which nothing was quite the same again – for Mike Gatting or for Micky.

On the day before the match – as in Bombay, before the World Cup semi-final – Micky paid out generous quantities of rupees to local spinners to bowl in the nets to the England batsmen. "The Pakistanis were practising on the other side of the ground, and suddenly all our spinners had disappeared." It transpired that Javed Miandad, the Pakistani captain, had ordered them to leave the English nets.

The umpires for the match were Shakoor Rana, Pakistan's most senior official, and Khizar Hayat. Were England by now in a state of paranoia about the decision-making, or were the odds being unfairly stacked against them? Micky's notebook entries suggest the latter:

1st Day

Gooch & Broad played spinners very well.

Gooch sawn off – Bat pad catch offside (middle of pad – bat behind pad) – Shakoor Rana.

Athey given out by Khizar Hayat. Same as Gooch – bat nowhere near ball.

Robinson given out by Shakoor Rana. Caught at wicket – above wrist – difficult decision?

2nd Day

Foster sawn off by Khizar Hayat. Bat pad offside.

French sawn off by Shakoor Rana. Stumped – back in ground some time.

This time, though, the damage was not so great, as Broad made 116, Gatting 79, and they reached a total of 292. Then on the second afternoon, according to Micky, "we bowled Javed, took four catches, and Pakistan came in with the score on 58 for three."

At one point, while all this was going on, Micky recorded an ominous entry in his notebook:

Shakoor loves centre stage.

Centre stage is indeed what Shakoor took as the day drew to a close.

"I didn't actually see the incident," Micky says. "I was making sure the twelfth man had got all the drinks ready for when they came off the field."

Pakistan, on 106 for five, were in trouble, with England trying to press home their advantage by squeezing in an extra over before close of play. Midway through what they hoped would be the penultimate over Mike Gatting, fielding at square leg, asked David Capel at long leg to come in closer to stop the single. As Eddie Hemmings ran in to bowl the next ball, Gatting made a further signal, indicating to Capel that he had come too far. Shakoor Rana, standing at square leg, interpreted this as moving the fielder surreptitiously behind the batsman's back and called 'Dead ball', thus kyboshing England's hopes of bowling a further over. Some say that shortly beforehand he had been looking closely at his watch.

Within moments a blazing row had developed between Shakoor Rana and the England captain, with pictures flying around the world of an angry-faced Mike Gatting standing close to the umpire and jabbing a finger towards his chest. Micky's notebook elaborates:

Gatt & Shakoor flare up – Last over
Shakoor calls Gatt "fucking cheating bastard"
Gatt responds !!

As *Wisden* put it, 'The language employed throughout the discourse was basic.'

It was not immediately apparent that a full-scale crisis was developing. The first point at which Peter Lush realised things were getting serious was when, back in the hotel, he took a phone call from Ted Corbett of the *Star*. "Are you aware," Corbett asked, "that the Pakistanis aren't going to be playing in the morning?"

A compromise of sorts, involving an exchange of apologies, was brokered, but it was scuppered, partly by the intervention of Javed Miandad, a street-fighter whom the England camp suspected of trying to delay the resumption because his team, one-up in the series, was in a bad position in the match.

Late in the afternoon of this third day that wasn't, Micky wrote a long letter home to Sheila, explaining what was going on.

> *The lines between Lord's and here have been red hot since last night, right the way through the night and resuming today. The reaction of the "establishment" was one of horror that the Captain could be involved in such an incident but Lushy and I soon made them aware of all the facts. I am sure that there are still some at Lord's who think that we should swallow our pride as Englishmen and show a stiff upper lip but in the longer term I am sure that our stand will serve the game better as far as future tours to Pakistan are concerned.*
>
> ...
>
> *Up to the present time we have lost 30 wickets in the series of which no less than 14 have been victims of umpires' "errors". In addition two blatant bat pad catches have not been given out when we have been in the field. Errors total = 16. 1 error has been made against Pakistan!! – It all sounds very petty doesn't it but I have never seen anything like it before in all the time I have known the game.*
>
> ...
>
> *I am now back at the hotel. ... Lushy has gone hot foot to Lahore to resolve the matter with their Board once he knew that their Board's Secretary had left an hour before him without having the courtesy to tell us beforehand! I have to stay in my room here to take all the calls that may come in from all over. It's like being in a cell.*

There he was, five thousand miles from home, sitting in a hotel room, in the thick of an international crisis that involved not just the whole hierarchy at Lord's but the British High Commission as well as the government of Pakistan. All over a game of cricket.

It was a ghastly time for Micky. No one took the game of cricket more seriously than he did. But this was something else altogether. He thought back to his playing days at the Oval, when he had set off from home each morning full of eager determination, and he remembered the cheerful way Sheila's brother had wished him well.

I can still hear Bill saying "Have a good game" – it helps to keep me sane.

On the next day, the official rest day in the match, feelings were running as high as ever, with the England players voting at a meeting to go home. Then later John Emburey, among the most vocal, was worrying about the consequences of the decision.

"You've got to look wider than what's happened here," was Micky's message to the players. "What will the repercussions be if we go home now? The best way to solve this is to get out there and finish the game."

"Micky had a difficult line to steer," Mike Gatting says. "He knew full well what he'd seen, and he knew what he'd been told. It was difficult for him to be constructive when it came to team meetings because the last thing he wanted was for all the players to know what had been said. He couldn't say anything. It would have caused a huge, huge rift."

Micky's notebook entry provides a summary of his day:

MJS by phone all morning.
Meeting after meeting when Lushy returns.
Instruction received from Lord's for Gatt to apologise if no other solution can be reached.
MJS talks to players at 11 p.m. Feeling very strong about Gatt's apology. Players will not take field. – Full meeting with players. Goochy, Dill, Billy all have their say. – UNANIMOUS that players won't take field if Gatt's is only apology. – It looks like a STRIKE !!
Embers in my room 1.15 a.m. Worried about young players.
Gatt to see all players individually at 7.30 a.m. to get them into field no matter what.
Bed 2.30 a.m.!! Very sorry for Gatt.

The match was finally resumed, without the extra day that England would have needed to force a victory, and it petered out as a draw. Then, before the final Test at Karachi, the Pakistanis announced that Shakoor

The game restarts

Rana would be umpiring again, and there was another row. "Well, you didn't agree to our request not to have David Constant," they countered when Peter Lush and Micky objected. A brief attempt was made to fly in umpires from India, then Shakoor Rana was replaced. The game was played out with little goodwill, but there were no significant flare-ups. By this stage, in the words of Milton, all passion had been spent, and the teams agreed to settle for a draw at teatime on the final day.

During the match Raman Subba Row and Alan Smith, chairman and chief executive of the TCCB, arrived from London, instructing Peter Lush to tell the players that, as a result of their ordeal, they would each receive a hardship payment of £1,000. In its way it was a well-meant gesture, but nobody was impressed, with some of the players arguing that they should refuse the offer. The matter was not helped when somebody at Lord's leaked news of the payment ahead of the official announcement. To the outsider it looked tacky, as if the players might have bargained for it during the dispute and it had all been hushed up.

"Hopeless," Micky calls it. "There wasn't much money in the game, and suddenly you're awarding the players a grand for hardship. It was absolutely ridiculous."

*

Mike Gatting had never been everybody's cup of tea at Lord's. Peter May, chairman of selectors, was an admirer, greatly preferring his bulldog spirit to the more laissez-faire approach of David Gower. But there were plenty who saw the captaincy of the England cricket team as about more than winning matches, and for them Gatting was not the sort of chap to uphold the right image of English cricket.

"All you could criticise Gatt for," Micky says, "was that as captain of the England side, no matter what happens, you shouldn't lose control. But in those conditions, after what had happened over the previous two or three weeks, that wasn't an easy thing to do. He knew what the form was politically, but he had principles and he was none too good at taking a step back. Someone like Goochy might have dealt with it differently."

"It was probably my fault more than anybody else," Mike Gatting says now. "But I don't know which is the worse, me having a ruck with the umpire or him calling me a 'fucking cheat'."

Christmas at home was a brief interlude, with post-mortems at Lord's preventing much relaxation for captain and team manager. Then came the tour of New Zealand and Australia, and the mutterings about Gatting's suitability started up again. The press had a story, England's indiscipline, and they were quick to highlight every instance of poor behaviour on the pitch. At Sydney, in the Bicentennial Test, Chris Broad, after scoring a masterly 139, hit his wicket in irritation after he had played on. At Christchurch Graham Dilley swore loudly after having several appeals turned down. Both were fined, but the press's view was that too little in the way of genuine apology was forthcoming from the tour management.

Was that the case? Was Micky too close to the players, accepting things that might be all right on a football field but not at cricket? Or were the press putting too strong a slant on it all?

Mike Gatting is certain which explanation he prefers, quoting Bob Vance, the chairman of New Zealand cricket whose son in England had written to him about press coverage of the series: 'Jesus, Dad, you must have the worst England team of all time out there.'

"Micky, what's your press doing?" Vance asked. "Your boys are a good bunch of lads. What's the problem? I've had a chat with the umpires. They say they're better behaved than our lot."

Vance, along with the umpires, wrote along these lines to the Test and County Cricket Board, but at a post-tour meeting at Lord's Gatting was admonished. "We told you to be whiter than white," was the message, "and you haven't been."

"Gatt wasn't the most popular person with some of them," Micky says. "It was the same when Brian Close was captain. They took the first opportunity to get rid of him. Even Illy, when he won the Ashes in Australia. I sat next to him at a celebration dinner, and David Clark the tour manager was speaking. After a bit I said to Illy, 'We did win the Ashes, didn't we?'"

Several at the TCCB were keen to replace Gatting as captain forthwith. "I wasn't in the room," Micky says, "but he'd obviously spoken his mind and it hadn't gone down well."

The crisis was averted. With Peter May firmly of the same view as Micky, that Mike Gatting should stay in position, the Board agreed to leave things as they were.

*

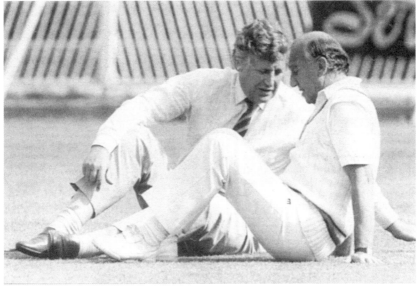

Peter Lush and Micky

"Lushy took the brunt of the pressure in Pakistan," Micky says.
"It was all hugely demanding on him. He was travelling off
to meetings hundreds of miles away. But he was a strong character,
and he stuck by his principles, our principles, the principles of the game.
He had a great sense of humour, and he was well liked
by all the players, as was Lawrie Brown, the physio,
who was a lovely man and a great support to me.
I was very lucky to come into a management team like that."

It had been a bad winter for English cricket, but the nightmare was far from over.

The visitors in 1988 were the mighty West Indians, who had beaten England 5-0 in each of their previous two Test series. So great was their dominance that Micky's first challenge was to convince his players that they were capable of competing with the visitors.

"In all my time in sport I'd never experienced top players, really top players, speaking in such awe of their opponents. Having been thrashed twice like that, you can get into a state but you've got to get over it. "

One symptom of their inferiority complex, in Micky's view, was the way the England players spoke of their opponents. "I don't want to hear you referring to 'Viv' and 'Gordon'," he told them.

"It was my way of trying to reduce the aura the West Indians had. Out in the Caribbean I think the England players, even the experienced ones, had got to the point where they were going into games accepting that they were going to come second. It was terrible."

At one press conference Micky tried the same line – "Viv? Viv who?" – and was ridiculed in the *Daily Mirror* under a headline which read 'What mental Micky asked yesterday':

> *England team boss Micky Stewart claimed last night, after a day of mayhem for his bowlers, that he didn't know the name of Viv Richards. "Viv?" asked Stewart. "Viv who? … The opposition are just 11 players as far as we are concerned. They don't have any names. If you think any other way, you're in trouble."*

"It wasn't just Viv Richards and Gordon Greenidge. It was almost the whole West Indian team. They would talk about the pace of Patrick Patterson. Well, he did have pace, but he gave you scoring opportunities. That was what we had to focus on."

The summer started exceptionally well for England. They beat the West Indians convincingly in all three Texaco Trophy games. Then in the first Test at Trent Bridge, after the visitors had taken a first innings lead of 203, England fought their way back to an honourable draw, with Graham Gooch hitting a defiant 146. Micky's first ambition, the restoration of some self-belief against the West Indians, was starting to be achieved.

The game ended on Tuesday evening, after which Micky drove from Nottingham to Swansea, arriving late at his hotel and going straight to bed. His plan was to watch a Benson and Hedges Cup match next day, to have a look at some players who might come into consideration for England, notably Kim Barnett, Matthew Maynard and Devon Malcolm.

"In the morning I came down to breakfast, and there were a couple of journalists sitting there. 'What do you think of this then, Micky?' one of them said, and he held up the front page of the *Sun*. I started my breakfast about an hour and a half later."

The headline article, a 'Sun Exclusive', concerned a 'sex orgy', involving three unnamed players, which was supposed to have taken place in the Rothley Court Hotel, where the England team had been staying during the Trent Bridge Test. The next day's headline was even worse: 'Gatting Made Love to Me'. The story told of the England captain alone in his room with a local barmaid.

Mike Gatting himself is adamant that nothing of consequence happened in the room, that it was his birthday and that others in the team were going to join the two of them for an entirely innocent drinks party. He had been the victim of a classic tabloid sting, with money changing hands before the story appeared. To prove the truth of what he was saying, he even hired a private detective.

Nevertheless, Micky was livid. He had fought on his captain's behalf through all the travails of the winter, and he had been rewarded with this. Whatever had or had not happened in the room, in Micky's eyes Mike Gatting had been an idiot.

It was not as if the players were unaware of the dangers. On the Australian tour they had had a tip-off that three girls in the hotel bar had been put there by an English tabloid. Micky told the team to stay in their rooms while he looked after the situation.

"When are the boys coming down, Micky?"

"They're not, I'm afraid. They're having an early night."

It was a world to which Micky was not accustomed – "I was amazed that any Englishman would want to write a story that was harmful to English cricket" – but it was now a fact of life, and from time to time Micky issued warnings to the players.

'The England cricketers of today,' Alan Lee wrote in *The Times*, 'behave no more outrageously than their predecessors. Nothing has changed except the amount of exposure the game receives. Like show-business personalities, the leading cricketers are now under a spotlight which was never trained upon the likes of Compton and Edrich.'

Micky was furious. His partnership with Mike Gatting, so successful in Australia, had been destroyed – and for no good cricketing reason.

Micky loathed the new journalism, and he would have loathed it even more if he had known at the time what he has only discovered during the writing of this book: that the editor of the *Sun*, Kelvin Mackenzie, who had just done English cricket so much damage, was an old boy of Alleyn's School.

*

The TCCB accepted Mike Gatting's assurance that no sexual impropriety had occurred in the hotel bedroom. Nevertheless, they concluded that he had 'behaved irresponsibly' by inviting the girl into his room and withdrew their invitation to him to captain England in the second Test at Lord's.

It was a decision that was not met with universal approval. 'Which is the greater evil?' Mike Brearley asked in the *Sunday Times*. 'A possible sexual laxity in an England cricket captain, or a sneaking, vicious, malicious and possibly libellous account in the popular press? To my mind, the TCCB has got hold of the stick at the wrong end.'

The politician Roy Jenkins, appearing on the BBC's *Question Time*, put it more simply: 'If he didn't do it, why isn't he captain? And if he did, why did they accept every word of his denial?'

Micky's understanding was that Gatting's suspension was only a temporary one. That was certainly how Peter May saw it. "He's got to be taught a lesson," the chairman of selectors said to Micky, "but he must come back as captain." So they opted to put vice-captain John Emburey in charge for the time being.

At the weekend the waters grew muddier for Gatting when some extracts from his forthcoming book *Leading from the Front* appeared in the *Sunday Times*. Under the terms of his contract with the TCCB he was not permitted to comment on the Shakoor Rana affair for two years, though he had attempted to get round this by having that chapter written not in his own name but in that of his ghost-writer Angela Patmore.

For some at Lord's this was seen as a much more serious matter than the tabloid headline about the barmaid. Robin Marlar, the former Sussex captain, expressed their view, writing in the *Sunday Times* of Gatting's 'unbalanced, almost lunatic determination to tell his side of the finger-wagging story in Pakistan':

> *If the book goes on sale, the board will be justified in suspending Gatting from all full-time cricket sine die, which is a terrible fate to contemplate for a fundamentally jolly cricketer who means no harm to the game he loves, or anyone in it.*

In the event, the book was published. It was not unbalanced, and the TCCB, after a six-hour hearing, fined Gatting £5,000. More significantly, for Micky as England team manager, feelings at Lord's hardened further against Gatting.

Meanwhile the Test series against West Indies continued. England under Emburey lost badly at Lord's and humiliatingly at Old Trafford, where they were all out for 135 and 93. Emburey's own form suffered a dip and, with the selectors deciding that a spinner was not required for the fourth Test at Headingley, a new captain, the third of the summer, was now required for the final two Tests. After that, there was a single Test against Sri Lanka and a winter tour of India.

"I was still hoping to have Mike Gatting back," Micky says. "We saw things very similarly, and we got on well. But, if it wasn't going to be Gatt, then for me it had to be Graham Gooch. The way he felt about playing for England, and about England as a team, was the same way I thought, the same way Mike Gatting thought. But unfortunately Goochy wasn't flavour of the month at Lord's, either."

The first problem for Gooch was that he had served a three-year ban for captaining a rebel tour of South Africa in 1981/82. He had spent the following two winters playing for Western Province, and all this led to his being a controversial figure in certain countries. Furthermore, he had acquired a reputation as a reluctant tourist, wanting to come home early from the Caribbean and, on family grounds, sitting out Mike Gatting's tour of Australia in 1986/87 as well as the trip to New Zealand in the early months of 1988. He had also made it known that he would not be available for that winter's tour of India. On top of all that, he had resigned the Essex captaincy at the end of the previous summer, saying that it had affected his batting form.

If not Gatting, Emburey or Gooch, then who? With Peter May as chairman of selectors there was a reluctance to return to the style of David Gower's captaincy, while all the other candidates were outside the current team. Some, such as Kim Barnett of Derbyshire and Mark Nicholas of Hampshire, had never played for England. Others, such as Chris Cowdrey of Kent and Paul Parker of Sussex, had played very little and not recently.

A large meeting was held at Lord's, with not only the selectors present but many from the TCCB. Micky argued once more for Gatting, then for Gooch, but eventually the meeting opted for Chris Cowdrey, appointing him for the final two matches of the series. "He was having a successful time with Kent," Micky says, "but he was always going to be a limited batsman against the West Indies because he was a front-foot player and he wasn't going to get too much in his own half of the pitch."

Poor Cowdrey. It was the chance of a lifetime, and nothing went right for him. The press ridiculed him as Peter May's godson. The car park attendant at Headingley refused to accept that he was anything to do with the England team and sent him packing. He scored 0 and 5 in another crushing defeat, this one by ten wickets, and in the run-up to the final Test at the Oval he had his foot badly bruised by a ball from Somerset's Adrian Jones and had to withdraw from the team.

By default Graham Gooch was now the captain, England's fourth in five matches. The result was another defeat, by eight wickets, but this time, against expectations, Gooch stirred England to a livelier display, in which they gained a first-innings lead. Batting for the second time, Gooch himself hit a determined 84, but the curse of the summer returned when, fielding in the slips, Gooch dislocated a finger and had to retire. So for the final hours of the ill-fated series the England captaincy was passed on once more, this time to Derek Pringle.

Botham had missed the summer with back problems, Edmonds had retired, and injuries had caused other disruptions to the team. Only Gooch had played all five Tests, and by the Oval the only men left from the triumph in Australia eighteen months earlier were Jack Richards, Phil DeFreitas and Neil Foster, none of whom had been in the side three matches earlier at Lord's.

"There was no stability," John Emburey says. "The players didn't have any confidence. Every match you went into, you were looking over your shoulder. It was a dreadful, dreadful feeling."

"The players' view at the time," Gladstone Small says, "was that there were too many people at the TCCB who wouldn't leave the playing of cricket to the cricketers and the coach. There was far too much politicking going on in the background."

"For the Ashes tour and the World Cup," Bill Athey says, "we had a really good feeling as a team. Everyone got to know each other. But then in 1988, with all the changes, people constantly in and out, you started to think, 'Is it me next?' And that bred selfishness. People started to think, 'I'm just going to look after myself.'"

After the West Indies came a single Test against Sri Lanka where, with several new players blooded, victory brought a brief respite, but soon the politics were starting again. With Micky still trying in vain to reinstate Gatting, Gooch was persuaded to make himself available and was appointed captain for the tour of India. The South African issue was not thought likely to create a problem, as the previous winter Gooch had been granted entry to India for the World Cup. Nevertheless the Indian government did object, and the tour was cancelled.

The only time Micky had previously encountered the South African problem had been when Gooch had been a member of the England party who visited Sharjah in the spring of 1987. On that occasion the TCCB had taken care to replace any passports with South African stamps on them. Even this, however, did not eliminate all difficulties.

"We arrived at the airport," Micky recalls, "and there was a request for us to have a team photo. So we all lined up, and Lawrie Brown, our physio, was missing. I went to look for him, and it turned out they hadn't let him through. Nothing to do with South Africa. He was the physio for Manchester United, and he'd been with them to Israel."

"You'll have to buy him a new passport," the British Attaché advised Micky.

"How much will that cost?"

"Fifty pounds."

Micky laughed. "Leave him there then."

Eventually Brown was let in, but the problems did not end there. England were due to play India, and the night before the match, at nine o'clock, one of the local officials appeared. "We will not have Gooch, Emburey, anybody who has been to South Africa."

"But this was all agreed."

"Well, we haven't seen any of the letters."

The matter was to be referred up the line to a higher authority, a man who was discovered to be "asleep" and "not to be disturbed" in his flat in Knightsbridge.

At midnight the matter was still unresolved. A meeting of the organisers was in progress, and they sent for Allan Border, the Australian captain. "What's going on?" he said. "I've been woken up and told that, if you're not allowed to play, we play. All our lads are asleep now."

Eventually, in the early hours, the man in Knightsbridge gave his approval, and England took part as planned. Politics, it seemed, was now an everyday part of cricket.

Peter May had had enough by the end of 1988. He retired as chairman of selectors, to be replaced by Ted Dexter, who in the spring sat down with Micky to discuss the options for the captaincy. Dexter was not a Gooch fan, having publicly referred to him as 'a wet fish', so the choice came down to Gatting or Gower. As far as Micky and Ted Dexter understood, there would be no problem if they opted to return to Gatting.

"I wanted Gatt back," Micky says. "Ted listened to what I had to say and, after a long conversation, he went along with me."

Perhaps it was not what the key people at Lord's had expected to happen. Dexter as a player had been a dashing cavalier, and they might well have assumed that he would see Gower as a kindred spirit. But he did not. He preferred to support Micky, who was clear that his plans for English cricket could best be realised by reviving his partnership with Mike Gatting.

Ossie Wheatley, the TCCB's chairman of cricket, along with Raman Subba Row, the chairman, were most unhappy with the decision and, after some telephone soundings, Wheatley exercised his veto. Then, after Micky had argued unsuccessfully for Gooch, it was announced that they had chosen David Gower, who at this stage was unaware of the initial preference for Gatting.

For Micky this was a major setback. After two and a half years in post he had a clear view of the way forward for English cricket, and it did not fit in any way with the outlook of the newly appointed England captain.

*

The previous August Micky had written a seven-page paper, 'Views and Comments on Present Structure of Cricket in England'. It contained a set of recommendations: on grass-roots cricket, the first-class county clubs, the domestic programme and England team cricket.

The section on grass roots cricket begins: 'I firmly believe that the standard of England's "grass roots" cricket is the lowest of all the major cricket playing countries in the world.' The emphasis, he argues, is too heavily placed on participation rather than the achievement of high standards. To change this, each county should establish a major league comprised of its best clubs, playing as long a format of game as possible, and these 'elite' clubs should also run age-group sides to bring the most talented youngsters to the top more speedily.

The section on first-class county clubs begins: 'I believe that the standards of control and organisation of administration and marketing in the county clubs have risen enormously over the last twenty years but by comparison the control and organisation standards of the product – i.e. CRICKET – have stood still.' Unlike in other sports, he argues, there is too little coaching of first-team players. If the admin and marketing can benefit from new technology with the relevant training of staff, why are there not similar developments in the coaching of players? This section ends with two further complaints: the poor quality of pitches being produced by counties and the surfeit of overseas players.

The section on the domestic programme argues that higher standards would be achieved if the programme eliminated 'the depressing "grind" outlook that many players have adopted to it', allowing players more time to work on their technical faults between matches. He recommends a championship based on 16 four-day games on 'true pitches', an unchanged NatWest trophy, a reduced Benson and Hedges Cup and a new format for Sunday cricket.

The final section on England team cricket begins: 'I have worked with 37 players since October 1986 covering five tours and two seasons at home. They have played 22 Test matches (Won 2, Lost 7, Drawn 13) and 38 one-day internationals (Won 26, Lost 12).' Then he outlines the two areas where he would like to see major change:

a) *Techniques and Fitness*

I have been surprised at the number of players with basic faults in their technique and also the lack of knowledge of the good habits that have always been associated with top players.

We have competed against all the other major cricket playing countries in one form of cricket or another and with the possible exception of India I would say that as a side England have been less fit, less strong, less athletic and less mobile than our opponents.

I make these two points because I believe that neither aspect of the game receives sufficient attention in our domestic cricket.

b) *Tours and Fixtures against Tourists*

I believe that regular reciprocal age group tours would be enormously beneficial towards producing a consistently successful England team. A restricted number of "over age" players could also be included.

Age group representative XIs should also play against the senior country touring England every season.

Much of this is now accepted practice, but at the time it was a visionary paper, arguing for greater professionalisation in a game that was lagging behind developments not only in other countries but also in other sports.

*

For Micky, David Gower was not a good match of captain and manager in the way Mike Gatting had been. Micky admired Gower as a richly talented batsman, but their views on cricket were not at all in harmony.

"David was a deep thinker about the game," Micky says, "but he thought of it more as an individual sport. He didn't see the team ethic as essential in the way I did – or as Mike Gatting did. He was very competitive; you have to be to achieve what he did. But his view was that each player had been picked for what he'd achieved and, when it came to the game, it was all down to that player. He didn't see himself as somebody who could contribute to other people's performances."

Gower also had little time for Micky's ideas about improving fitness. Again he thought that was the responsibility of each individual in the side.

Gower's captaincy had brought success against Australia in 1985, but in four years much had changed. The Australians had themselves acquired a team manager, Bobby Simpson, who had introduced a greater team ethic with much concentration on the fielding, and they approached the 1989 series with a fiercer, less convivial attitude than they had adopted in 1985.

Allan Border was the Australian captain, and Micky remembers him before the one-day Texaco Trophy match at Lord's. "We had been practising at the Nursery End and were walking back to the pavilion, past where the Australians were practising. Allan Border was very pally with several of the England team: 'Both', David Gower, Allan Lamb and, from his time at Essex, Goochy. But as we approached somebody heard him saying, 'Don't talk to them at all as they go by.'"

From the first moment of the series, when Gower put the Australians in at Headingley and watched them score 601 for seven, England were on the back foot.

But for a dismal batting collapse on the final afternoon, England might have left Headingley with a draw, and they competed on even terms for two days at Lord's. Then a bad Saturday, when Australia's last four wickets added 263 runs, left England in a losing position in that Test, too.

At the end-of-day press conference the journalists, led by the mischievous Phillipe Edmonds, grilled the England captain about his bowling strategy. Gower, after enduring several minutes of it, got up and walked out, saying that he had tickets for the theatre. It did not help when the journalists discovered that the show he was off to see was called 'Anything Goes'.

"You have to understand that he's experienced a bad day," Micky said valiantly in his absence. "There's precious little to say until we put it right."

It was a bad day, and it reflected a weakness in Gower's approach to captaincy, a weakness that came to a head in the afternoon session when Geoff Lawson, the Australian number ten, scored 74.

"We were always three or four overs behind in the field," John Emburey says, "and that has to come from the captaincy. I got a wicket just before lunch, and I was expecting to bowl. But I didn't. The seamers came back on, and they were at the wrong ends. I had dislocated a finger so I was down at third man, but in the slips we had Gooch, Lamb and Gatt, three experienced players. I was waving at them: 'What's going on?' Then David put me on at the Nursery End where in nearly 20 years at Lord's I'd bowled about 25 overs. By then I was pissed off. We were behind the run of play in our thinking on everything, and everybody just let David get on with it. Nobody wanted to get involved."

Cricket always has its bad days. The problem for Micky as manager was that he was struggling to find a way to get involved and have influence.

"Micky and Gatt talked the same talk," Neil Foster says. "They were men of action. David may have found Micky too focused, because he didn't want to appear too committed to anything. I know how committed he really was as captain, but he liked to let things sort themselves out whereas Micky wanted to be doing stuff about things. Micky thought that the harder you worked, the better you became, so he was always going to get on better with people who shared that attitude."

"Gatt, Goochy and I came from similar backgrounds to Micky," John Emburey says. "Yes, Micky went to public school, but we were all Londoners, we had decent cricket brains and we had a workmanlike approach. David was more easy-going, a bit flippant when things didn't go well, and that didn't appeal to Micky."

In the second innings at Lord's Gower redeemed himself with a century, but the Test was lost. In a six-match series England were already 2-0 down, and Micky was at his lowest ebb. "I knew working with David would never work in the same way, and I started asking myself, 'Am I wasting my time?' It was the only time when I thought I would give the job away."

He telephoned Sir George Edwards, the aircraft engineer who had led the British half of Concorde's manufacture, a great friend of the Bedsers and the President of Surrey when Micky returned to the Oval in 1979. "He had been a bit of a mentor to me," Micky says, "when I started as manager. He had so much basic common sense in everything he said."

Edwards invited Micky to his home to talk it all through.

"I've always felt strongly about the job," Micky explained, "but I feel I'm whacking my head against a brick wall. And I'm not enjoying it now. I'm thinking strongly about giving it away."

"Oh yes? So you don't care about English cricket any more."

"Of course I do."

"Well, how do you think you're going to influence it if you resign?"

Micky soldiered on. Rain prevented a third defeat at Edgbaston, but now the popular press was at fever pitch. The England captain, recording his inner thoughts in a summer-long diary, was sinking as deep into the slough of despond as his team manager:

> *A section of the press has become openly belligerent. Hardly a day goes by without sackings or resignations being demanded. Some of the tabloids have taken to insulting drawings of me and others in dunce's caps. I find it pretty offensive and I must say the whole aspect of dealing with the media has got to me more than I expected.*

During the fourth Test at Old Trafford there was another manufactured furore when an ITV camera caught Gower making a playful v-sign to the crowd.

> *The press has over-reacted laughably and now I have Ted on the phone to do his duty ... It has depressed me enormously and, in this black mood, I can see no reason for trying to maintain a relationship with the media. I cannot believe there is any justification for what is becoming a witch hunt. If they want me out so badly, I might just give them satisfaction.*

The match was lost comprehensively, and with it the Ashes. But this paled into a minor story when on the final day another bombshell hit English cricket: the announcement that 16 players, including nine who had played for England that summer, had signed up for a rebel tour of South Africa that winter.

Micky had heard whispers that a trip was being planned. Jack Bannister and David Graveney, officers of the Professional Cricketers' Association, were known to be involved in the arrangements, but Micky had no idea that the current England team had been so extensively recruited.

"I'd said to Ted Dexter, 'If there was any truth in the rumours about the England players, I would know,' and I didn't. I remember confronting Dilley and Emburey, and Tim Robinson. Neil Foster was almost in tears about it. I said, 'You've let me down.' I knew I had a good relationship with the players, and I thought they would have confided in me. But they were sworn to secrecy. They were all fed up with the hierarchy, and they were being offered so much money."

Another press conference – this time the Ashes have gone

The constant changes in the team had made most of them insecure about their Test futures, with the spirit in the England side in free fall. Gatting, in particular, had reason to feel thoroughly disenchanted by the course his own career had taken, so even he, the great patriot, signed up for the rebel tour, agreeing to take on the captaincy.

"Do I wish I'd said no?" Gatting asks himself now. "I suppose all I will say is that I'd been cast adrift by England, I'd been lied to, I'd been dragged through the mud unnecessarily, I'd not had the support of the board when I needed it. What was my next port of call? My family. Middlesex." He pauses, then finally answers his own question: "I wish I hadn't had to go. I loved playing for England."

*

The comedians were well and truly enjoying themselves at the expense of England's cricket, and they had further material when Micky took a second-string side for a 55-over match against Holland at Amstelveen.

273

Micky's understanding was that the party would spend a night at the hotel at Heathrow, then fly into Holland for a day's practice before playing the match, but on arrival at the hotel they were informed that a 40-over contest had been added to the schedule, to be played the next day. There was no time for preparation, and in the game England, batting in near darkness in the closing overs, contrived to lose by three runs to Holland. Even *The Times* rubbed in the embarrassment, calling it 'as historic and shattering a defeat as any setback at this level since the West Indians were defeated by Ireland in 1969'.

Among the young cricketers under the spotlight that day was Micky's son Alec, who began his England career with a duck.

Peter Roebuck of Somerset was the captain, and Micky still recalls the look of bewilderment on the faces of the team during the captain's off-beat pre-match talk in the dressing room: "We need to know exactly what the structure is going to be over the next six hours, what we're all here for ..." There was more in similar vein at the post-match press conference. So that was another captaincy option that would not be pursued.

The next day amends were made with a 98-run victory but, as far as the comedians were concerned, the damage had already been done.

For the final Test at the Oval, with England 4-0 down, the selectors raised to 29 the number of players to appear in the six-match series, the last of them the Kent fast bowler Alan Igglesden whom Gower had never seen bowl.

Before the press conference Micky undertook a calculation. Of the first-choice opening bowlers around the 17 counties, nine were overseas players, five had been banned for signing up for the rebel tour and a further seven or eight were out of action with injuries. He explained all this to the assembled journalists, not meaning to suggest that Igglesden was lower in the pecking order than every one of those who were unavailable. Nevertheless his explanation led Jim Swanton in the *Daily Telegraph* to comment that it could not have done Igglesden's confidence much good to know that he was there as the fifteenth choice.

The game was drawn, leaving England's Test record since their Boxing Day victory at Melbourne as Played 25, Won 1, Drawn 13, Lost 11. And next up was a tour of the Caribbean.

Could things get any worse?

16

STARTING AGAIN

"We had a talented side," Micky says, reflecting on those turbulent years in the late 1980s. "If everything had gone smoothly, if all those incidents had not happened, I could see how we were going to take it forward. I was looking to a situation where we would have, say, six batsmen, four of them experienced, two learning the trade, and the progression would be smoothly managed. I'd started thinking in that way."

At Slazenger he had dealt with unforeseen difficulties, including a recession, and he had learnt how you had to face the new realities, not go back to what had worked previously. "That all stood me in good stead with the England job. The only big difference was that with England you had to handle the public knowledge of it all – working with the press."

By Micky's own admission it was his greatest failing, not coming to terms with the way the media had changed since his own days as a player. "You can only be as you are, but you've got to be a bit shrewd in the way you project yourself."

The team was now under the captaincy of Graham Gooch, with neither Ian Botham nor David Gower selected though both had made themselves available. The South African rebels were missing, too, so there was a new, less experienced look to the side. Apart from Gooch and Allan Lamb, the other 14 players had only 65 Test appearances between them.

Four had yet to make their England debut: the Essex batsman Nasser Hussain, the Surrey left-armer Keith Medlycott, the Leicestershire all-rounder Chris Lewis, and Alec Stewart, whose 1,633 runs in the county championship that summer were second only to Jimmy Cook, Somerset's South African. Alec heard about his selection in the same way as every other player, with no advance tip-off from Micky.

The failure to pick Botham and Gower caused some shock, which Ted Dexter addressed at a press conference. "Ian's form has not even remotely approximated to Test standard this year," he said. Then in relation to Gower: "David's shoulder has been troubling him, and it was felt that a winter off would be the best thing." Both these statements were true – in the autumn Gower had an operation on his shoulder – but, from Micky's point of view, they were not causes for great regret.

There were considerable advantages to starting afresh with a younger party. "We were going out with people who hadn't experienced coming second to the West Indies so many times." Also, with Gooch in charge: "We were creating the nucleus for a new England team, all of whom would fall into line with the approach and attitude we were wanting to adopt: the team ethic and the preparation."

It helped Micky greatly that Graham Gooch was also a firm believer in improving the team's fitness. Gooch, no natural athlete, had become a convert to fitness training eleven years earlier, in 1978, when Essex had promoted him to open the batting. "I realised that I had to be a fitter, stronger, more mentally alert type of player, and I had to change my weight a bit."

"From early on," Micky says, "he was the sort of lad who, if he had a pint of beer in the evening, it showed on his body the next day."

So by the time he was appointed England captain at the age of 36 Gooch was a veteran of road running and gym work. At one stage he became so fanatical about it that, when Essex played at Ilford, his journey to the ground each morning was by way of an eight-mile run along the A12 from his home in Gidea Park, Romford.

"Looking back now," he says, "it was a bit mad. But I absolutely know that all that work in those years helped me to perform to my best to an age when most other people would have retired."

Apart from the long-term stamina he built up, there was an unexpected side effect, one that he did not discover till later. "I didn't engage a coach. I probably should have done. So I had to push myself. And when you do push yourself, to the limit, on your own, that helps to build a strength of character. The hardest part of training is getting out of bed at six o'clock, or whenever, and putting your stuff on. It's so easy to say, 'Not today.' If you're doing it on your own, you have to motivate yourself, and that self-motivation was very good for me when I was out in the middle."

For the first time England had a winter in which there was time to build in preparation work before the main tour. In October there was a three-week trip to India to play in a one-day tournament. Then, through November, December and January, Micky supervised a programme of activities to prepare both physically and technically for the challenge that lay ahead in the Caribbean. There were regional centres to which the players reported, where they worked on their individual games with coaches and former England cricketers. There were medical examinations, which led to the players individually undertaking schedules of circuit training, devised by a fitness guru from the University of Kent, Colin Tomlin. Then there were team get-togethers at Lilleshall.

Graham Gooch reflected on it in his diary of the winter:

Micky has been the ideal man to run our fitness programme. He has all the zip and enthusiasm from his days as a professional footballer with Charlton. He buzzes around, advising here, cajoling there. He will never be angry if somebody fails just because the other man is too good for them on the day – but woe betide anyone who doesn't give his all. He never bawls you out, but relies on a little joke and a quiet comment to let you know what he's thinking. He doesn't miss a thing, either.

"Micky had put a lot of thought into it," the Middlesex bowler Angus Fraser recalls. "It was a young, exciting England side, and we were making a fresh start. Being on that tour was a new experience for me. I'd played at Middlesex where there were plenty of big name players and they all knew their job – so, coming into that, you had to be self-reliant. England was coming together as a much younger side, and Micky created a real sense of togetherness."

"You could see a difference in the way things were going to be run," Gladstone Small says. "We did a lot more preparation before we left: the batsmen facing short-pitch bowling, the bowlers practising bowling straighter to cut out the boundary balls. There was much more discipline around the whole trip. There weren't as many of the big players who had won the Ashes, and I think that helped Micky."

This was all positive stuff, but they also had to have a strategy for playing the West Indies. At Headingley the batsmen assembled for two days of indoor nets during which local fast bowlers were told to let go of their deliveries at 17 yards, to prepare the batsmen for the pace they would face in the Caribbean. Mike Atherton, who was not in the tour party, joined the group, where Micky was assisted by Geoffrey Boycott. "He was excellent," Micky says. "He didn't change. He just stood there at the side of the net."

With a limited budget from the cash-strapped TCCB, Micky's attempt to meet Boycott's proposed fee was not so successful, with the Yorkshireman ending up giving his time for nothing. "I offered him a hundred pounds a day, and he said, 'Don't even bother sending it.'"

It was also necessary to devise a strategy for the games. "The West Indies had a formidable attack," Micky says. "Four quicks who bowled their overs at 12 or 13 an hour, with two bouncers every over. They didn't give you many scoring opportunities. The England policy was always to pick two opening bowlers, an all-rounder and two spinners, almost regardless. So we'd face 13 overs an hour, then bowl 18 back at them. We'd struggle to make a total. Then, unless you knocked them over for a low score, they'd get their runs much more quickly, then come straight back at you in the second innings."

It was decided that England would play the series without a spinner, "which didn't go down too well in some quarters", and they would bowl their overs at the same rate as the West Indies. At the start of the tour they tried to negotiate a 15-an-hour agreement with the West Indian manager, Jackie Hendriks, but it was refused. "We can't have that," he said emphatically. There was supposed to be a minimum of 90 overs a day in the series but, with the evening sun low and casting shadows, that was almost never achieved.

England went into the first Test at Sabina Park, Jamaica, as planned, with four pace bowlers: Devon Malcolm, Gladstone Small, Angus Fraser and David Capel. The keeper was Jack Russell, and the six front-line batsmen, preparing to take on the fire of Patterson, Marshall, Bishop and Walsh, comprised two veterans Gooch and Lamb, two with little Test experience Robin Smith and Wayne Larkins, and two debutants Alec Stewart and Nasser Hussain.

The wicket was a true one, and Viv Richards opted to bat first. His openers, Greenidge and Haynes, saw off the new ball and were looking in control with 62 on the board as lunch approached. Then came a moment that in its way defined England's new regime. Greenidge clipped a ball down to fine leg where the outfield was rough and the man on the boundary was Devon Malcolm, comfortably the worst fielder in the England side. The ball bobbled when he attempted to pick it up, and Greenidge turned for a second run.

"The day before the Test," Micky says, "I'd had a 20-minute one-to-one fielding session with Devon – and another shorter one on the morning itself. His catching was hopeless. If I knocked a ball up into the sun, his hands would be like that, shaking."

Gladstone Small remembers the occasion. "Micky was sending up these skiers for him, and Devon wasn't getting anywhere near them."

"For Christ's sake, Devon, what's the problem?"

"The sun's in my eyes."

"Well, get the other side of it then."

"How can I? It's a hundred million miles away."

For all this, Malcolm had a strong arm. The ball from Greenidge bobbled and hit him on the knee, and almost in one movement he grasped it and sent it fizzing into Jack Russell's gloves for a sensational run out.

Better still, the four England bowlers stuck rigidly to plan, sending down over after consistent over on an off-stump line. The result was that the West Indian batsmen, deprived of their accustomed flow of runs, lost

Graham Gooch and Micky – on the seafront during their wet stay in Guyana

patience and took unnecessary risks. By early evening they were all out for 164. Small, Malcolm and Capel accounted for the top order, and Fraser went through the tail with a spell of five wickets for six runs.

Suddenly they had turned the tables on the West Indies, but could the batsmen make the kind of total that would put the match firmly in England's hands? The answer was clear by the close of the second day: England 342 for eight. Larkins 46, Smith 57, and Lamb 132.

"It was a typical Allan Lamb innings," Micky says. "Physical, brave, gutsy. He would never let the bowlers dictate to him. I admired him a lot, the way he played the quicks. He'd worked out this way of playing, always letting the short balls go to the off side of him.

"Smithy was a similar character in many ways, very brave. A great dictator with the bat in his hands. But I used to give him stick. He was too unassuming, too humble. He never stood there with presence. The exact opposite of Viv Richards.

"Wayne Larkins was a fine player, technically outstanding and a magnificent striker of the ball. Goochy was a great admirer of him. Goochy's reasoning was that, if we were going to beat the West Indies, we had to score runs. It was no good batting for three quarters of an hour, scoring six, then falling to one that lifted and took the glove. And, for all his faults, Wayne would always look to play his shots."

By the end of the third day West Indies were eight wickets down in their second innings, only 29 runs ahead, and a famous victory was drawing close.

Then came the rain, all through the rest day, and the field did not recover in time for any play on the fourth day. By seven o'clock on the fifth morning Micky was on the ground, making sure that the staff were hard at work, and finally the game resumed, England winning by nine wickets. Sixteen years and 29 Tests had passed since they had last beaten the West Indies.

The Test in Jamaica was forty years on from the famous series when the West Indians, with 'those two little pals of mine, Ramadhin and Valentine', came to England and won for the first time. By way of celebration, several of the England team of 1950 had been invited to Kingston, including Len Hutton, Alec Bedser and Godfrey Evans. Their presence gave Micky the opportunity to take a couple of his bowlers, Fraser and DeFreitas, for a meal with Alec Bedser.

"The idea," says Angus Fraser, "was for us to pick his brains. The good thing about Micky was that you could have a joke with him, you could take the piss a little bit and he wouldn't take offence – so, after a bit, we said to Bedser, 'What sort of cricketer was Micky, Alec?'"

Bedser looked down at his plate, frowned and rubbed his chin. They sat in silence, expectant. Then eventually the great man spoke: "He was a bloody good short leg."

"It was brilliant to see the way Micky's face dropped. After that, that was always the line we used to take the p--- out of Micky. 'He was a bloody good short leg.'"

It rained and rained in Georgetown, Guyana, where the second Test was abandoned without the bowling of a ball. So they reached Port-of-Spain in Trinidad still one up. Viv Richards was out of action so Desmond Haynes stood in as captain for a match as pulsating as any during Micky's time as England team manager.

West Indies, put in to bat, were 29 for five, then 103 for eight, before recovering to 199 all out. In reply Gooch and Larkins, batting with great watchfulness on a difficult pitch, put on 112 for the first wicket, but the West Indians battled their way back with hostile fast bowling and only a hard-fought 40 from David Capel allowed England to achieve a first innings lead of 89.

All England's fitness work seemed to be paying off on the fourth day. Greenidge and Haynes cleared the deficit, but the England bowlers stuck to their task and none was more impressive than Devon Malcolm, bowling with pace and fire, who got through 24 overs in the day. In all he took ten wickets in the match, and England were left almost the entire final day to score 151 to take a 2-0 lead in the series, with only two Tests to go. The new-look England was rapidly coming of age.

Alas, their luck ran out. Gooch had a bone in his left hand broken by a nasty lifting delivery from Ezra Moseley that reared up off a crack in the pitch. Then at lunch, when the score was 73 for one, a local thunderstorm flooded the field. "We'd got the game on toast to win it," Micky says. "It was very frustrating."

Eventually the match was resumed. Officially there were 30 overs to be bowled, 30 overs in which to score 78 runs, but there was little prospect of that much play, especially when Desmond Haynes slowed down the over rate further than ever. "I was seething a bit inside," Micky says. "I knew it would happen, but I was willing the umpires to step in."

Gooch had his fracture confirmed by X-ray, but the decision was taken not to tell anybody, not the West Indians and certainly not the press. The psychology of the game required their opponents to believe that it was only a bruise and that he was padding up, ready to return to battle.

"It's good news," Micky told the reporters. "He'll be going back out."

Unfortunately Gooch had a close relationship with David Norrie of the *News of the World*, who heard the truth ahead of the others, and that caused ill will, most of it directed once more at Micky who had "lied" to them all.

"Yes," he said afterwards, "and, if it happened again, I'd do the same thing. I wouldn't do anything to give the West Indians any advantage."

Only 17 of the 30 remaining overs were bowled. England reached 120 for five. Then it became too dark to continue.

It was the day on which the whole tour turned. Gooch, leading batsman and captain, was unable to play again, the tour party sustained further injuries, most crucially Angus Fraser, and in the final two Tests West Indies regained their old mastery, winning the series 2-1.

Yet, for all the disappointment, there was a feeling in the England camp that things were moving forward once more. 'At worst,' Alan Lee wrote in *Wisden*, 'England merited a shared series, and at best an unimaginable upset of the world champions of Test cricket.' Gooch, he thought, 'was in his own way the most impressive England captain since Brearley.'

*

Graham Gooch was England captain throughout the remaining two winters and three summers of Micky's time as team manager. The results were a mixed bag: won 8, lost 7 and drawn 10. A 3-0 defeat in Australia was the lowest point, a 2-2 draw with West Indies in England among the highs. There was acute disappointment when England, for the second time under Micky, reached the final of the World Cup, only to lose in Melbourne to Imran Khan's unpredictable Pakistanis. And in Micky's last summer, 1992, there was another difficulty with Pakistan, captained now by Javed Miandad, when allegations of ball tampering flared up in the Lord's Test.

Gooch was the driving force of England's recovery, leading from the front with batting of the highest quality. In the summer of 1990, in six Tests against India and New Zealand, he scored an unprecedented 1,058 runs including an innings of 333 against India at Lord's. Then in 1991, in the first Test against the West Indies at Headingley, he carried his bat in the second innings for a match-winning 154. "It was a bowler-friendly pitch," Micky says, "and he played magnificently. The whole way he went about the innings was superb, and it was so important. In my time in cricket I wouldn't rate any innings above it."

Gooch was in his late thirties, a batsman with a modest Test average of 37 at the start of 1990. Yet in those two and a half years, by sheer hard work and strength of character, he scored 2,721 runs at an average of almost 65. In so doing, he was an inspiration to the young men batting at the other end, notably Alec Stewart and Mike Atherton.

It can be argued that the 1990 tour of the Caribbean was the start of the modern age for England cricket. It was the first tour covered by *Sky* television, bringing into the game unprecedented sums of money, and it saw the start of a new approach to preparation and team work.

"We laid the foundations for what you see in the England set-up now," Gooch says. "The fitness, the monitoring of fitness, the nutrition, it was the birth of all that on a team scale. Before then, individuals had sorted themselves out."

Yet the Gooch/Stewart approach was not to everybody's taste, and in Australia in 1990/91 they were unable to generate the same unity of purpose that had been present in the Caribbean the previous winter.

It did not help that Gooch broke a finger early on the tour and had to watch from the side while the first Test at Brisbane was lost by ten wickets. It did not help that the Australians, still under Allan Border, had become a tougher, more confident team than they had been four years earlier. And it did not help that the tour party now included two men who were reluctant to go with the flow of the new regime: the newcomer Phil Tufnell and the returning David Gower.

"Goochy was all or nothing," is Mike Gatting's view. "There were no grey areas. That would have been fine with the younger ones, but I don't suppose he was good at sitting down with David, coming to an agreement with him."

"I talked to David," Micky says. "I said to him that so many of the younger players looked up to him as an outstanding cricketer and with his image. The more he could contribute to those players, by setting an example, was invaluable, but he didn't quite see it that way. He was right to an extent. It is down to the individual, but there comes a time, especially if things aren't going quite right, when everybody's working hard, if there's one of the top players not joining in wholeheartedly, it affects the rest of the side. In that situation I felt he could have influenced them for the good."

Gower was the most successful English batsman in the first three Tests, scoring 353 runs in six innings, but the faultline between him and the tour management became public in the fortnight between the third and fourth Tests. England failed to reach the three-match final of a one-day tournament involving Australia and New Zealand and, in the unexpected gap in the playing schedule, the tour management opted to set up a four-day game against New South Wales. Gower was, in fact, given a break, but it did not stop him from expressing his hostility to the decision in an autobiography he wrote a year later with his friend Martin Johnson:

> *The Stewart–Gooch argument was that you must keep practising in order to get better, but if you keep hammering away at it you are actually driving people into the ground and making things worse. Jankers games rarely do anyone any good because the whole psychology of the match is wrong. I felt at the time that we would have been far better served as a unit to say, 'We've lost this one-day thing, and we have not been playing very well. However, we are still in with a chance of levelling the Test series, go away and do what you want to do for the next four days.'*

The next match at Carrara, against Queensland, brought matters to a head. On the third day, having been dismissed for 13, Gower opted to leave the ground without permission, taking with him the young Derbyshire batsman John Morris, who had just made his only century of the tour. Seeking to inject a lighter note into proceedings, Gower acquired the use of a Tiger Moth aircraft, in which the two of them flew low over the ground, waving mischievously. It created a tremendous storm, and at the disciplinary hearing Gower was stunned by a fine of one thousand pounds.

Micky was most upset, more than anything because the escapade took all the attention away from a batting performance by Robin Smith. "Robin had been out of nick, and he got a hundred. Everybody likes reading about themselves, it's a real confidence booster and Robin's a confidence player. But everything in the newspapers was about the aeroplane and nothing about Smithy's hundred. That really annoyed me."

Phil Tufnell was another who did not fit into the Gooch/Stewart team ethos. Gooch was instinctively uneasy about the young spinner's irreverent antics, finding them deeply disrespectful. Micky, however, came to realise that he had misunderstood Tufnell's reluctance to conform. "I always made a point of finding out as much as I could about a player's background. I did the same whenever I employed people at Slazenger. But for some reason I slipped up with Phil Tufnell. I was saying to him things like 'Look, son, I've known plenty like you when I was carrying the goalposts on Blackheath,' and it turned out his father was a silversmith and he'd been to public school. If I'd known all that, I might have handled him differently. Not that I'd have been any less hard on him!"

At some point Doug Insole, chairman of the international committee of the Test and County Cricket Board, arrived, and it did not take him long to observe to Micky what a difference there was in atmosphere from the tour of the Caribbean – and with so few changes in personnel.

The fourth Test was drawn, the fifth lost, and England's poor winter ended in New Zealand where they lost a one-day series 2-1. Gooch, Atherton, Lamb and Smith all played important innings but David Gower, after his plane ride in Carrara, made a series of low scores.

Had the Gooch/Stewart regime taken things too far, destroying the enthusiasm of the team's most naturally talented player? Had it, in the words of Ian Botham, become too 'regimented, inflexible, robotic'? Or was it a case of changing the old habits that had seen England fail to keep pace with developments in other countries?

"It was a time of change," Graham Gooch says, "and for some people the change was unpalatable. You still had a bit of the attitude of 'I play cricket to get fit.' And that's important. You do need to get the right amount of cricket. But I've never seen a cricketer become a worse player by being fitter and stronger."

"Micky and Graham sang from the same sheet," Angus Fraser says. "The professionalism, the fitness, they were things that moulded my career a lot. David had been successful doing things his own way, but Micky and Graham felt this sense of responsibility because they were dealing with a young group of players. You had players with five-year bans for South Africa so Micky knew that what he had in front of him was the team he had to build things around. He had to get us playing the game in the right way. The modern way.

"Obviously David was more laid back and could fall back on the fact that he was so naturally gifted. So he didn't have to work as hard at his game as many of us. And that did test Micky. It certainly tested Graham. I always chuckle when I remember that Botham said we lost the World Cup Final in 1992 because we'd done too much training and were knackered. He failed to mention that one of the reasons we may have made the final in the first place was because we were so fit."

"I enjoyed playing under Micky," Mike Atherton says unequivocally. "I bought into the fitness and the greater professionalisation that he was trying to bring to the England team. You'd be stupid not to at 21. And I enjoyed him as a person. I felt I could talk to him. I thought he was a good bloke to have in charge."

*

Back in 1989 Ian Botham, already struggling with his back, had driven to a crucial Test match at Old Trafford from Hove, where he had bowled 40 overs on Monday and 25 on Tuesday. And he was expected to be at his best again on Thursday morning. Micky told him not to net, only to be grilled by the press afterwards: "Why wasn't Botham practising like the rest of them?"

So for the summer of 1991 Micky pressed through a change in the county championship schedule, enabling the England team to have two days together before each Test.

"That extra day was a great help," Derek Pringle says. "You had time to get your mind off county cricket, and you had longer to bond with the people you were playing with. Before then, we used just to turn up on Wednesday afternoon, have a net, then we'd have a three-course meal where we'd stuff ourselves, have lots of wine, then play the next day."

That summer, when they drew against the West Indies, there were two new faces in the England side: the young Middlesex batsman Mark Ramprakash and the long-awaited Graeme Hick, the Zimbabwean who had finally completed his period of residential qualification. Both in time would pass 100 first-class hundreds, the outstanding run-scorers of their generation, yet neither would fulfil their potential in Test match cricket.

"I'm sure I could have done more for Graeme," Micky says. "Technically, against the best bowlers, he got caught on the crease too much; he got done for pace. Years earlier I remember Robin Jackman, when he was coaching in Zimbabwe, telling me, 'I've just seen the best kid I've ever seen at twelve.' And he came to Worcester, got stacks of runs and became the Big White Hope, with all the publicity and expectation. With his personality, quiet and unassuming, he'd struggle to cope with that. Then he got an agent who, I was told, was arranging for him to go on the *Terry Wogan Show*. It was the last thing he wanted. It was bad enough for him with all the newspaper publicity. It was unfortunate that his debut was against the West Indies because, after all the fuss, they targeted him. And for the first time in his life he experienced failure. He had to play himself out of adversity, and he'd never done that before. It was very difficult."

Ramprakash was a different case. "He was a fine player, but he was very uptight. He wanted so much to achieve his ambition, and that didn't help him in his career with England. On his second day in the England side, at Headingley, he took an outstanding one-handed catch at cover, and he pulled off a fine run-out, too. The press wanted him to be at the end-of-day conference, and I said no. They moaned about it, but I said, 'It's too early for a lad making his debut.' At the end of the series, when he and Alec Stewart knocked off 60-odd to win at the Oval, he displayed his real ability."

In nine innings that summer, against the testing pace of Marshall, Ambrose, Patterson and Walsh, Ramprakash batted with patience and great determination. All nine times he got into double figures, seven times he reached 20, but he never got to 30. Then, against the friendlier bowlers from Sri Lanka, he was out for a duck. In New Zealand, battling to hold on to his Test place, he failed to make an impression in the warm-up matches. In his last chance at Nelson he was bowled for a duck, and his frustration boiled over.

"The dressing room was divided into three," Micky recalls. "Goochy and I were sitting down, discussing the next Test, and, when Ramps got out, we heard the clatter of studs coming into the next section. Then silence. Then suddenly crash, bang, wallop, whoosh. It was like World War Three had broken out."

The noise went on and on, testing Micky's tolerance.

"I'm going in," Micky said eventually. "I'm not having that."

"No, don't go in there yet," Gooch advised.

Later on the tour Micky's long-standing difficulties with the press flared up once more. In the third Test at Wellington the heavily built Gloucestershire fast bowler 'Syd' Lawrence, running in to bowl, collapsed in agony, letting out an almighty scream. His left kneecap had cracked in half, horrifically. "I've never seen someone in such excruciating pain," Micky says.

Micky ran out to the middle with Lawrie Brown, and they carried him off. As they tried to minister to him, a television cameraman pushed into their midst, ignoring repeated requests not to come so close. It became too much for Micky and, along with Lawrence's close friend Jack Russell, he shoved the cameraman away. "Actually," he says, "it was Jack who gave the biggest shove."

An ambulance arrived, and Micky demanded that a path be cleared, with no cameras filming the departure. "The police tried to clear a path, but the New Zealand television crew had a girl producer and she started to argue. 'I'm just doing my job,' she said. 'I've just told you,' I said. 'Get out of the way.' The English press wrote it up that I'd bullied her. There was talk of my being charged with obstruction."

The argument between Micky and the journalists continued. "Somebody in the press conference said that it was the same as the IRA bombing of the Brighton hotel, when they took pictures of Mrs Tebbit being brought out."

It was a moment which for Micky crystallised his dislike of the invasiveness of much of the media. "So what would you do if your son wanted to be a journalist?" a reporter had asked him once, and back came the reply: "I'd sling him out of the house."

Later, when emotions quietened down, Micky issued a statement: 'The way I conducted myself was to ensure that the people close to Syd, his family and friends, were not greeted on their televisions by pictures of his suffering. Whatever I did was from a human point of view. As a last resort I believed it necessary to push the camera away.'

There was little sympathy from the press corps, with Alan Lee writing that Micky had been overcome by 'emotional mists', had 'struggled to compose himself' and had 'helped create an over-blown scandal where there should have been only sadness.'

It was heartfelt stuff from Micky, but maybe his years as England team manager would have received a better press if, as the ECB do now, the TCCB had employed a press relations officer.

Eventually, in the face of legal threats from the New Zealand television company, the tour manager Bob Bennett issued a statement regretting the events surrounding the injury: 'I am sure that in the cold light of day many of those involved would have acted with much greater restraint. The situation was extremely emotional.'

It is doubtful, even twenty years on, whether Micky does regret his stand against such insensitive intrusion into the agony of one of his players.

*

Alec Stewart established his place in the England side during Micky's last three years as team manager. "The Gooch/Dad relationship was perfect for me," he says. "Work hard, train hard, then play. That was second nature to me. I played eight winters of Australian grade cricket, and it was just like that there."

His early matches for England suggested promise without producing any stand-out scores, but in Australia in 1990/91 he hit 79 and 91 in successive Tests. Then came a decision, taken in part by Micky, that would alter the course of his Test career. Needing to win the final two Tests to level the series, England decided to play not four but five bowlers – so, with no all-rounder in the side, they dropped Jack Russell, probably the best wicket-keeper in the world, and gave the gloves to Alec.

The peculiar aspect of this was that Alec had never been a regular wicket-keeper in first-class cricket. While growing up, for no reason that he can recall, his cricketing hero had been the Kent and England wicket-keeper Alan Knott: "I must have got his autograph more times than any other boy." Yet Alec, though he often kept in school and club cricket and for Surrey second eleven, was never more than the occasional behind the stumps for the first team. However, Micky encouraged him to work at it, realising that in the modern game such a second string might do him no harm.

It is one of cricket's curiosities. Alec played for Surrey for 23 years, keeping for them in just 81 first-class matches, one fewer than the number of times he kept wicket for England.

The change of strategy in Australia was not a success, with the five bowlers no more effective than the four had been. Also, whether as a consequence or not, Alec had two poor games with the bat, hitting only 29 runs in four innings.

The following summer, against the West Indies, he made way for Hick and Ramprakash, returning for the final Test at the Oval when once again he replaced Jack Russell, this time scoring important runs in a famous victory. "He caught Richards off Tufnell," Micky remembers. "A difficult catch, standing up." Then in the next five Tests, freed of the gloves and promoted to open the innings, he came of age as a batsman, scoring four centuries.

He was no longer 'Micky Stewart's son'. Indeed, Micky was fast becoming 'Alec Stewart's father', as he is for most people now.

Man of the Match, The Oval, May 1992
"That was the first time I agreed to be photographed with Alec," Micky says.

By choice Alec would rather have played for England as a specialist batsman, preferably opening the innings, but he was too loyal a professional to say no when pressed into wicket-keeping duty. "He always blames me for making him keep wicket," Micky says.

We shall never know if it was the right decision. Alec played 133 Tests, more than any other England cricketer, remaining a regular in the team beyond his 40th birthday. As he admits himself, "I might not have played that many if I had not kept wicket." Yet the statistics of his career – a batting average of 34.9 when keeping wicket, one of 46.7 when not – suggest that he could, perhaps should, have been the outstanding England batsman of his generation. He remains, with the Indian Sunil Gavaskar, one of only two opening batsmen to score a century in each innings of a Test in the Caribbean.

Between the retirement of Ian Botham and the emergence of Andrew Flintoff, England lacked a genuine all-rounder, and it fell to Alec as wicket-keeper-batsman to fill that role. In so doing, it almost certainly diminished his contribution as a batsman. As he puts it, "England weakened a strength in trying to strengthen a weakness."

Micky was no longer manager when Alec became the settled first choice as keeper. "At the time," Micky says, "my view was that we didn't have many strengths in the side, but one was the opening partnership of Mike

Atherton and Alec, the way they complemented each other. It was a great pity to lose that."

Yet, for all that, Alec Stewart was an outstanding Test cricketer: a stylish and aggressive batsman, with a great gift of timing, a wicket-keeper whose mistakes were rare, and a positive character with an unflinching loyalty to the cause. For a year in the late 1990s he was England captain.

"The biggest influence on my career from start to finish," he says, "was my dad: the way he brought me up and, as a coach, the way he was my second pair of eyes. Even after he finished with England, I always went back to him for help. I was very lucky."

Alec articulates the values Micky drilled into him: "Be the best you can. If you're going to do something, do it properly or don't bother. Have good manners. Be honest and straight. If you're a liar, you've got to have a good memory – so deal in facts."

It is almost the same advice which Micky received from his own father, and there is a further echo when Alec says, "He's my best mate as well. Even now."

*

Micky's last day as team manager was Monday 24 August 1992 at Old Trafford when England beat Pakistan by six wickets in the final Texaco Trophy match of the summer. It was a trophy that England had won six times out of seven during his years in charge.

The newspapers all ran farewell tributes to Micky, with Martin Johnson in the *Independent* as acerbic as ever:

> *Stewart has certainly not found it easy to adapt his own simplistic outlook on harnessing talent – hard work, clean living, and what he himself would describe as 'giving it 120 per cent' – to individuals. If he had got hold of Beethoven at an early age, some might say, Ludwig would have become so bored with Stewart making him practise his scales, that he would have packed it in and taken up the tuba instead.*

The most perceptive piece, reflecting on Micky's family background, came from Simon Barnes in *The Times*:

> *Stewart himself, often spikey and adversarial when dealing with 'the press' – we are all tarred with the same brush – is a different man if you ever catch him relaxed. I managed this once, when we had a couple of beers in Delhi. He told me that his father had been a professional gambler and told the story vividly. I was much struck by the apparent incongruity. Later I realised that this was not incongruous at all. The term 'professional gambler' seems to imply a splendidly dashing character, one who lives by the sword, a man*

prepared to run great risks, a man for whom life is a great adventure. A professional gambler, one feels, is a man with immense panache.

But this is nonsense. Panache is a matter for a gilded aristocrat with a fortune to burn. A professional gambler must be single-minded; he must, above all, be professional.

The word is important to Stewart, as it is important to Gooch and virtually all the England cricketers who play under them. England cricketers have been professional, in the sense that they have been paid to do the job, for a long time. But professionalism as a creed has only been part of the England set-up in recent years.

One might define professionalism as achieving everything possible, within your limitations. Stewart was talking on Saturday about making your thirtieth over of the day as accurate as the second: of never getting out because you are tired. An intense emphasis on physical fitness, part of the West Indies set-up for the last decade, has always been Stewart's way, and Gooch's. Professionalism, in short. How else did Gooch manage a triple-century when in his late thirties?

... Cricket, like everything else, has changed since the war. It is just that cricket has been slower to realise this than most other concerns. Stewart has not changed the face of cricket, but he has forced the England team to come to terms with the fact that the face of cricket has changed forever.

*

Doug Insole sounded out Micky about staying in post for a further 18 months, but he declined to do so, thus becoming the only England manager up to now to have left at his own time of choosing.

His successor, from Graham Gooch's county Essex, was Keith Fletcher, who made an inauspicious start: losing all four Tests in India and Sri Lanka, then losing 4-1 at home to Australia and 3-1 away to the West Indies. At this point Ray Illingworth succeeded Ted Dexter as chairman of selectors, and he soon assumed powers that rendered Keith Fletcher redundant. Yet results did not greatly improve, and Illingworth gave way to Lancashire's David Lloyd, who himself was replaced by the Zimbabwean Duncan Fletcher during the summer of 1999.

Each manager had his own style, appealing in different ways to the individuals in the side. Angus Fraser played under four England managers and is well placed to compare them:

I liked Keith Fletcher. He had a great cricket brain on him, but he wasn't a great manager of people. I didn't feel as relaxed and as comfortable in his company as I did in Micky's.

I struggled with Illy, full stop. I had a couple of run-ins with him.

I enjoyed 'Bumble' Lloyd, but he was bloody mad. He was the opposite of Micky, who was always very calm and level. With Bumble, it was an emotional roller-coaster ride because he just couldn't contain himself. His frustrations kept coming out.

Without doubt Micky was my favourite England manager, and it wasn't just because he was my first. I am very, very fond of him. He was always communicating, making sure everything was alright, working on your game with you. He took a real interest in you. It was his job to get the best out of you, and he did it very well. Also, he handled all the players the same. He didn't have any favourites, even with Alec. Neither of them took advantage of the situation. It was very professional.

At the end of Micky's reign Robin Smith was one of the top half dozen batsmen in the world, with a Test average over 50, an even more impressive figure when one considers that he had played over half of his 36 Tests against Australia and the West Indies. Yet he never achieved these heights in the years that followed, losing his England place during Ray Illingworth's time at the helm:

Once you get near to Test cricket level, it's not so much about discovering new things but harnessing the skills you already have. Micky taught me to play within my limitations, not to try and play every shot I knew. So we worked on the four shots I had that were most productive and concentrating on using them in your first forty runs. Then you could get a few of the more rarely-used shots out of the locker if you wanted to.

Not only did he help with my technique, he helped me with my confidence. I've never really been someone with an abundance of confidence. What you see is certainly not what lies beneath. Micky was fantastic with me, and that continued with me throughout his time as England coach.

Look, everyone knows how to play a square cut if they're good enough to play for England, so that wasn't what Micky did. He made us understand more about the game, about what you can and can't do in various conditions, the reasons why spin bowlers go over or round the wicket, what to look out for if you are batting against Ian Bishop on a fast Antigua wicket.

He was like a father to me. That's not to say he didn't come down hard on me, he's a tough man from the old school. But he seemed to know and understand more about the psychological areas of different people. And we shouldn't forget Sheila in all of this. She was like a second mother to me. She would come up and put her arm around me if Micky gave me a hard time and say, "Actually, he thinks you're doing really well."

Micky cared. And he rated me. He made me believe I was good enough to succeed at international cricket.

Micky was 'a tough man from the old school' but, in the words of one England tour manager, 'he had a young heart'. He was not one who was always testing the players mentally, to see who was strong enough. That was more the style of Raymond Illingworth, a no-nonsense northerner who had no time for the gentler side of man-management, as Robin Smith discovered:

If you want my honest opinion, the coaches who came after Micky just didn't grasp who Robin Smith was. They didn't understand that I had very little self-esteem. For example, with Ray Illingworth in South Africa before the first Test, I was reduced to tears because of the way they handled me in the nets. Now Micky would never, ever have said the things that were said because he knew deep down how sensitive and quiet I was. Discipline is one thing, but the sharp, cynical comments of that time just tore me apart. I was never the same player again.

Mike Atherton has a different viewpoint:

I've never been someone who looks at a coach and gives them too much credit or too much blame. I've always thought that as a professional cricketer you sort yourself out. You don't blame others.

However, I do remember I was struggling at the beginning of the 1990/91 tour, and Micky was very good talking about the extra bounce of the Australian pitches and how you should counter that. It was talk, rather than him telling me to move my hands on the bat or move my feet or whatever.

Gladstone Small:

There wasn't a lot of coaching; it wasn't as scientific as it is now. You were left to your own devices so long as you stayed in shape. Micky did a lot of talking individually, not so much technical stuff but he could make you see and think about the game more than I had done. During the game he would say to you, 'What should be happening now?', and in the nets he would get you focused and have little games to help you when you bowled.

And Graham Gooch:

Micky was an anchor for England: a stable character with lots of experience, excellent ideas and good man-management. The word 'manager' would be right. He dealt with everything that's needed to run an international cricket team.

I immensely enjoyed my time working with him. He guided me, helped me, encouraged me to move forward, even though I was in my mid-thirties. They were my best years. I was near the end of my career, and the sun shone for me. I've so much to thank Micky for. He's been a great friend to me.

The most common thread in their memories of Micky is the side of him that the press rarely saw, the side of him that did not come out enough in his fraught relationship with David Gower: his sense of fun.

John Emburey:

Micky was someone who could quickly work people out. Then once he got to know them, he'd have a laugh and a joke. He could be very, very amusing and he was good fun to be with. Very open, very honest. Wasn't frightened to say things to people when they needed to be said, and he was very trusting.

Robin Smith:

Micky has a great sense of humour. Even now I remember him giggling madly, uncontrollably, and it was just so nice to see our coach having a lot of fun on the field in practice and in the dressing room afterwards. He was a great guy. Someone I'd do anything for.

Mike Atherton:

Micky was a good bloke. Trustworthy and loyal to those around him. And fun, too, around the dressing room. After a couple of glasses of wine he was good value. I should imagine that he would have been a good team-mate in his day. He was certainly a well-respected coach, somebody I enjoyed playing under.

And lastly Phil DeFreitas, constantly in and out of the England side, yet the only man who played in every one of the Test series during Micky's time as manager:

Micky was fun, always taking the mickey out of me. Loveable, friendly. He cared. He did care about what happened to me. That's how I see him. He cared about me and my family. Also Sheila, she was always asking after me, so I suppose Micky must have talked to her about me when they were at home. Sheila used to tell me off when I did things wrong off the pitch. They were both like parents to me.

*Micky's last innings –
with Graham Gooch,
Portugal, September 1992*

*"Goochy wanted to say that
he'd opened the batting
with both father and son."*

Micky's first duty after stepping down was to sit in on the selection of the 16-man party for the winter tour of India and Sri Lanka. The outcome was a further rumpus in the world of English cricket.

The bans imposed on the South African rebels had expired, and as a consequence Mike Gatting and John Emburey, among others, were available once more. During his ban Gatting had been the stand-out English batsman in county cricket, and there was agreement that he should be returned to the side. Seven batsmen were required in all, and Gooch, Atherton, Stewart, Smith and Hick were certainties. So that left only one place and three strong candidates: Neil Fairbrother who was enjoying great success in the one-day side, Mark Ramprakash who had been a disappointment in the recent Tests, and David Gower who after the difficulties in Australia had been discarded but who had now won back his place, averaging 50 in the final three Tests of the summer.

Ramprakash was the first to be eliminated. Then it came down to a choice between Fairbrother and Gower, and the selectors plumped for Fairbrother. The crucial factor was age, Keith Fletcher told the press. All three of Gooch, Gatting and Gower were now 35 and over, and three was too many. English cricket needed to be looking forward.

To many observers it looked bad. There was David Gower, the most charming of men, the highest run-scorer in English Test history, a gifted and elegant batsman who warmed the hearts of spectators whenever he made runs. He had never turned his back on England as Gooch, Gatting, Emburey and others had done. Now they were all back in the fold and he, a misfit in 'the grim Roundhead culture', had once more been thrown aside.

Such was the strength of feeling that MCC members requisitioned a special meeting to call for a vote of no confidence in the England selectors. Their anger about the treatment of Gower was compounded by the non-selection of Jack Russell, the specialist keeper, and Ian Salisbury, the promising leg-spinner. It seemed to these MCC rebels that too much of the traditional charm of English cricket was being destroyed.

It did not help that, in the days before the selection committee met, an autobiography by Gower appeared on the book stalls two weeks ahead of schedule. Written with Martin Johnson during Gower's year in the wilderness, when his Test career seemed to be over, the book had a somewhat angry tone when describing the problems of Gower's ill-fated Australian tour under the captaincy of Graham Gooch.

In particular, Gower tore into Micky and his style of management: 'I like to treat people as individuals,' he wrote, 'while Micky would prefer a team of Subbuteo players all programmed to do things by numbers.' He wrote of the team manager's 'limitations at bringing the best out of individuals', giving as an example Micky's handling on the Australian tour of Robin Smith.

There was undoubtedly a faultline, created by the changes Micky had made in the England team set-up. The outcome, the jettisoning of Gower, was sad for everybody involved and for English cricket. Some thought that Gooch and Micky were too like-minded to be a good combination. 'I feel,' Mike Brearley wrote, 'that Gooch needs a close adviser whose attitude complements rather than coincides with his own earnest and occasionally morose style.'

For Micky there was the additional difficulty that, amid the selectorial controversies, there was at the time a public perception, wholly false, that his son Alec was getting preferential treatment. Various letters to this effect were sent to Micky, as this one from a Yorkshireman when Alec was recalled for the Oval Test of 1991:

> *Dear Sir*
>
> *I was at Old Trafford last Sunday, a full house, and the England squad was announced over the P.A. system. It may interest you to know that, apart from the general astonishment at the absence of David Gower, there was a chorus of boos when your son's name was included.*
>
> *It appears that if one scores 3 centuries in 6 Tests and also manages to be top scorer in 5 innings then this is not as good as scoring 29 runs in 4 innings. One can only come to the conclusion that nepotism is rife in the selection committee. There are also grounds for believing that Messrs Dexter, Titmus and yourself are jealous of Gower's talent and gentlemanly conduct at all times.*
>
> *Allowing for your undoubted loyalty to your family and the many years service you gave to Surrey (but not England) I still cannot believe that favouritism should play a part in selecting the England team. Please announce your retirement, along with Messrs Dexter and Titmus, and hand over to Raymond Illingworth or Brian Close who both have proved themselves in the big arena.*
>
> *In closing I feel sorry for your son Alec as he has had nothing to do with his selection. It is a shame that he is being placed in a position beyond his competence.*

*

There lingered in the background of all this the whiff of the old Gentleman-Player divide, an issue that flared up again in 1993 when Graham Gooch, broken by repeated losses to Australia, resigned the England captaincy. Who would succeed him: Alec Stewart, the current vice-captain, or Mike Atherton?

Simon Heffer, a political journalist writing in the *Sunday Telegraph*, was quick to spot a wider significance in the choice:

> *The current edition of the 'Cricketer's Who's Who' gives a clear picture of the two men that cricket correspondents have decided are fighting for the privilege of captaining England.*
>
> *Alec James Stewart (nickname: Stewie) is the captain of Surrey. He is 30 years old. He was educated at Tiffin Boys' School, where he passed four O-levels. He likes "most other sports" and is a Chelsea supporter. His principal relaxation is "eating out". Before the season started, when he filled in his 'Who's Who' questionnaire, he was particularly "looking forward" to playing in coloured clothing on Sundays.*
>
> *Michael Andrew Atherton is 25. He was educated at Manchester Grammar School and Downing College, Cambridge. He has 10 O-levels, three A-levels and a BA (Hons) Cantab after his name. He likes golf and squash, and his principal relaxation is reading "decent novels (Heller, Kundera, etc)". This last indulgence would be lost on most of his team-mates, the majority of whom would imagine Kundera was the chap who owned the Tandoori in the Harleyford Road.*
>
> *In case you were not aware of it, the succession to the England captaincy is becoming a class issue.*
>
> *... The real case against Stewie, as one long-serving cricket correspondent put it to me, is that he is "an oik". ... In their Athers-for-Captain campaign the old school are motivated by their belief in cricket as a civilising force. They look at society and see where oikishness has led.*

Sheila was furious, so furious that Micky conveyed her feelings to Heffer, who replied to her in a hand-written letter. He defended his article on the grounds that he was only reporting the views of others and that cricket had 'acquired a political dimension' and could no longer be confined to the sports pages.

> *The game has changed so much and become so commercial that the greater attention it attracts has become inevitable. Like Micky, I like to think it is the game it was; but I am afraid it is not.*

Sheila's reply was short and to the point:

> *I have noted your comments, but you will understand that I still feel very hurt that you could repeat a description of my son as "a cad, an ignorant, inferior person" – the dictionary's definition of "an oik".*
>
> *I do feel it is not cricket that has changed so much, but the way it is reported, and the people writing those reports.*

17

STILL LOOKING AHEAD

In the autumn of 1992 Micky moved from the role of England team manager to that of National Director of Coaching and Excellence, working within the National Cricket Association which was responsible for all cricket below the first-class game. His brief was to implement some of the changes he had recommended in his 1988 paper on the structure of cricket in England.

Tony Lewis, the former England captain, welcomed the appointment, writing in the *Sunday Telegraph*:

> *He will do more for England cricket within a month of his new job with young cricketers than he was able to achieve with the older ones. ... When the Board decided they had to do something about England's poor record in international cricket, they began at the wrong end, at the top not at the bottom.*

"I don't agree with that," Micky says. "That would have taken too long. We had to do something straightaway at the top, and there was enough talent in the England team to do that. That was the shop window of the game. If you can get that into a healthier state, it gets easier to sort out the grass roots because a successful England side will inspire youngsters to play."

In his first year Micky travelled around the country, observing coaching schemes, age-group representative sides, minor county cricket and much more, and he wrote regular reports on his activities. Always he was impressed by the dedication of so many volunteers and by the number of people playing cricket, as he stated in a report at the end of his first year:

> *Thanks to the thousands of individuals who work so hard for the game of cricket ..., the amount of participation in the game is immense, from the introduction to the veteran stages. Excluding India there is possibly more cricket played in the UK than the whole of the major cricket playing countries in the world put together. Arguably there may be more cricket activity in Yorkshire than in all of Australia.*

He was less impressed by the overall standard, compared with other countries, and his principal explanation for this lay in the lack of an appropriate organisational structure:

> *At present it is written down that we have <u>TWO</u> games of cricket in the UK – the "First Class" game and the "Recreational" game. The TCCB is responsible for the former and the NCA for the latter.*

That appears to be straightforward but it isn't. It is a mass of fragmentation that includes a clash of interests and activities of the main organising bodies. At present these arms of control of the different areas of cricket activity, instead of resembling something like the tentacles of an octopus, all leading into and being controlled by one body, are more akin to a plate of spaghetti with none of the strands attached to one another.

I believe that we need to reform our STRUCTURE so that we have ONE game that is controlled by ONE national body through a COUNTY BASED STRUCTURE that deals with all levels of the game. The areas of control and the lines of communication, all leading to the centre, must be clear and concise.

"In our small country," he says, "there were hundreds and hundreds of cricket clubs, thousands and thousands of players, with no emphasis on the quality of the cricket played. The best players were spread out in so many clubs, in direct contrast to what went on in Australia where it all revolved around relatively few clubs in their grade and district system.

"It annoys me when people say, 'I play cricket but only …'. The cricket people play on Saturdays and the cricket that's played in a Test match, it's all the same game. You don't have Australians saying, 'I only play Fourth Grade.'

"It's part of being English, part of our character. You take the average golfer in South Africa or Australia. Their outlook is far different from the English golfer. It's all about competition. In England so many people just go out for a round of golf: 18 holes of walking, sunny day, nice conversation. A lot of club cricket was like that, and it was lovely. But in the world today you don't create a strong national side if the game doesn't have a harder edge than that."

For Micky the challenge was to maintain the traditional qualities of English club cricket while injecting a greater competitiveness for those young players capable of progressing to the highest levels of the game. The challenge was also to sustain a healthy county game without allowing the narrow self-interest of those counties to get in the way of what was needed to create a strong England team.

Micky's first step was to place greater emphasis on the England youth sides, where results had historically been very poor. The England Under-19s, for instance, played 51 matches between 1970 and 1992 and won only six of them. The profile of these games was much lower than in other countries, and many counties were not happy to release their young players, even from second-eleven games.

*Working with England Under-19s: Micky with a young Andrew Flintoff
– emphasising the importance of presenting the full width of the bat*

Micky, however, insisted on the priority not only of the matches but of the preparation sessions for them. As a result the England Under-19s, featuring Michael Vaughan and Marcus Trescothick, beat the West Indians in a full-length game for the first time since 1978.

Micky also encouraged counties to deal with the decline of cricket in schools. Playing fields had been sold off, teachers were less inclined to undertake out-of-hours activities, and a national curriculum, emphasising academic subjects, had been introduced. The situation was at its worst in inner-city areas, and he argued for counties to follow the example of Surrey where his former team-mate Mike Edwards was undertaking pioneering work.

Edwards, an old boy of Alleyn's, was something of a radical politically, an early activist in the Professional Cricketers' Association. It was an organisation which, Micky recalls, did not meet with everybody's approval in the strike-ridden 1970s. "Alec and Eric Bedser were totally against the unions. They used to call Mike 'The Surrey Communist'."

Edwards, with a Cambridge degree, went to teach at Tulse Hill Comprehensive in Brixton. "His ambition was to develop pupils for Oxbridge, and he was very successful. He became Second Master there. But I bet him he wouldn't stay in the state sector. 'You'll finish up in one of the top public schools,' I used to tell him."

After many years of such jibes Micky's telephone rang. "With all the stick you're going to give me, boss," came the voice down the line, "I thought you should be the first to know. I'm going to Tonbridge."

In fact, he did not go. He became Surrey's development officer, introducing cricket to thousands of children in state schools. For Micky, his work was a shining example of the way a county club, rather than just looking after its own short-term interests, could be the driving force for the promotion of cricket throughout its geographical area.

The National Coaching Scheme, placing the emphasis on increasing participation, had encouraged armies of enthusiastic volunteers to go into clubs and schools. Micky wanted to supplement this with a greater focus on the coaches who worked with the most talented young players. Within six months of his appointment he had summoned the top 45 coaches in the country to a get-together at Lilleshall where they engaged in practical sessions as well as discussion forums. Micky had visited the FA as well as learning about the set-up in the Bundesliga in Germany, and he was keen to introduce into cricket the equivalent of football's elite coaching qualifications.

By 1996 Micky's characterisation of English cricket's structure as a plate of spaghetti, with an inappropriate distinction between the first-class and the 'recreational', had been accepted. The Cricket Council, the TCCB and the NCA were amalgamated into the England and Wales Cricket Board, which began life in January 1997 under the chairmanship of Lord MacLaurin, a cricket-loving businessman who had transformed a declining Tesco into Britain's leading supermarket.

In August of that year MacLaurin launched a paper, *Raising the Standard*, full of radical proposals, several of which flowed out of Micky's thinking. In particular, he argued for a streamlining of club cricket within each county, with a pyramid that brought the cream more rapidly to the top. "The best players were spread out in too many clubs," Micky says. "Not enough of them were playing with and against each other, as they would have been in Australia."

"Micky made a great contribution to that paper," Ian MacLaurin says. "Even now, at the age of nearly eighty, he is still looking positively to the future, coming up with ideas. That's why he looks so young, thinks so young. He's not stuck in the past. Cricket would be very much better served if there were more about like him."

"There were always people," Micky says, "who would say things like 'We won the Ashes in the '50s without any of this' or 'I got a thousand wickets and I didn't do that'. But the game was changing. Other countries were moving ahead of us."

The key change during MacLaurin's chairmanship of the ECB occurred after Micky's retirement in 1997: the decision by Chris Smith, minister for culture and sport, to agree to the removal of Test cricket from the list of sporting events that had to remain on terrestrial television. This brought in *Sky* television, and suddenly the game at all levels had the funds to introduce the improvements it wanted.

How things would have been different if Micky had had access to such money. "It took me the best part of five years to get £60,000 from the board to introduce and establish a qualification for people involved in the cricket management of a county club. We worked with the School of Management at Bradford University, and we finally ran a course that was attended by one person from each county. There was plenty of cricket content, but there were also sessions on man management, on budgets and on general business matters."

One whom Micky targeted for the course was the Lancashire captain Mike Watkinson, who was nearing the end of his career. "I was always impressed by him," Micky says. "He was working in the winters as a draughtsman in the steel industry, and I said to him, 'If you can maintain your enthusiasm, you'd be just right for this.'" Watkinson agreed to attend, and in time he became a highly respected cricket manager at Old Trafford. "But for that Bradford course he could have been lost to the game."

Micky undertook a revamping of the coaching courses, upgrading the old Teaching and Coaching Awards into new Level One and Two qualifications and introducing into the Advanced Award some of the latest developments in sports science and technology to create a Level Three that was aimed at coaches who were working with young professionals and representative age-group sides.

Micky was certainly not one to pooh-pooh the modern ideas. "When I was manager at Surrey I remember watching a promising youngster in the field. His father was on the boundary with a bottle, regularly offering him a drink. I said to the father, 'If he's going to be a first-class cricketer, he'll have to learn to last two hours without any liquid.' I was totally wrong, as sports science has now shown us."

After the introduction of the Level Three, the next challenge was to create a Level Four, aimed at the very top coaches. Time did not allow Micky to complete this task before retirement, but he was keen that his successor be somebody of vision capable of taking the work forward.

Micky was not initially on the selection panel nor was the candidate he favoured on the original short list. But he corrected both those things and, to the surprise of many, Micky's job of National Director of Coaching and Development went to Hugh Morris, the 33-year-old Glamorgan batsman.

"I had met him a few times," Micky says. "I did some research on his background, and I had a bit of a gut feeling about him. We had a long chat one day at Worcester, and he was a bright lad. A good organiser. A visionary sort of fellow. I wanted somebody like that, not just somebody who would look after what we had already put in place."

They worked together from September till the end of the year, mapping out the new Level Four award and planning improvements to the age-group cricket, and time has proved the perspicacity of Micky's 'gut feeling'. Morris has become a pivotal figure in the rise of English cricket in recent years, taking on major responsibilities. "It's no coincidence," Micky says, "that, since Hugh took over, England's cricket has gone from strength to strength. And he showed his strength of character when he fought off throat cancer."

*

In 1998, shortly after his retirement, Micky succeeded Stuart Surridge's widow Betty as President of Surrey County Cricket Club, and he was persuaded to stay on for a second year when his designated successor, John Major, needed more time to complete his autobiography. This extension of his presidency proved to be fortunate because in 1999 Surrey, under the captaincy of Adam Hollioake, won the championship for the first time since Micky had led them to the title in 1971. It was the last year in which there was one division, with all of the 18 counties playing each other once, and Surrey dominated from start to finish, with 12 victories and no defeats in their 17 games.

As in 1971 they had as their overseas player a Pakistani spinner who joined them halfway through the summer: Saqlain Mushtaq. Also, as in 1971 and in the 1950s, they had a team the great majority of whom had roots in the county through birth or schooling and through the county's youth system: Mark Butcher, Alec Stewart, Graham Thorpe, Alex Tudor, the Bicknell brothers

Darren and Martin, Alistair Brown, Ian Ward, even the Hollioake brothers Adam and Ben who had migrated from Australia to Weybridge as young boys.

Micky was the link in a special chain that connected the 1950s through 1971 to the side that went on to win the championship three times in four years at the turn of the century, a side which included his son Alec. It was a great delight to him to discover that some of the team, notably Mark Butcher, were well aware of, and inspired by, the club's history. Such knowledge did not, however, extend to the burgeoning marketing department. Two of the girls working there approached Micky one day during his presidency. "Mister Stewart, could you help us?" one asked. "You don't know the name Peter May, do you?"

*

Micky has remained active in the game. In 2007, in the wake of a humiliating Ashes defeat in Australia, he was a member of the commission, chaired by the golf administrator Ken Schofield, which examined the state of English cricket, and he still spends most Saturdays watching club cricket in Surrey on behalf of the Bernard Coleman Charitable Trust, looking for young players who have the potential to step up into the professional game.

It is typical of the man that, in working on this book, he is concerned, above all else, to set down his thoughts on the future direction of English cricket.

He is wholly positive about the current set-up of the national team: "I am so pleased that Andy Flower has done so well. As the first England manager, beginning in totally different circumstances, I always had the view that the England cricket side should be run as it is now. If I hadn't set things in motion 25 years ago, it may have taken a lot longer for Andy to achieve the success he has. From where I stand, as an England supporter, I have every admiration for him. There's one thing that's certain. He handles the media better than I did."

Micky is enthusiastic about all the technological and scientific advances which have been introduced into the game, though he admits to a certain wariness about the way they are sometimes applied. "The most difficult thing of all is how you progress natural talent. There are so many systems being introduced, so much emphasis on physical development, and that's all to the good for the young cricketer. But it's a waste of time if people can't play naturally. Results have to be all-important in assessing players. At the top level it's not 'how' that counts but 'how many'."

He is less enthusiastic about the way both international and domestic cricket are being scheduled. "So much of it is put together to generate the maximum revenue. In my view the programme should be written down with a view to producing the best quality cricket possible, and only after that should it be adapted to meet the financial considerations. It would be better, for example, to take £75 million and have the game as it should be than £100 million and have a schedule which is so demanding that the top players are not at their best and are at risk of serious injuries – or they are being rested when people have paid out good money to watch them."

Yes, if it were 75 million against 100, but what if it were 10 against 100? Would he still argue the same way?

"I might," he replies. "Everybody would have to go back to being amateurs." He pauses and laughs. "Oh no, that would be no good. The amateurs were more expensive than the pros."

It bothers him greatly that so much money is spent, by counties and by clubs, on hiring overseas players, cricketers who are not qualified to play for England and who block the progress of those who are. At the NCA he conducted a survey of club cricket, and he estimated that there were 10,000 overseas players across the country. More recently, he has calculated that, including those playing for counties, they are costing the game in the order of £35 million.

At county level he would run a four-day championship and a 50-over competition, in both of which the counties could field only one player not qualified for England – but in the Twenty20 cricket they could have eleven if they wanted. "It concerns me," he says, "that the television money coming down to the counties seems to have encouraged some of them to pursue success by spending on players as if they were Premier League football teams. Cricket is nothing to do with all that. I can't believe, with all the cricket played in Surrey, that you have to search around the world to bring in players who will do the county good. They take places in the side, and they slow up the progress of the players in the county's development programme. With young players the only way you can know whether they are going to be major contributors is for them to play. Sometimes you have to sacrifice the immediate results to ensure that you have long-term success."

He makes the same criticism of the top club sides in Surrey, some of whom not only import overseas players but make payments to local players. "The league system has made club cricket more competitive, and that is to be welcomed. But the problem is that clubs respond to the leagues rather than to the county boards. Some see the county board as nothing more than a vehicle for getting a grant to improve their facilities, but at the same time they are spending large sums on paying players. It's a criminal waste of money."

If Micky had his way, each county would have a top tier of clubs, with no promotion or relegation affecting that tier. Those clubs would be located around the different population centres of the county, and they would be represented by the best players living there. In that way the money being spent on club cricket would not drain away into players' wages, and the best young cricketers would have a clearer route into the top club sides and on into the professional game.

Micky is an admirer of the way the Australian grade system was until recently, where the best talent rose rapidly to the top, but he does not want to lose the level of participation that exists in the English game. To that end, he is keen that coaches not only nurture the best young talents but spread the joy of cricket up and down the land.

"Participation is absolutely vital," he says. "All the various schemes that introduce the game to youngsters, they not only produce players, they produce future county cricket club members, club secretaries, scorers, people who paint the sight screens – people who enjoy the game, even if they haven't an ounce of ability in their body."

It is the theme to which he returns again and again. Cricket is one game, from the grandeur of Lord's to the artificial, pockmarked pitch in Ruskin Park, and it should all be joined up. The path to the top should not be blocked, and the game at all levels should be respected.

"In Australia the grade cricketers see themselves as on the first rungs of a ladder that leads towards playing for Australia. But in England there's more than one ladder. So there is a disconnection between club cricket and the England side. Some of that disconnection is because there's a gap between the clubs and the counties. We're the only Test-playing country in the world where our first-class game is played by private clubs. It would all work much better if the county clubs were the pinnacles of the cricket which was played in their part of the country."

*

Micky has been a progressive in cricket, at the forefront of change, but in one respect he is an unshakeable traditionalist.

"I may be looked on by many people as a hard-bitten professional, associated with bringing in aspects of football, but in actual fact my view of how cricket should be played is very Corinthian – as the game was in most of the years I played it. It was a special game, an honest game with very few incidents of cheating or sharp practice.

"Some of what I see now hurts me. I don't expect it to be exactly as it was. People have changed; society has changed. But I watch club matches, and I'm appalled by some of it: lbw appeals where practically every fielder on the ground joins in; appeals for catches that the fielders know are not out; players charging at the umpire as they appeal; then the reaction when the decision is not out. I hardly see a weekend game when I don't see dissent. Even in the Under-15 matches, they're all shouting the odds in the field. You can be just as competitive and aggressive without any of that. It makes me sad to see it.

"Football is different. It's a physical contact sport. Cricket isn't. It's like golf, and it should hold on to its finer points as golf has done. When I played, there was a respect for the game that had been handed down the generations. I wish we could get that back."

*

For 75 years cricket has been at the heart of Micky's life: from that brick wall in a South London side street where he developed his catching skills to the hotel in Melbourne where, with Elton John in support, they celebrated England's Ashes triumph, a victory to which he had quietly contributed as England's first team manager. He played in the greatest county side of them all, becoming one of the best close catchers in the history of the game, and he managed his son Alec's development into one of the finest players of the modern era, the most capped England Test cricketer of all time.

He has never stopped, never been happy to rest on his achievements. He has seen so much change, he has been responsible for some of it, and he is still looking ahead, still wanting to make sure that future generations have the best possible chance of success and that the game remains at the heart of our national sporting life.

On the last Sunday before this book was completed, he visited his daughter Judy where her four-year-old boy Max had just been given his first cricket bat. In the hallway Micky bowled to him, with a semi-hard ball.

"It's going to bounce once, and you're going to hit it," he told Max. "But you've got to watch the ball."

The ball was duly hit, a cross-batted heave, so Micky took the lesson one step further: "Now try to hit me with it."

Again Micky bowled the ball. It landed on an off-stump line, and Max hit it with a whack that saw the ball whistle like a rocket past Micky's ear, straight into the sitting room where it missed the television screen by inches.

"Maybe he'll play," Micky says with a happy smile.

ACKNOWLEDGEMENTS

This book has come about as a result of many hours of conversation with Micky. Over a period of two and a half years we have been meeting regularly at the Grosvenor Hotel in Stockbridge, so regularly that the woman behind the bar greets each of us now with the words "Your usual?". Sheila has also attended many of these sessions, and I would like to thank both her and Micky for their patience as I painstakingly gathered everything I needed to write this book. I would also like to thank Micky for the care he has taken to ensure that what I have written is correct: not just the facts but the impressions created by the words I have chosen. It has not been hard to understand why his attention to detail and his concern for people have been held in such high regard within the cricket community. It has been a pleasure to work with him. I hope I have done his story justice.

Micky and I spent a day visiting the scenes of his childhood, and I would like to thank Susie Schofield and Neil French of Alleyn's for showing us round the school and for digging out the old magazines.

I would like to thank the following for giving up their time to talk to me: Geoff Arnold, Bernie Coleman, Mike Gatting, Graham Gooch, Roger Harman, David Harrison, Jacqueline Hooper, Doug Insole, Roger Knight, Peter Lush, Ian MacLaurin, Derek Newton, Ian Peacock, Pat Pocock, Alec Stewart and Derek Ufton.

I would like to thank Simon Lister for his help in interviewing a number of former England cricketers. I would also like to thank those he interviewed: Michael Atherton, Bill Athey, Chris Broad, Philip DeFreitas, John Emburey, Neil Foster, Angus Fraser, Derek Pringle, Gladstone Small and Robin Smith.

I have also used material from interviews I have conducted for other projects – with Michael Barton, Alec Bedser, Harry Brind, 'Buzzer' Hadingham, Geoffrey Howard, John Pretlove, Roy Swetman and Michael Willett.

I have been exceptionally lucky in having the manuscript read by several people whose opinions I value highly: Scyld Berry, Stephen Brenkley, Ron Deaton, Simon Lister, Douglas Miller and David Smith. Their feedback was most perceptive, and I am enormously grateful to them.

Just before completion of the book, my usual printers went out of business, but I have been most fortunate in retaining the help of their pre-press specialist, Robert Taylor. His design of the jacket and his remedial work on the photographs have been, as always, first-rate.

Finally I must thank Susanna Kendall who has had to live with me through all the ups and downs of this project. The scope of the book has made it a challenging undertaking, and I have owed much to her contribution: not just her emotional support but her sensitive and intelligent editing.

I have made regular use of the following reference books:
Wisden Cricketers' Almanack
Playfair Cricket Annual
Bailey, Thorn & Wynne-Thomas, *Who's Who of Cricketers* (Newnes, 1984)
Swanton, Plumptre & Woodcock, *Barclays World of Cricket* (Collins, 1986)

I have also read and occasionally quoted from the following books:
Ken Barrington, *Running into Hundreds* (Stanley Paul, 1963)
Rob Cavallini, *Corinthian-Casuals* (Dog N Duck Publications, 2009)
Arthur R. Chandler, *Alleyn's – The Coeducational School* (Gresham Books, 1998)
John Clarke, *Cricket with a Swing* (Stanley Paul, 1963)
Peter Dobereiner, *Maestro: The Life of Henry Cotton* (Hodder & Stoughton, 1992)
Dickie Dodds, *Hit Hard and Enjoy It* (The Cricketer, 1976)
Mike Gatting, *Leading from the Front* (Queen Anne Press, 1988)
Graham Gooch, *Captaincy* (Stanley Paul, 1992)
Graham Gooch, *Test of Fire* (Robson Books, 1990)
David Gower, *Gower – The Autobiography* (Collins Willow, 1992)
Wes Hall, *Pace Like Fire* (Pelham Books, 1965)
E.R.T. Holmes, *Flannelled Foolishness* (Hollis & Carter, 1957)
Robin Jackman, *Jackers* (Don Nelson, 2011)
Jim Laker, *One-Day Cricket* (B.T. Batsford, 1977)
Jim Laker, *Over to Me* (Frederick Muller, 1960)
David Lemmon, *The History of Surrey CCC* (Christopher Helm, 1989)
Peter May, *A Game Enjoyed* (Stanley Paul, 1985)
Pat Pocock, *Percy* (Clifford Frost, 1987)
David Smith, *Larger than Life* (Two Heads Publishing, 1995)
Rob Steen, *David Gower – A Man Out of Time* (Victor Gollancz, 1995)
Alec Stewart, *Playing for Keeps* (BBC Books, 2003)
E.W. Swanton, *Sort of a Cricket Person* (Collins, 1972)
David Tossell, *Tony Greig* (Pitch Publishing, 2011)
Simon Wilde, *Ian Botham – The Power and the Glory* (Simon & Schuster, 2011)
Ian Wooldridge, *Cricket, Lovely Cricket* (Robert Hale, 1963)

also from a number of newspapers and cricket magazines, notably:
The Times, Guardian, Daily Telegraph, Nottingham Evening Post,
The Cricketer, Playfair Cricket Monthly and *Wisden Cricket Monthly*
and from the yearbooks of Surrey County Cricket Club.

Most of all, though, I must thank Micky for agreeing to undertake this book.
It took him a long time to make the decision, but I hope you will agree with
me that the wait has been worthwhile.

Stephen Chalke
Bath, June 2012

A BRIEF STATISTICAL DIGEST

Michael James Stewart, O.B.E.

Born: 16 September 1932

BATTING AND FIELDING IN FIRST-CLASS CRICKET

Home

Year	Matches	Innings	Not Outs	Runs	Highest	Average	Catches
1954	14	22	2	580	134	29.00	26
1955	24	42	5	1085	118	29.32	52
1956	28	48	1	1586	166	33.74	28
1957	34	54	5	1801	147*	36.75	77
1958	34	52	4	1230	118	25.62	61
1959	33	62	6	1849	140	33.01	52
1960	30	51	6	1866	169*	41.46	40
1961	31	57	4	1415	120	26.69	39
1962	30	55	9	2045	200*	44.45	28
1963	24	41	2	1148	169	29.43	29
1964	24	44	5	1980	227*	50.76	24
1965	34	55	4	1588	143*	31.13	33
1966	30	49	7	997	102	23.73	30
1967	23	31	3	1184	112	42.28	21
1968	31	55	11	1145	91*	26.02	19
1969	23	37	7	1317	105	43.90	9
1970	22	39	5	1246	128	36.64	16
1971	23	41	3	959	108	25.23	21
1972	16	27	3	463	79	19.29	10
Overseas							
1955/56	4	8	-	265	68	33.12	3
1959/60	2	4	-	65	39	16.25	1
1962/63	3	6	1	107	42	21.40	3
1963/64	6	6	-	307	119	51.17	5
1967/68	4	7	-	119	44	17.00	6
1970/71	3	5	-	145	93	29.00	2
TOTAL	**530**	**898**	**93**	**26,492**	**227***	**32.90**	**635**

ONE-DAY CRICKET

Matches	Innings	Not Outs	Runs	Highest	Average	Catches
75	72	2	1172	101	16.74	24

TEST CRICKET

Matches	Innings	Not Outs	Runs	Highest	Average	Catches
8	12	1	385	87	35.00	6

CENTURIES IN FIRST-CLASS CRICKET (49)

For Surrey (48)

109	Pakistan, Oval	1954	145*	Lancashire, Oval	1962
134	Essex, Colchester	1954	200*	Essex, Oval	1962
118	Kent, Blackheath	1955	110	Oxford Univ, Guildford	1962
105	Leics, Oval	1955	143	Middlesex, Lord's	1962
106	Hants, Guildford	1956	169	Essex, Oval	1963
155*	Camb Univ, Guildford	1956	130	Kent, Oval	1964
166	Essex, Clacton	1956	130	Yorkshire, Bradford	1964
100	Derbyshire, Derby	1956	166	Hampshire, Oval	1964
114*	Combined Serv, Oval	1957	104	Glamorgan, Oval	1964
147*	West Indians, Oval	1957	227*	Middlesex, Oval	1964
140	Warwicks, Edgbaston	1957	155	Sussex, Oval	1964
103	Warwicks, Oval	1957	107	Leics, Oval	1965
118	Northants, Oval	1958	118	Gloucestershire, Oval	1965
123	Glamorgan, Oval	1959	143*	Yorkshire, Oval	1965
104	Somerset, Oval	1959	101	Leics, Oval	1966
140	Essex, Oval	1959	102	Sussex, Eastbourne	1966
107*	Leics, Leicester	1959	112	Northants, Northampton	1967
107	Northants, Oval	1960	100*	Gloucestershire, Oval	1967
112*	Somerset, Oval	1960	105	Scotland, Oval	1969
169*	Kent, Oval	1960	100	Notts, Trent Bridge	1969
147	Notts, Oval	1960	128*	Sussex, Hove	1970
116*	Somerset, Taunton	1960	110	Sussex, Guildford	1970
120	Camb Univ, Fenner's	1961	101	Warwicks, Edgbaston	1971
137*	MCC, Lord's	1962	108	Glamorgan, Oval	1971

For MCC (1)

119	Indian Board President's XI, Bangalore	1963/4

CENTURIES IN LIMITED-OVER CRICKET (1)

For Surrey (1)

101	Durham, Chester-le-Street	1972

BOWLING IN FIRST-CLASS CRICKET

22.4 overs, one wicket for 99 runs

His victim was his old friend Brian Taylor of Essex, caught at the wicket for 47 in a match at the Oval in 1965 which on the last afternoon had drifted into a draw.

Micky is keen for it to be recorded that he also took a wicket for the Army against Oxford University in 1951, bowling the Alleyn's old boy Jimmy Crisp. The three-day fixture had not long lost its first-class status.

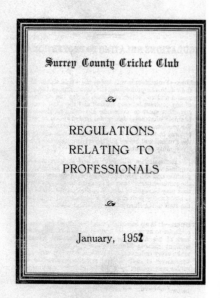

Surrey County Cricket Club

REGULATIONS
RELATING TO
PROFESSIONALS

January, 1952

Surrey County Cricket Club

REGULATIONS RELATING TO PROFESSIONALS

Duties—Professionals will devote the whole of their time to their duties as professional cricketers during the cricket season and no professional shall during the continuance of any contract between himself and the Club engage in any other sport or undertake any other employment or business whatsoever during the cricket season or without the previous consent in writing of the Committee. The consent in writing of the Committee must be obtained by the Professional before playing cricket otherwise than for the County or Club.

Professionals will bowl at the practice nets when required whenever the Club nets are open for Members to practise and will play in matches when selected. During the summer period they will perform any work or service that may be required of them by the Committee and which is customarily performed by a professional cricketer on the staff of the Surrey County Cricket Club.

Fitness—It is an essential part of the duty of a professional cricketer to be proficient and skilful and fit to play to the best of his ability throughout the cricket season and without causing himself injury. Professionals will make every endeavour to fulfil this duty and will submit themselves to such medical examinations as the Committee may require by a Medical Adviser nominated by the Club. The Committtee shall be entitled to suspend any Professional who is not fit subject to the provisions below regarding "accidents" and "sickness."

3

Qualification—Professionals are required to retain their qualification to play for the County under the "Rules of County Cricket" for the time being in force.

Commencement of Season—The Cricket Season commences on the 15th of April or such other date as may be dertermined by the Committee and Professionals will be required to be fit for cricket by that date. The cricket season ends on 15th September or such other date as may be determined by the Committee.

Hours—Professionals selected to play or act as twelfth man in any match whether at home or away must be present on the ground where the match is to be played at least one hour before the advertised time at which play is due to commence.

On days when first class matches are being played at the Oval, Professionals not selected to play elsewhere will report to the Secretary or his deputy and be ready for practice at 10 a.m.

On all other days Professionals not selected to play elsewhere will report to the Secretary or his deputy at 11 a.m. and be ready for practice at 11.30 a.m. Practice will continue until 7 p.m. except on Saturdays when the ground is closed for practice at 5 p.m.

Professionals will not be absent from the Oval during practice hours without the special permission of the Secretary. In the event of a match at the Oval in which the Professional is taking part being finished before the due time, the Professional will not be absent from the Oval unless he has obtained the special permission of the Secretary.

4

Match Money and Expenses (additional to Weekly Wages)—

FIRST ELEVEN. Players taking part in three-day matches will be paid match expenses of £8 for each match away from the Oval and £4 for each home match. For each match against tourists of Test Match standard additional expenses of £2 will be paid.

WIN MONEY. For every first eleven match won outright in the County Championship or against touring teams of Test standard £5 win money shall be paid to each professional playing in the match. £2 win money will be paid for a win outright in other three-day matches. Players taking part in a two-day match won outright will receive 10/- win money.

SECOND ELEVEN. Professionals taking part in two-day matches will be paid £7 for each match played away from the Oval and £4 for each home match. For every match out of Surrey, except Lords, entailing absence from home on Sundays an extra £2 will be paid to those taking part.

FARES. Railway tickets (or the equivalent value) will be provided from London termini for all away matches but only on condition that the player travels by such trains as is prescribed. Fares or the equivalent will not be paid in respect of three-day and two-day matches played in Surrey or at Lords.

5

TWELFTH MAN—

3 DAY MATCHES. Will be paid at the rate of "3 day" match expenses.

2 DAY MATCHES. Will be paid at the rate of "2 day" match expenses.

ONE DAY MATCHES. Match fees at the rate of 20/- for a match played at the Oval, and 25/- for an away match will be paid to players taking part (Scorers and Umpires).

HALF DAY MATCHES. Match fees of 10/- each will be paid to all players taking part. Tea will be provided.

EXTRANEOUS EMPLOYMENT. When a player is detailed to take part in a match not organised by the Surrey Club he will be paid at the appropriate rates.

HOTELS. Except as provided for above no hotel expenses will be paid.

BAGGAGE MONEY FOR AWAY MATCHES. An allowance of £3 per three-day away match and £2 per two-day away match will be made. No allowance will be made for other matches.

SELECTION TO TAKE PART IN ANY MATCH IS IN THE ABSOLUTE DISCRETION OF THE COMMITTEE.

6

Talent Money—Talent money will be awarded at the discretion of the Committee and will not be reckoned as part of the Professional's earnings for the purpose of arriving at any guaranteed minimum earnings.

Insurance—The Club will effect a Policy of Insurance whereby legal liability under the Workmen's Compensation Acts and the Employers' Liability Act will be covered.

Accidents and Sickness—If a Professional is injured in or falls sick as the result of the execution of his duties under these rules he will be paid his wages for so long during the currency of his contract with the Club as he is prevented from playing on account of such injury or sickness. The Committee shall be the sole judge of what is included in the expression "in the execution of his duties under these rules." The payment will only be made on the understanding that the Professional in the opinion of the Committee makes every effort on his part to become fit to play. Professionals receiving payments under the National Insurance Acts will only be entitled to such wages as will make up the payments so received to the normal amount of their wages.

If as a result of injury or sickness incurred otherwise than in the execution of his duties as aforesaid a Professional becomes unable or fails to perform his duties the Committee may dismiss him by giving him a week's notice or the equivalent of a week's wages in lieu of notice. The Committee may however in their absolute discretion suspend the Professional during his inability or failure to perform his duties.

7

Doctors' Accounts—All Doctors' accounts (except of any doctor nominated by the Club to examine the Professional) shall be the responsibility of the Professional concerned unless the Committee determine otherwise.

Misconduct and Suspension—If at any time a Professional absents himself from his duties without the consent of the Committee or the Secretary or neglects or refuses or for any reason whatever fails to perform his duties or is guilty of any misconduct or behaviour which in the opinion of the Committee of the Club (who will be the sole Judges) is detrimental to the interests of the Club, the Committee through the Secretary shall have the power to dismiss the Professional by giving him a week's notice or the equivalent of a week's wages in lieu of notice. The Secretary shall have the power to suspend a Professional for misconduct or misbehaviour pending consideration of the matter by the Committee at its next meeting. Whilst suspended from this or any other cause a Professional shall be entitled only to receive wages during the period of suspension at half the rate to which he is normally entitled.

Benefits—The Committee is under no obligation of any kind to grant any benefit matches and Professionals must clearly understand that no expectation of being granted a Benefit Match is held out to them as an inducement to become members of the staff, or as a term of their employment. If a Benefit Match is granted the Professional will enter into a special agreement with the Club which will state the terms and conditions upon which such Benefit Match is granted.

8

Winter Tours—The Committee reserve discretion in granting permission to any Professional to go on a winter cricket tour. The Committee also reserve the right in granting such permission to impose such conditions as they may think fit regarding insurances against accident or illness for the benefit of the Professional and/or the Club.

General—County and Second Eleven caps are awarded at the discretion of the Committee.

Professionals must not write for the Press, grant interviews to the Press or broadcast on any subject directly or indirectly connected with cricket without first obtaining the written permission of the Committee.

On Sundays during the Cricket season Professionals are expected to rest and shall not without special permission from the Committee play Cricket.

Players of the Surrey XI or those likely to be included in the XI shall play NO extraneous cricket whatsoever during the season except those matches authorised by the Committee to be played for the Benefit of any Surrey player.

Professionals must obtain the permission of the Secretary to travel to and from away matches otherwise than by train or other public conveyance.

The Committee reserve the right to alter, extend or rescind any of the above regulations.

Signed on behalf of the Committee,

B K Jardine.

Secretary

INDEX

Micky Stewart and his family, with the exception of son Alec, have been omitted

316

INDEX

Micky Stewart and his family, with the exception of son Alec, have been omitted

INDEX

Micky Stewart and his family, with the exception of son Alec, have been omitted

INDEX

Micky Stewart and his family, with the exception of son Alec, have been omitted

INDEX

Micky Stewart and his family, with the exception of son Alec, have been omitted